Monograph 46
The American Ethnological Society
June Helm, Editor

HILL FARMERS OF NIGERIA

Cultural Ecology of the Kofyar
of the Jos Plateau

Robert McC. Netting

University of Washington Press
Seattle and London

To my family

Preface

FIRST FIELD WORK is often compounded much more of hap-
penstance and luck than we are willing to admit in our more
"scientific" moments. When I arrived in Nigeria in September of 1960, it was for the stated purpose of doing a study of
political acculturation in a tribe of the Jos Plateau, probably
the Angas. My research turned instead to the Kofyar, a people largely innocent of either ethnography or a common
name, and to problems of subsistence and social organization. Perhaps it was the relative paucity of modern politics in
the area or the omnipresence of traditional agriculture
which altered my course. No doubt the attraction of an
isolated escarpment and palmy, terraced slopes played a part.
Most of all, there was a sense among the Kofyar of quiet
independence and easy courtesy—they were their own men,
and they felt at home in a world big enough to share with an
outsider. I came upon a people and a place that seemed
right, and they showed me what was significant in their life,
what I should study. A wise anthropologist had told me this
would happen, and that I should accept the freedom to feel
which our humane discipline still affords us. The choice of
the Kofyar was lucky, and the problems of understanding
their culture were absorbing.

Shifts in the focus of research may satisfy the researcher while bringing consternation to those who support him. Fortunately for me, Ford Foundation's Foreign Area Training Fellowship provided both ample financing and the leeway to define and pursue a new task on the spot. This grant also enabled me to take preliminary language training and conduct documentary research in England and to complete the writing up of the material for a dissertation. During this period, I relied on the efficiency and understanding of Miss Dorothy Soderlund and others of the Foundation staff. From 1960 to 1962 I spent eighteen months in Nigeria of which I lived fourteen months in Kofyar country. The manuscript on which this book is based was finished in 1966 before returning to the field, but revisions and additions were made with new information gathered between November, 1966, and July, 1967. The invaluable second period of research was made possible by a Social Science Research Council grant under its Committee on African Studies. Though my topic and venue did not shift this time, the coups, riots, and civil war which have so sadly rent Nigeria made field work anxious and precarious. For bearing with us during that difficult time, I must thank Rowland L. Mitchell, Jr. of SSRC.

Friends and cohorts in Nigeria contributed directly to the pleasure and productiveness of my two visits to the country. Dr. P. C. Lloyd and Dr. Robert Armstrong of the University of Ibadan and Mr. Bernard Fagg, then Director of Antiquities, gave me encouragement during my preparations and in the intervals of field work. The administrative and technical officers with whom I came in contact were uniformly helpful, and I especially appreciate the knowledge shared with me by Mr. Humphrey Wimbush of the Forestry Department, Mr. Lotringer of the Agriculture Department, and Mr. Yonge of the Geological Survey. Mr. John Palmer of the Agriculture Department made several excellent maps of Bong village and the surrounding hill area from aerial photographs and gave them to me. I enjoyed the hospitality of Dr. and Mrs.

Pendleton in Pankshin, of Mr. and Mrs. Ifan Williams at Divisional Headquarters in Shendam, and of Mr. and Mrs. Robin Jagoe in Kaduna. I owe a special debt of gratitude to Hamo Sassoon and his wife Caroline for their continued interest in my work, their sympathetic and graphic knowledge of the peoples of the North, and their willingness to open their home to me, whether sound or sick.

My nearest expatriate neighbors within the Kofyar area were the Roman Catholic Fathers of the Société des Missions Africaines. It was they who provided me with everything from mail deliveries to window frames. The mission church of St. Brendan at Kwa was my half-way house to the outside, a place for relaxation, restoratives, and unfailing Irish humor. Father Patrick Rooney first introduced me to the Kofyar, and his friendship was a major factor in making my days there such happy ones. Fathers Meehan, McAuley, and MacNeely all showed me special kindnesses. During the more recent trip, the presence of my wife and two-year-old son with me in bush made such good offices particularly valuable. Father James Smyth helped us in countless ways. Bishop Reddington of Jos and Father Hourihane graciously made available the mission house at Kwande for our use. When visiting Jos, we looked forward to the company of Fathers Smith, Shevlin, and Aje. Indeed without the unstinting assistance of these men and indeed the entire Jos Diocese, our field work would have been immeasurably more difficult.

At a time when uncertainty, suspicion, and the threat of violence clouded Nigeria, we were especially grateful for the personal concern and administrative aid of Mallam Liman Ciroma, then Secretary to the Military Governor of the North. Though directly involved with the crises of government, he took time to affirm his continuing interest in the science of man.

The Kofyar individually and as a group were always affable and polite, tolerant of my endless questions and bad grammar, and glad to welcome me to the fields, the dance, the household circle, and the sacred grove. The list of the considerate and cooperative is too long to begin, but I particularly appreciated my talks with Danaan, former chief of Bong, and my neighbors, Dashe and Dagot. Kofyar schoolboys and teachers who proved conscientious and capable assistants were John Alkali, Albert Dakogal, Daniel Dayok, Ambrose Longkwang, Kieran Daber, Simon Dakop, Anthony Bala, and Augustine Damar. Literacy does not divide them from their traditions, and they are assuming new and necessary roles in their communities. Louis Dagar, a lad of seventeen in 1961 who was with me almost daily, proved a sensitive interpreter of his people's language and customs and developed a real feeling for the work I was doing. After he became a thriving tailor, his place was ably filled during the second period of research by Alphonsus Dashe. I liked the Kofyar and their country, and one of the highest compliments I have ever received was their expressed belief that I was a reincarnation of one of themselves. The things which I do not yet know about their culture stem from my failure to ask rather than any unwillingness on their part to answer.

I have incorporated in this manuscript a number of suggestions made by my dissertation adviser, Dr. Lloyd A. Fallers, and I have profited from discussions with other members of the Department of Anthropology at the University of Chicago. At various stages of preparation, these pages have been read with thoroughness and thought by Dr. Thayer Scudder and Dr. Edgar Winans. As perceptive students of cultural ecology, their comments were of great value to me. The data cited, the interpretations advanced, and the final form of the manuscript are, of course, entirely my own responsibility.

The jobs which must be done and which the writer cannot do spell the difference between manuscript and book. For their diligent typing I am indebted to Claire Cosgrove and Rose Antipin. Eve Kemnitzer and Barbara Baker made the maps and diagrams. Dr. June Helm encouraged me to undertake a revision which was larger than either of us suspected. Final editing owed much to the knowledge and tact of Phoebe Miller.

Through the alarms and excursions of the field and the much longer times of plodding study and writing, it was my family who did most to keep this work in progress. From the beginning, my parents provided strong moral support for my work as well as timely financial help. Jacqueline, my wife, brought a new dimension of awareness with her into the field and radiated the steadfast warmth at home that books and people need in their tentative early days. This, then, is their book too.

R. M. N.

University of Pennsylvania
Philadelphia
March 15, 1968

Note on Orthography

THE PHONEMES of Sura, which is obviously closely related to Kofyar, have been summarized by Jungraithmayr (1964), and Wolff (1954) has proposed orthographies for the neighboring Sura, Angas, and Ankwe languages. A word list of Kofyar is in Netting (1967). For purposes of convenience in typing and agreement with the local usage of the administration and literate Kofyar, I have represented Kofyar phonemes in transliteration by the following symbols:

Vowels	*Consonants*		
i = i	p = p	š = sh	
ɛ = e	t = t	v = v	
a = a	č = c	z = z	
ɔ = o	k = k	ž = zh	
u = u	b = b	m = m	
ə = oe	d = d	n = n	
	j = j	ŋ = ng	
	g = g	w = w	
	ɓ = ɓ	r = r	
	ɗ = ɗ	l = l	
	f = f	y = y	
	s = s		

Although Kofyar is characterized by phonemic tones, they are not indicated in words transcribed in the text. Length is indicated by the doubling of vowel symbols.

Contents

Plates

Figures and Tables

Hill Farmers of Nigeria
*Cultural Ecology of the Kofyar
of the Jos Plateau*

1

Introduction

TERRACING THE LAND is an impressive human achievement. A hillside serrated from top to bottom in successive steps is a symbol of effort carefully applied, of a difficult environment modeled to man's own proportions. It usually occurs with a highly developed agriculture that can profit from such a major investment of time and energy. The Kofyar are hill farmers, practicing intensive agriculture on the flanks of the Jos Plateau in Northern Nigeria. Their widespread use of terracing suggests at once a special adaptation to their habitat and raises questions about the mobilization of labor and the social organization of production reflected in this cultural landscape. These dual interests, involving on the one hand the description of a unique and highly integrated traditional farming system, and on the other an attempt to analyze the interrelations between agriculture and the sociocultural background of the cultivators, form the basis of this study.

Terracing, together with the system of permanent, intensive agriculture that makes terraces both possible and advantageous, is more prevalent in tropical Africa than one might

3

suppose.[1] It has been reported among hill pagan peoples in Adamawa and Sardauna provinces in northeastern Nigeria (S. White 1941) and adjoining Cameroun (Gardi 1956), as well as among the Maku Ibo of the Eastern Region (Floyd 1965). The Kabre of Northern Togo (Froelich, Alexandre, and Cornevin 1963) till their massif in this manner. Because of these and other similarities, German ethnologists formerly lumped all of these hill people together as the remaining fragments of *altnigritische Kultur* (Baumann, Westermann, and Thurnwald 1940:50ff.). In East Africa, numerous groups such as the Nuba (Nadel 1947:16) and the inhabitants of Ukara Island in Lake Victoria (Thornton and Rounce 1936, Allan 1965:199–206) maintain terrace cultivation, and the remains of terraces from Ethiopia to South Africa indicate a wider occurrence of intensive hill agriculture in the past (Davidson 1959:219–20). Most of these accounts are brief, treating terrace farming as a curiosity in a continent where shifting agriculture is the rule, and giving minimal technological and sociological data. Elsewhere in Africa, terraces have been introduced by European administrations, often in the face of considerable local resistance (Young and Fosbrooke 1960). In more level areas, there are occasional occurrences of intensive agriculture in which land may be cropped continuously. Soil fertility is restored either by annual deposit of alluvial materials, as with the Gwembe Tonga (Scudder 1962), or by the use of animal manures, as with the Chagga, the Turu, and the Hausa (Grove 1961). Irrigation systems that may make possible intensive land use are known among the Sonjo (Gray 1963) and the Pokot (Conant 1965), but again much of the relevant material has not yet been published. From scattered references (Meek 1925:120; Findlay 1945; Fairbairn 1943), it appeared that terracing was present among the Angas and other groups on the southeast border of the Jos Plateau in northern Nigeria. This circumstance along with the isolated nature of the

[1] See map in Floyd 1965:92.

country and the existence of relatively traditional and unreported societies there stimulated my interest in the area.

In the context of general ethnographic research, it is particularly important to understand the methods and practical knowledge by which a human group gets its food. For this reason I chose to work with a hill society that appeared to have a particularly high development of cultivation and where traditional practices were still followed. In Kofyar country I was impressed not only by the terraces, the cleverly designed ridges, the stone corrals for stall feeding domestic stock, and the luxuriance of homestead farms but also by the fit, sturdy aspect of the people and their statement that they did not have an annual period of food scarcity. Their mastery of their environment was such that hunger was rare and serious famine was known only in legend. Moreover, there is in the study of food production a sense of grappling with basic human realities, the stuff of life and the cornerstone of cultural evolution. As De Schlippe (1956) says:

Originally every human group has built its culture "from the ground up." Food production, which in all except the most primitive societies takes the form of agriculture, is its foundation. Agriculture is one of the main links between a human group and the "landscape" in which it lives and which it exploits. Through agriculture every environment has taught its inhabitants a certain way of life. The teacher of a culture is its environment and agriculture is its classroom (xii).

I would perhaps be more cautious, remembering that human beings enter an environment bearing culture and that this superorganic heritage may lead different people to "learn" varying adjustments to the same set of external factors. Yet the fundamental nature of this adjustment can, I believe, be demonstrated.

Modern cultural anthropology has been slow in devoting its attention to inclusive problems of securing livelihood from the environment. Tools could be collected and classified, gross adaptations such as plains bison hunting or Northwest Coast salmon fishing could be isolated and compared, all without going beyond a loose theoretical framework of anthropogeography. From general field reports, museum collections, and tribal maps came the information that Wissler and others synthesized in the culture area concept. Similarities of subsistence type within particular habitats were more than mere classifying devices. Wissler saw the possibilities for a scientific ecological analysis: "The method usually followed in ecological studies is to seek correlations between the characters of life forms and the specific characters of the environment and, if it be found that these usually happen together, it is assumed that some causal relation exists between them" (1926:212). The correspondence of cultural and natural areas was further demonstrated by Kroeber (1939), but his emphasis was on the *limits* that environment set to the historic diffusion of specific complexes of traits. He followed Franz Boas in maintaining that culture was adapted to the environment at many points but was not directly produced by it. Indeed it was American anthropologists along with the French human geographers, Paul Vidal de la Blache and Lucien Febvre, who effectively criticized geographical determinism and substituted for it the less doctrinaire approach of possibilism (Thomas 1925). The growing weight of cross-cultural documentation clearly indicated the inadequacy of tracing simplistic connections between geographical causes and cultural effects (Forde 1934).

American ethnographers were well suited by training and taste to the task of systematic debunking, but their materials were often insufficient to provide alternate ecological explanations in place of the discredited environmentalist hypotheses. It was difficult to tell how much meat a Cheyenne brave needed to support his family, or the extent of Delaware maize fields. The student often lacked the direct experience of the culture operating on a traditional subsistence base, and his informants could not reconstruct certain types of data having to do with production and consumption. There was a marked paucity of economic data to correlate with what was known of social structure, political organization, and religious patterns. Functional statements dealing comprehensively with the purpose and integration of human institutions could not be supported. In most cases, the anthropologist also lacked the historical depth in a given culture that would include a knowledge of successive adjustments in habitat and type of exploitation over time. Only with the accumulation of comparative research, a knowledge of geologic, climatic, and biotic phenomena, and material from archeological and documentary sources on culture history could solid ecological propositions be advanced. To describe properly both environment and the human activities connected with it requires a long period of direct observation of a very mundane sort. Routine censusing, counting, measuring, and weighing provide quantitative bases that are as necessary as they are unexciting. To get a clear conception of agriculture, for instance, its processes must be watched and recorded over at least a year, whereas a single technological process or ritual may be thoroughly investigated in a short period of time (De Schlippe 1956:27).

Anthropologists began to approach such problems as they embarked on extended field research in functioning societies. Yet "Environment" and "Subsistence" remained often little more than chapters that set the scene for the, to them, more absorbing questions of kinship organization or legal systems. It seems to me that the social scientist became interested in the area of subsistence only when he began to perceive it as a *system* with a rational plan, a complex regularity, and a set of interrelated ideas and activities. For example, agriculture conceived as a set of cultural patterns could be reduced to elements and systematically analyzed by the same methods that had yielded new understanding of language, lineage relationships, child rearing, and other human activities. Practices and beliefs that in isolation seemed misguided or accidental took on form and meaning as their functional ties with environment, technology, and one another became clear. Malinowski (1935) traced the relationships of Trobriand coral gardens with a master ethnographer's skill. He was, however, chiefly interested in the "sociology of garden making" (56), and he admits in a concluding *mea culpa* (459) that he collected no quantitative or specialized botanical material. Thus he can make important social statements about magic organizing and timing native gardening but not about the material advantages in terms of environment and production of such regulation of the agricultural cycle. The production of a crop surplus makes possible an elaborate system of prestige giving, but it is a necessary rather than a sufficient condition.

Another factor stimulating anthropological investigations of agriculture was the damage done among native peoples by outside authorities who wished to bring about changes without reference to local environment or traditional practice. Richards (1939) saw in the Bemba *citimene* system of pollarding trees, burning branches, and planting crops in the ashes a viable adaptation to the dry woodlands of Central Africa. To misdirected administrative efforts to "improve" native agriculture and popular views of the Bemba as "unenterprising" and "lazy," the anthropologist countered a description of local techniques and skills coupled with explanations of nutrition, the effects of migrant labor, and historically acquired values opposing farm labor. She also noted that the European after thirty or forty years in the country had not discovered a better way of producing millet in the environment, or even anything as good (289). Richards outlined the anthropologist's contribution to the study of native agriculture as the provision of information on "the methods by which the people of a particular district produce their food, their economic motives, and the rules that govern the use of the land's resources" (289).

In more recent years a number of studies have appeared whose primary emphasis is on agriculture. Attention has been concentrated on shifting or swidden (slash and burn) cultivation because this means of exploiting the environment was little known in industrial countries and revealed a different but highly integrated equilibrium. The delicate adjustment of men to land, the evidences of system and order in agricultural production, went far to answer the charges of "experts" from the temperate climates that slash and burn cultivation was always wasteful and ultimately destructive. Conklin (1957) was able to show that an "integral" system of shifting cultivation in the Philippines both protected the soil while it was being cropped and meshed with natural regeneration cycles so well that no permanent harm was done to the land. The demonstration from Hanunoo vocabulary of the minute and precise categories into which subsistence farmers classify soils and useful plants showed the existence of a deep interest and understanding of the environment. Freeman (1955) discussed the skills involved in tree felling, burning, weeding, and reaping by the Iban of Borneo. The seemingly haphazard association of food crops in African Zande plots was shown by De Schlippe (1956) to fall into certain categories or "field types," each one corresponding to a named ecological variant of the local environment. His insistence on treating shifting agriculture as a rationally organized activity is seen in the use of the word "system" in the title of each of the book's parts.

All of these studies contain quantitative data on area cultivated, yields, and man-hours employed, thus providing objective standards of comparison. Each contains a considerable volume of detail that impresses the reader with "the great complexity which is typical of a technology at subsistence level" (De Schlippe 1956:99). It is interesting to note the scientific convergence implicit in the publishing of three works on shifting cultivation in successive years by scholars of different countries working in three separate areas and coming from the disciplines of social anthroplogy or practical agronomy.

These studies reflect only one aspect of the marked increase in anthropological attention to problems of human culture and its environment. Work in this area has been subsumed under the general heading of ecology, a term used in biology to designate the interrelations of living organisms and their environment (Odum 1959:4). Several useful papers summarize the intellectual background of ecology, the development of anthropological theory on environment, and recent contributions using ecological data (Bates 1953, Helm 1962, Geertz 1963, Vayda and Rappaport 1968). As Bates (1953) points out, ecology might well be regarded as a pervasive point of view rather than a special subject matter. Its growing popularity in anthropology stems perhaps from dissatisfaction with explanations couched solely in terms of culture or social structure and the desire to test hypotheses with quantifiable data. Programmatic statements of future research goals often include specific attention to man's bio-physical nature and his ecology (Wallace 1961, Gluckman 1963:38).

Steward (1937) early pointed out the difficulties in analyzing social institutions merely as the result of culture contact and diffusion. His alternative to trait collecting and historical speculation was the ecological approach:

An "explanation" of human behavior patterns explains in proportion as it traces determinants to ultimate sources. These determinants or factors are necessarily stated in different terms. Some are innate human drives, which, though overlaid and obscured by culture patterns, must sometimes be stated in psychological and even physiological terms. Some are more or less arbitrary behavior norms to be treated in terms of invention and borrowing. But both are adapted in varying ways and degrees to the requirements of existence in a particular natural environment. The adaptation must be stated in ecological terms. (Steward 1938:260)

Gray has noted that as anthropology looked beyond static structures and fixed configurations to questions of change and process, it became apparent that cultures are not closed systems (Gray and Gulliver 1964:11). In discussing evolution, Sahlins (1964) emphasizes that a culture is embedded in "fields of forces," and that ecology offers a new perspective by shifting attention to the "relation between inside and outside," the "interchange between culture and environment." It has been recognized that only an understanding of extracultural contexts could illuminate cultural persistence and alteration.

To characterize the nature of this investigation I prefer the term "cultural ecology." This neither denies the validity of a unified science of ecology nor asserts the notion of an autonomous science of culture (cf. Vayda and Rappaport 1968). Rather, it calls attention to (1) the unit of study as a culturally defined population of human beings, (2) the focus on cultural rather than physical adaptations, and (3) the direct debt in theory and method to Julian Steward who thus named the approach. I shall be concerned with standardized or institutionalized modes of socially transmitted behavior that are interdependent with features of the environment.

Man is obviously an animal who can be studied as an organism influenced genetically and physiologically by selective pressures from his surroundings. We might call this biologically oriented subdiscipline human ecology. Anthropologists can indeed achieve significant results by combining physical and cultural data, as in Livingstone's analysis (1958) linking the presence of malaria, the adaptive value of heterozygosity of the sickle cell gene, and the disturbance of the West African rain forest by shifting agriculture. Alland (1966) has suggested that "medical anthropology" should be developed as an approach to problems of this kind. A study that concentrates on culturally adaptive mechanisms and does not deal fully with physiologic factors is incomplete. I am aware, for instance, of potentially important environmental relations with disease among Nigerian populations, but I am not trained in this aspect of ecology and cannot now provide useful data on it. The material I shall present is a contribution toward the understanding of certain functionally related factors in the total ecology of the Kofyar. It is neither a complete ethnography nor an exhaustive statement of ecological relations. I have also avoided the use of concepts from biological ecology such as "food chain," "niche," or "succession." It is dangerous to reason by analogy from biology to the social sciences (Bartholomew and Birdsell 1953). A tribe is, after all, not a subspecies; invention is not the same as mutation. Though several scientific disciplines are concerned with the same universe of ecology, it is helpful to recognize that their starting points differ. The biologist works outward from communities of plants and animals, the cultural geographer begins with landscape or places (Febvre 1932:64; Sauer 1963:320), and the cultural anthropologist looks first to human groups for his material. The anthropologist's work has many acknowledged points of convergence, and encourages cooperation, but because of the scientific division of labor, neither his problems nor the relevant data for their solution will ever be identical with those of other sciences. The term cultural ecology reflects both the anthropological tools and the distinctly cultural approach used here.

The model I shall use in analyzing the cultural ecology of the Kofyar derives essentially from the writings of Julian Steward. The method was developed in important publications on the Indians of the Southwest and the Great Basin (1937, 1938) and given a more general theoretical formulation in the 1955 volume, *Theory of Culture Change*. Steward emphasized functionally related aspects of the environment, subsistence activities, and culture. For example, he demonstrated the connection of (1) dry climate and sparse, scattered occurrence of plants and animals with (2) a bow-spear-club hunting and seed gathering technology, and (3) low population density, nomadic movements, bilateral kinship organization, and the lack of exclusive territories. Perhaps the most significant characteristic of this approach, as Geertz (1963:6) points out, is its restriction to those aspects of both the natural setting and the local culture where interdependence is most explicit. Neither the total habitat nor the whole of culture is considered. The crucial features of the environment are those which directly affect man's subsistence quest or threaten his physical well-being. *What is rele-*

vant in the environment depends on man's devices for coping with it. Underground water or uranium were present but not part of the Paiute environment because devices for exploiting them, such as deep wells and atomic reactors, were not part of the cultural equipment of hunter-gatherers. On the other hand, the fact that grass seeds grew erratically in small clumps and required harvesting during a short period of ripeness was a central condition in the irregular wandering of families, the small size of their groups, and the absence of cooperation among female collectors. A change in either the key potentials of the environment or the existing methods of exploitation would create a situation in which different forms of organization would be adaptive. The "constellation of features which are most closely related to subsistence activities and economic arrangements" is called by Steward the "cultural core" (1955:37). He distinguishes the social, political, and religious patterns that are closely connected with subsistence from "secondary features" that are determined to a greater extent by purely historical factors.

Steward's formulation of cultural ecology has proved stimulating and influential in current anthropological thinking. This can be traced to its ready application to the data from specific societies, its emphasis on standards of proof, and its clear and logical procedures. Instead of looking at wide-ranging geographic and general evolutionary theories, he focuses on cultural adaptations to particular local environments.[2] He demands that the connections between a limited number of variables be "empirically determined." The implication is clear that various types of evidence including quantitative material should be submitted in support of ecological propositions. His statement of method is simple and direct:

. . . human ecology is not postulation of a general or novel theory. It is essentially a manner of stating a problem. The problem is first to ascertain what behavior patterns are required when a certain environment is exploited by certain economic devices. Second, how, if at all, such patterns affect other activities and institutions and the latitude

[2] For a strongly worded reaffirmation of this stand, see Steward 1965.

allowed them. In short, it entails an equation of culture process involving the interaction and mutual adaptation of both historically and
environmentally determined behavior (1938:260).

The crucial terms of the ecological equation appear to be
environment, exploitative techniques, and the cultural core.
I have (1965b) attempted to incorporate these terms in a
model suggesting the relation of environmental, technological, and social variables among the Kofyar (cf. Conklin
1961). In Figure 1, the outer ring of the diagram represents

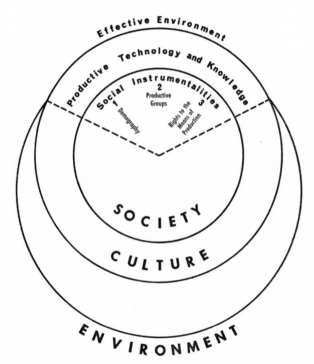

Fig. 1. A Trial Model of Cultural Ecology

the total environment of which certain features are *effective*
(in Steward's terms "relevant") as directly involved in man's
subsistence efforts. These environmental properties are significant for the process of maintaining life to the degree that
changing any one of them would have repercussions on the

cultural system (Wagner 1960:6). The variables may include not only climatic, edaphic, and biotic factors of the physical habitat but also the "intercultural environment" (Sahlins 1961), the influence of neighboring groups. As biologists have always emphasized, "living things are themselves part of the environment of other living things" (Sears 1957:8). Works by Barth (1956), Harding (1960), Oliver (1962), Lehman (1963), and Sahlins (1964) all stress the setting of societies in fields of cultural as well as natural influence. Helm suggests the comprehensive term *oecumene,* "comprehending not only space and habitat but the sociocultural resources and groups beyond the society but within its experiential field" (1962:633). Local resources and other human groups both call forth adaptive responses.

Some students may contend that processes of acculturation and social contact should not be included in discussions of the relations of man and physical environment. I would agree that there is a danger in indiscriminate piling up of presumably functional connections that may end by calling everything ecology. It will be useful, therefore, to restrict the intercultural environment to those factors which bear directly on the maintenance of life. Thus we might include the annexation by a neighboring group of agricultural land on the border, or a slave raid by the cavalry of a distant state. Military weapons, scarce natural resources, and craft specialization may all modify relations with an adjoining group and the resulting ecosystem. On the other hand, the benefits of new water conservation techniques or a more effective fishhook may spread through trade or migration. The diffusion of a cosmological idea or a feathered headdress, though possibly useful as an indicator of contact, would not figure directly in this analysis.

It is the culture's store of technology and knowledge that define the sphere of effective environment. A herd of elephants may represent desirable big game for hunters with appropriate weapons, a threat to the growing crops of agriculturalists, and a neutral or irrelevant part of the environment to fisher folk living in the same area. The traits of material culture and associated activities that fall into this category are those oriented toward production and protection. Means of securing subsistence, of providing warmth and shelter, of escaping floods or invasion are all included. Using a single method, stone walls may be built to support an agricultural terrace, to erect a permanent house, and to build a defensive barrier, thus meeting the requirements of survival as dictated by various sectors of the environment. The technological sector of the total culture that concerns us here embraces not only tools and their use but also knowledge of soil potential, plant characteristics, and construction techniques that are important in satisfying physiological needs. Other cultural traits such as designs for decorating pottery or spells used in love magic are not immediately related to ecological questions and may be omitted from consideration here.

The inner circle in Figure 1 represents society, or more properly social organization. I have called those institutions which appear to be ecologically adaptive *social instrumentalities*. This sector includes Steward's "cultural core," but it also suggests some order of priority, indicating which social factors are most frequently and most demonstrably related to the system of environment-cum-technology. We begin with the functionalist notion that "institutions are instrumentalities fulfilling certain ends" (Goldschmidt 1959:120) and focus on those institutions whose purpose is production or protection and which show most clearly the links of reciprocal influence with exploitative activities. For instance, the composition of a voluntary work group is more likely to be governed by standards of labor efficiency than that of a funeral party. The following factors seem to be regularly and instrumentally related to ecological considerations:

1. The size, density, and aggregation of the population.
2. The division of labor and the composition of productive groups.
3. The rights to the means of production.

The basic demography of a population should perhaps be regarded as a condition of other social institutions such as settlement pattern and community organization. The nature and extent of the sexual division of labor, occupational specialization, and cooperative production by households, lineages, secret societies, or *corvées* are included in the second category. Rights to the means of production refers to ownership or control of resources and capital goods. This might also be extended to cover systems of distribution and exchange, but I will touch on these only peripherally.[3]

There are certainly other potentially adaptive sociocultural variables that might be discussed. Goldschmidt (1959:150–180) considers the instrumental aspects of values, authority systems, and ideological development. I will mention possible influences in these areas among the Kofyar while suggesting that their functional relationships to the ecosystem are more speculative and less open to empirical test. It now appears possible to correlate certain attitudes and personality types with ecological factors (Edgerton 1965), but this requires cross-cultural data gathered under rigidly controlled conditions with a variety of psychological tests. I am stimulated by such research but painfully aware

[3] Most anthropological works on "primitive economy" are ethnographic descriptions of material culture and subsistence activities, as well as modes of exchange. There is certainly no precise line separating ecology and economics (with their shared stem meaning "household"), and the division that exists is largely an artifact of the division of labor between natural and social scientists (Bates 1961). Theoretically there is considerable overlap, as when the biologist sees man's economics as but a special case of the broader subject of ecology (Clarke 1954:2), while the economist includes both subsistence techniques and exchange in his definition of substantive economy (Polanyi 1953). My use of the term ecology is meant to emphasize the systematic interaction of specific environmental, cultural, and social factors and the process by which adaptation takes place. This centers principally on productive and protective activities. The emphasis is due partially to the fact that the self-sufficient Kofyar were traditionally little dependent on exchange, and large-scale market allocation is a recent innovation. Thus the starting point of the inquiry and the characteristics of Kofyar society largely determine the relative attention given in succeeding chapters to productive as opposed to distributive activity.

of the random nature of my own psychological observations and the dangers of inferring relations between subsistence type and character structure in the reports of others.

Steward points out that adaptation is most evident in the density and distribution of population, the roles of the sexes, family, and communal groups in productive activities, the territory occupied and exploited, and the size, composition and permanency of villages (1938:2). He also deals at length with the political direction of cooperative activities (1938:246) and the relation of rights in resources to the ecological situation (1938:235, 253, 254).[4] I will concentrate on the same aspects. Functionally, the variables of demography, productive groups, and rights to the means of production may be no more important or closely integrated than other cultural traits. Yet, within the ecosystem certain linkages seem to be more frequently present and more clearly defined. These relationships must be empirically demonstrated by various lines of evidence such as logical explanation of correlation, cross-cultural comparison, and historical change whenever this is possible. The investigator also has a responsibility to indicate the extent of inference in each case.

In seeking the instrumental role of certain institutions I am not suggesting that they are shaped solely in response to subsistence demands or that the same social factor viewed cross-culturally has in every case a similar ecological connection. Certainly the institutions that are found most widely are multifunctional, and their ubiquity alone points to a high degree of flexibility in purpose. If I discuss the household as a labor group, this does not minimize its role as a socializing mechanism or a group uniting in sacrifice to an ancestor. I wish merely to point out the probable selective advantages of certain social features under conditions laid down by a particular system of exploitation in one specific environment.

When ecological limits are plain and the relationship to

[4] It is also interesting to compare these factors with those discussed by Sauer in 1925 as the "cultural landscape" (Sauer 1963:342).

social instrumentalities is crucial, we may speak of *determinants*. In most instances, causality will appear circular, and we will be able to speak only of reciprocal influences and systematic interconnections (Vayda and Rappaport 1968). It must be emphasized that ecology examines the dynamic interrelations of organisms in a biotic community. As energy is transferred from unit to unit and material is taken up and discharged, no single factor can be seen as fixed or stable. For example, annual burning by man has probably contributed to the creation of savanna grassland in many parts of Africa whose natural climax vegetation would be dry forest. The loss of tree cover may bring about changes in soil composition, ground temperature, evaporation, wind, and precipitation (Stewart 1954). This in turn may make a formerly arable area less suited for crops and better adapted to herding (Dale and Carter 1955). Because of an environmental change that they themselves have set in motion, local agriculturalists must then either emphasize stock raising or give up their land to better adapted pastoralists. A climatic pattern of increasing desiccation might produce the same effects of cultural succession. Functional linkage shows itself in correlated environmental, technological, and social changes that may in theory begin anywhere in the system, evoking adjustment and readaptation among other elements.

The method of cultural ecology has been used with conspicuous success in studying peoples with a simple technology whose dependence on their environment is immediate and compelling. Steward's own examples come from family-level food collectors in the Great Basin, patrilineal band hunters of nonmigratory game, and composite band bison hunters (1955). Detailed studies in the relation of California Indian populations to resources of fish, acorns, and game (Baumhoff 1963), and of the shift to bison hunting by Plains tribes with accompanying common development of mobility, emphasis on war, and status based on the horse (Oliver 1962) have indicated the value of comparative ecological analysis of existing data. It is perhaps less obvious that the ecological approach will yield equally useful results when applied to agricultural societies.[5] Steward was not particularly optimistic about the possibilities in this direction: "When . . . ecology allowed latitude in subsistence activities, non-economic factors such as warfare, festivals, ceremonies, etc., became determinants of sociopolitical patterns" (1938:257). My purpose in this monograph is to pose ecological questions in the context of a traditional, self-sufficient society with relatively efficient agricultural techniques. Does the increased material security and greater population of such a group mean that more aspects of culture are historically borrowed and that social organization may be understood as a self-contained, relatively independent system? Or are certain institutions still closely tied to subsistence and defensive requirements and subject to rapid adaptive pressure in situations of change?

I have not attempted here to extend conclusions from Kofyar ecology to a cross-cultural sample of intensive cultivators or even to neighboring tribal groups in Nigeria. I regard such comparative material as extremely useful, but in most cases the relevant variables are not adequately documented, especially as regards quantitative material. The relationship of environment, technology, and social instrumentalities is complex, and even the more convincing hypotheses such as the nonmigratory game, bow-spear-club, and patrilineal band linkage have a way of disintegrating in light of more complete data.[6] For example, it would seem at first glance that hoe agriculture and a common set of cultigens are characteristic of all the tribes of subsistence farmers occupying a single environmental zone on the southern margin of the Jos Plateau. The striking cultural diversity among these groups would then be explained by nonecological factors. Yet when one walks through what appears to be a homogeneous area

---

[5] Beardsley (1964) has raised this issue in reference to historical and ecological interpretations of community life in a national society.

[6] Citations in Vayda and Rappaport 1968.

on the map, the variations in microenvironment are marked. Oil palms yield suddenly to long grass or silk cotton trees. Waterlogged alluvium occurs alongside volcanic slopes. Annual precipitation differs significantly between two spots a thousand yards apart. Even preliminary investigations indicate that various methods of agricultural production are possible with the same tools and crops, and that these methods have differing requirements for the spatial and cooperative organization of population. Therefore, I have avoided generalizations and offer merely a case study of a particular adaptation in the hope that others may find the data of comparative value or may themselves refine and apply the suggested approach with greater rigor and precision.

Functional relationships are often imputed by anthropologists but seldom demonstrated on a sound empirical basis (Kopytoff 1964, Collins 1964). Frequently the investigator describes a case of covariation and then "explains" the interdependence of the covarying factors in a plausible manner. While recognizing the difficulty of conclusively proving that given elements of environment, technology, and social organization interact as part of an ecosystem, I believe that functional relationships may be more convincingly inferred when several lines of evidence point in the same direction. Such potentially converging types of evidence are (1) a synchronic description of two or more factors in the same society that appear to interact in a regular, logically explicable manner, (2) a cross-cultural comparison of the same factors operating in contemporary societies, (3) a historic sequence charting the interaction of the factors through time. Functional connection can be postulated if a change in one factor of a system regularly coincides with change in another factor in such a way that their interaction appears to be purposeful. Thus the linkage of two variables may be suggested by the analysis of a single ethnographic case, but unless the variables may be altered in some controlled manner, either comparatively in separate cases or diachronically through historical means, the relationship remains hypothetical.

All these methods have been used by anthropologists in pointing out functional relationships in an ecological context, but, for want of adequate data, it has seldom been possible to combine them. The first approach involving description of synchronically correlated factors, especially those of environment and subsistence system, is evident in a number of recent studies (Conklin 1957, De Schlippe 1956, Carneiro 1961, Gulliver 1955). This same method is frequently extended to suggest links with territoriality (Hallowell 1949), division of labor (Freeman 1955), group size (Steward 1938), nomadic movements (Barth 1961), household composition (Stenning 1958), trade (Gluckman 1941), and political systems (Krader 1955, Wittfogel 1956). Cross-cultural comparison has been particularly effective in demonstrating adaptive social patterns with varying habitats and technological arrangements (Lattimore 1940, Eggan 1954, Murphy and Steward 1956). Variations within basically similar culture patterns which represent adjustments to local differences in wild food potential (Steward 1938), soil fertility (Scudder 1962), available building sites (Nicholas 1963), or seasonal climatic changes (Evans-Pritchard 1940) have also been well documented. Sound sources for charting historic changes in environment, in an exploitation system, or in both are rare, but valuable inferences can be made from archaeology (Wedel 1941), local traditions (Linton 1936:348–354), tribal distributions and origins (Oliver 1962), and colonial archives (Geertz 1963).

Perhaps the most useful studies of cultural ecology are those that combine a full synchronic description of an ecosystem with historical and comparative data indicating the way in which it came to be and the relative adaptive value of its elements. Using the concept of niche from animal ecology, Barth (1956) has shown that the relations of ethnic groups in North Pakistan depend both on the correspondence of particular cultures to natural areas exploited and on competition through time leading either to replacement or symbiosis. Where two groups use available resources with equal efficiency, one group's military strength may determine the occupation of land, and historical factors may thus necessitate readjustment of the ecosystem. Goldschmidt and his colleagues in the Culture and Ecology in East Africa Project (1965) appear to have focused not only on the contemporary functional integration of crucial factors in the environment, economic exploitation, and social institutions but also on the historical effects of contact on adaptation (Winans 1965a). Their method has been a broadly based comparison with factors of linguistic group, tribe, and subsistence type carefully controlled.

To the extent that my data allow, I will follow this approach to cultural ecology, using ethnographic description, functional analysis, comparison among contemporary cultures, and changes through time. This means that a complete ethnography of the Kofyar is not intended, and ethnographic material is included only in so far as it appears relevant to ecological problems. I have devoted particular attention to the physical and cultural environment, the techniques of intensive hill agriculture, the relation of this subsistence system to demography, productive groups, land tenure, and certain other institutions, and to the patterns of change accompanying migratory cash-crop farming. The data are not well balanced in quantity or of equal authority throughout. I did not have a carefully thought out plan of ecological study when I entered the field, and my findings came piecemeal in response to the elementary questions of why people lived where they do, what they did with their time, and how they got enough to eat. Many of my conclusions came in the analysis of quantitative material after leaving the field. I am aware that the professional geographer, climatologist, and botanist may find shortcomings in the environmental data. I must take refuge in my lack of specialized training in these fields and admit that I failed to recognize the value of precise observations of rainfall, plant associations, and soil types until late in my work. Government statistics and reports have been of little use because recording stations are distant and official visits to Kofyar country are rare. The Jos Plateau escarpment also shows a significant range of climatic factors within a small area. The paucity of comparative data will, it is hoped, be remedied by projected studies of neighbors of the Kofyar. Almost all cross-cultural data obtained in the study were the result of random inquiries, and only the internal contrast of hill and migrant Kofyar populations has substantial documentation. Documentary material of some historical depth will probably never be available for the Kofyar because of the past isolation of the area and its infrequent contacts with the Hausa kingdoms. We may hope that archaeological sampling will someday give us an idea of the age of individual settlements and the development of local traditions in the area. Fortunately, changes within the sixty years since British conquest of the Kofyar have been dramatic and important. Administrative records and living informants are both useful sources of this information. Even short-range descriptions of altered farming methods, economic goals, and social groupings can cast light on the processes of ecological adjustment.

Although, I have always been critical of anthropological works that dehumanized their subjects in order to make points of scientific interest, I find that in trying to deal with selected features of culture and society in a concise and meaningful manner, I have been guilty of this failing. For farms have been substituted land areas and yield figures. People are inadequately impersonated by property-owning, manually skilled creatures who combine to invest labor so that they may consume. The living Kofyar in the gaiety of a *koem* flute dance, in the hunt's excitement, in the solemnity of divination and sacrifice, in the taut atmosphere of a witch-craft accusation would never recognize the mechanical, bloodless apparitions I have portrayed. The rich fabric of culture demands a fuller treatment, which I look forward in time to providing. In the meantime, I offer this account of a signal achievement, the development of a unique and highly productive intensive agriculture, based on sound technology, supported by adaptive social institutions, and capable of transformation to fit new environments and different social goals.

2

The Environment

Location

THE KOFYAR PEOPLES live on the southern fringe of the Jos
Plateau in the Northern Region of Nigeria. They are usually
classified with Angas, Sura, Birom and other Plateau peoples
simply as "hill pagans," and in ethnographic notes they are
variously referred to as Kwolla, Dimmuk, and Mirriam. Traditionally the Kofyar practiced subsistence cultivation in a
territory of some 200 square miles. They numbered about
70,000 in 1963. The Plateau is a boot-shaped highland area
with its sole roughly paralleling the Benue River about
eighty miles to the south. The provincial headquarters and
trading center for the entire area is Jos, a European-created
city with a population of over 30,000. Because of its central
position and the needs of its tin-mining industry, Jos is a hub
of communications with rail connections to the cities of
Lagos, Port Harcourt, and Kano, and motor roads radiating
west, south, and east. On the Plateau itself a good system of
all-weather roads reaches across the high grasslands, but most
of these end at the edge of the escarpment. Only one quite
recently constructed road makes its precipitous way down the
southern and steepest flank of these uplands. Lowland Divi-

26

sion, the southeastern section of Plateau Province, looks toward Jos because of this road link and has little important contact with the Benue Valley and the Eastern Region. In 1967 Plateau Province became a part of the newly created Benue-Plateau State.

Except for the northernmost group of hill villages, all of the Kofyar are established in Lowland Division. Their territory, lying a little to the east of the geographical center of Nigeria, is a section of about twenty miles in length by ten in width, intersected by latitude 9°N and longitude 9°15′E (see map, Fig. 2).

It is roughly bounded on the west by the River Li and on the east by the Shemankar. It can be reached by a dry season road branching from the main Jos-Shendam road at Dokan Tofa and crossing a tributary of the Shemankar. This enters Kofyar country at Dokan Kasuwa (Doka) and there connects with a north-south road along the foot of the hills linking Kwang, Kwa, and Dimmuk. Unbroken plainland sweeps south from Dimmuk, and the road leaves traditional Kofyar territory at Kwalla. South of this point at Kurgwi an east-west road passes from Shendam to Namu and Lafia.

Geology and Topography

The Jos Plateau is geologically representative of the Pre-Cambrian Basement Complex, the ancient group of crystalline rocks which form part of the main African continental mass (Buchanan and Pugh 1955:1). Its surface has been identified with Gondwana and may be regarded as a remnant of the oldest surface found in the continent. The Younger Granites of which the Plateau is largely composed are particularly resistant, and the impressive surrounding scarps are evidence of erosion rather than faulting (Buchanan and Pugh 1955:18). The surface of the Plateau is tipped so that from an average altitude of 4,000 feet above sea level, it rises to some 4,400 feet on its southern margin. The fact that the northern part of the Plateau tails off into the high plains of Hausaland while the southern edge descends ab-

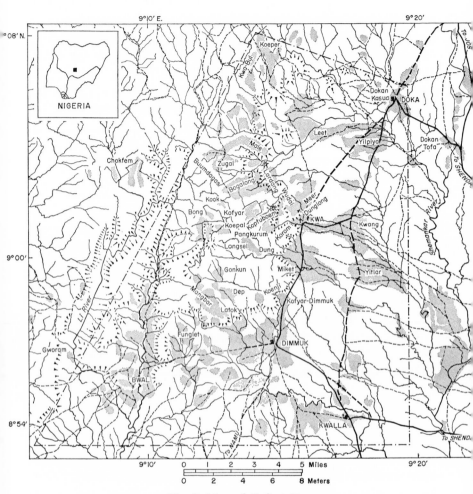

Fig. 2. Map of Kofyar Country

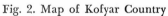

= settled areas

= edge of the escarpment

— = roads

━ ━ ━ = tracks

········· = paths

·—··—··—· = approximate boundary of Kofyar territory

ruptly to the Benue Trough also contributes to the impos-
ing aspect of the 1,400- to 2,000-foot southern escarpment.
At intervals, rising from the rolling grassy plains or among
the tumbled hills of bare rock, are the craters and flows
remaining from a period of volcanic activity.

No map is yet available that gives an accurate picture of
the topography of that part of the Plateau which borders and
then slices into Lowland Division. The major feature of this
area is a series of short ranges or buttress ridges stretching
south from the main body of the Plateau. They are divided
from each other by the broad valleys of the Shemankar and
the Li and the narrow V-shaped valleys of their tributaries.
Though the tops of the ridges are a little lower than the
Plateau surface, they do not fall off gradually to the plain
but preserve the rugged contours of the scarp. Thus the open
plain rises gently for over twenty miles from Shendam, at 900
feet, northwest to Kwa, at 1,500 feet. Immediately above is a
ridge with a 3,000-foot crest less than a mile from Kwa.
Settlements tend to cluster either on the plain proper or on
the hilltops, but a few hamlets cling to the less abrupt slopes
of the escarpment itself. Each major ridge system projecting
fingerlike from the uplands has its own tribal grouping,
the Tal-Montol, the Kofyar, and the Chokfem Sura, each
bounded by a stream bed and tending to expand southward
rather than laterally to the east or west.

The Kofyar country includes both a main ridge fifteen
miles long and five miles wide, seamed transversely by east-
ward-flowing streams, and a narrow belt of plainland extending three to four miles west and south from the base of the
ridge. The ridge is capped by the four-hundred-foot cone of
Moelaar (Bong Peak), the basalt plug or core of a volcano
whose crater is no longer visible. Volcanic boulders are
strewn about on the ridge's southern slope in the Latok area,
and small twin punchbowl craters are visible against the
edge of the hills on either side of Lardang village. Lava flows
from these volcanoes of recent age are clearly demarcated by
continuous heaps of pitted black rocks and red soil stretch-

ing eastward across the plain. Perennial streams fed by cold springs high in the hills follow rocky courses down to the plain, where they wind through wide sandy beds. The plains streams, especially the Shemankar, may rise suddenly with rains on the Plateau, and at times during the wet season fording is dangerous. Projected bridges have not yet been completed, and motor vehicles cannot enter the area for about five months during the year. During the rainless months, many of the smaller plains streams dry up completely, and water must be carried considerable distances from remaining pools and sinks.

Soils

Soils resulting from the weathering of granites and quartzites in the Kofyar hills are immature, having a relatively high mineral nutrient status because of the presence of decomposing rock fragments. Though rocky outcroppings and the thin, pebbly covering of some slopes make the area appear infertile, the soils are actually richer than the more mature soils of the plains, and local pockets among the rocks may be deeper also.[1] The color and texture of soil may indicate both its origin and its use by man. The prevailing color is tan or light brown when dry. In moist or swampy areas that support dense vegetation, it becomes darker in color, indicating the presence of humus. Soil that has been regularly composted for agricultural purposes is also of a darker brown. Areas of old lava flows show up plainly in reddish oxidized soil. This earth of volcanic origin becomes heavy and gluey when wet and very hard when dry. It is generally considered by the local farmers to be less productive than the tan soil. Agriculturists have described the heavy basalt soil around Dimmuk as of a "sticky, impervious nature." There are pockets of yellow clay present in the area which is used for pottery making, and some stream beds show the presence of a red pigment that is collected and used for body painting.

[1] James Jackson, personal communication.

Land cultivated with no accompanying restoration of organic materials becomes progressively lighter in color and sandier in texture. Worked-out soil is referred to by the Kofyar as *piya,* or white, and is said to be more granular than earth suitable for farming. Such soil has been largely leached of nutritive elements by water. The virgin area to the south around Namu has soil that is both reddish and sandy, though with considerable fertility. The sandy quality and the absence of rocks make it easily worked. Because of native soil conservation techniques, there is no large-scale erosion in either hills or plains, whereas the Garram Valley, thirty miles to the northeast, is riddled with deep gullies.

Temperature and Precipitation

The seasons in the Plateau area are well marked in terms of rainfall and wind direction. Throughout the winter months the harmattan blows out of the northeast. In December and January it often is quite strong, and wind-borne dust from the Sahara darkens the sky and blots out distant prospects. The Tropical Continental air mass which is then the controlling climatic factor is very dry, and from November into March there is negligible rainfall. The southern edge of the Plateau corresponds roughly with the division between predominantly four- and five-month dry seasons (Pullam 1962). Temperatures increase toward the end of the dry season. During 1961 the hottest month was February, with noon temperatures in Dimmuk averaging 93.2° F. The wet southwest winds from the ocean begin to be felt in Northern Nigeria in April with the northward movement of the Intertropical Front (Buchanan and Pugh 1955:21). The Kofyar remark on the moister air that "softens the skin." Almost all of the average 40 to 60 inches of rainfall come in the six months of April through October. Days of rain and overcast skies may be cool to the point of chilliness. Noon temperatures at Dimmuk averaged between 80° and 85° from June through September, and the 1961 mean for July was 79.3°.

There are appreciable climatic differences even within the

restricted Kofyar area. During the dry season, when the noon temperatures on the plains average 89.5° F., with a range from 80° to 97°, the hills are noticeably cooler and are seldom lacking a breeze. As a general rule, mean maximum temperatures fall by approximately 4° F. per thousand feet of altitude (Buchanan and Pugh 1955:30). The diurnal range of temperature in the hills is such that for most of the year, comfortable sleeping demands a covering of three

TABLE 1

KWA MONTHLY RAINFALL, 1962–63 *

	1962	1963
January	. . .	. . .
February	. . .	. . .
March	1.9	2.4
April	3.2	3.6
May	5.65	3.44
June	6.3	4.6
July	6.3	6.4
August	18.54	16.74
September	12.56	8.47
October	8.72	10.9
November	2.5	. . .
December	. . .	. . .
Total	65.67	56.55

* The Reverend Frank Meehan, Société des Missions Africaines, who kindly made these figures available, suggested that the 1963 figures were less accurate than those for 1962.

thicknesses of blanket. Night readings in the cooler months may drop below 50° F. Though specific data are lacking, it may be that the lower temperatures of the hills contribute to the maintenance of the humus content of the soil. The critical temperature at which humus remains constant is about 77° F., while higher temperatures bring progressive deterioration (Phillips 1959:243).

It is generally stated by the Kofyar that the hills have a more dependable and larger supply of rain than the plains.

There are no satisfactory records from the hills for comparison with those gathered by plains mission schools, but crop failures due to drought seem to be more frequent on the plains. During 1961, rainfall at the plains village of Kwa totaled 45.53 inches, ranging from a single peak high of 9.73, in July, to an October low of 4.79. Records from Dimmuk, five miles away on the plain, are incomplete, but there was a significant difference in early rains, Kwa having 11.33 inches during April and May, while Dimmuk got only 2.05. Monthly precipitation rates for Kwa in 1962–63 are given in Table 1.

During an eighty-day period of June–August, 1961, Bong, in the hills, received approximately 27 inches of rain by my count, compared to Kwa's 18.24. The larger precipitation in the hills is easily explained as the result of warm moist air being forced suddenly to rise and cool as the south winds encounter the plateau escarpment. The sheltered, well-watered, high valleys have abundant oil palms which are entirely lacking on the plateau uplands. Differences in rainfall are even noted among hill villages, with those such as Bong, perched directly above a steep incline in the path of the southwest wind, having more showers and frequent fogs, to the point at which basic farming patterns must be modified. Distribution of rain is markedly localized, and the time of first planting, which depends on a thorough drenching of the fields, may differ by several weeks in villages only a few miles apart.

Vegetation and Wild Animal Life

The borders of the Plateau and the immediately adjoining plainlands are classed as Northern Guinea Savanna, though the vegetation picture is complicated by locally higher rainfall, immature soils, and partial localized natural fire protection afforded by rock outcrops. The marker tree for this zone is the *Isoberlinea doka,* but *Vitex doniana, Lannea schimperi,* and *Uapaca somon* are more general in occurrence. Along streams are *Sysygium guineense* and *Berlinea,* with its white flowers.[2] South of the hills, in the Namu-Kwande-Kurgwi area, the forest is of the Southern Guinea type (Buchanan and Pugh 1955:35). In Phillips' typology (1959:177), most of Kofyar country would be rated sub-humid wooded savanna of the less luxuriant type. It is normally characterized by the releafing of the trees, which are largely deciduous, and the sprouting of grasses in the hot February–April period before the rains.

Though the Kofyar area climax vegetation may have been a continuous cover of broad-leafed species, long-continued agricultural use has turned much of the area around villages into open grassland. Annual burnings are probably not the cause of this treeless condition, since savanna trees are all fire tolerant to varying degrees. Intensive farming with short fallow periods and persistent firewood collection are the practices which prevent regeneration of tree growth. On fallow hill lands that have not been severely degraded by farming, a tree growth of fifteen to twenty-five feet in height may appear in the time of about twenty years.. Small sacred groves, which are never farmed, have dense thickets with a few tall trees. Stories of the original settlement of the hills often refer to an ancestral hunter or magical practitioner seeking out a "forest" in which to settle, and it is probable that the well-watered areas with soil deep enough to support substantial tree growth made excellent village sites.

The trees that continue to flourish in the Kofyar countryside are almost all economically useful species growing in tilled areas that are safe from fire. These include the oil and fan palms, the canarium, the locust bean, the papaya, the mango, all of which bear edible fruit, and trees of the fig genus (*Ficus*) which provide a rapid growth of straight poles for building purposes, as well as leafy branches for dry season fodder. Inhabited areas in both fields and plains are easily distinguished from a distance as parklike areas surrounded by grassland. Some of the useful trees are planted and then

[2] Mr. Humphrey Wimbush and Mr. James Jackson of the Northern Nigerian Forestry Division kindly furnished this information.

protected from domestic animals with fences. On the high
Plateau, where rainfall is lighter and farming has been
heavy, the rolling grasslands show hardly a trace of remaining tree growth.

Large tracts of sparsely inhabited bush lands adjoin Kofyar country in the eastern hills and on the plains to the
south, so that a great many different kinds of wild animals
are still to be found. Although a few men now possess muz-
zle-loading smooth-bore guns, most hunting is still conducted
relatively inefficiently by large groups of men armed with
spears and clubs and accompanied by dogs. Larger and more
valued game, such as bush cow (a type of dwarf buffalo) and
leopard, may have suffered somewhat from the inroads of
Tiv and Hausa hunters from outside the area. Elephant,
wart hog, hippopotamus, and hyena are rare, being encoun-
tered only on distant plains bush farms. From picture books
of Nigerian wildlife (Thistleton 1960, Booth 1960), hill
villagers were able to identify some forty-five mammalian
species. The most usual type of game killed on communal
hunts is antelope, ranging from the kob and reedbuck down
to the abundant duiker. Bush rats and mongooses of various
species are eagerly pursued along with genets, civets, and
squirrels. The red river hog is a hunting prize. Baboons,
patas monkeys, and the small green monkey are serious pests
during the period when crops mature. Bush and guinea fowl
are found in the hills, and almost all the common Nigerian
birds (Elgood 1960) are known. Snakes include the python
and such poisonous species as the puff adder, the spitting
cobra, and the carpet viper (Cansdale 1961).

The Kofyar and Their Neighbors:
Cultural Clines and Boundaries

To speak of the Kofyar peoples is to create an abstraction
from observed fact. The term is not used either by the people
themselves or by the government. Neither modern boundaries nor traditional divisions reflect the unity of this group. It
is quite certain that no single political entity ever embraced

more than a small portion of the Kofyar. Yet it is possible for the observer to distinguish these people from their neighbors and treat them as a single cultural group, even though in some cases the lines cannot be precisely drawn (see map, Fig. 3). Goody faced a similar problem in delimiting the peoples he called LoDagaba, and I will follow his usage by designating the Kofyar as "the inhabitants of a sociogeographic region of relative cultural uniformity which is recognized by the actors, though not directly by means of a "tribal" name . . ." (1957:97).

Perhaps the first indicator of the existence of a community is the sharing of a common language which can be grouped with Hausa in the Chad branch of the Afro-Asiatic family (Greenberg 1955). I call this language simply Kofyar. It is sometimes referred to as Mernyang, but that name more properly includes only the speech of the plains villages Kwa, Kwang, and Miket, and, by extension, the villages of Kofyar, Lardang, and Bogalong in the hills. To the Goemai, the neighboring, tongue is *lifwo pang*, the hill speech. Many Kofyar, when asked what language they speak will reply simply *lifwo lu mu*, "the speech of our house." They are also quick to point out dialectal variations within their own area. These consist mainly of differences in vocabulary and slight changes in the quality of certain vowels. Thus the people of Bong have a small but perceptible difference in dialect from Kofyar three miles to the east, and a slightly larger difference from Latok three miles to the south. Other minor but constant differences obtain in the villages to the north. Yet all of these groupings occupy a continuous hill tract and have a long history of intermarriage. Certain traits of speech are shared by plains communities and the adjoining hill villages, while other linguistic elements separate hill and plains. Despite these differences, and though the evidence of an exhaustive survey of linguistic geography is lacking, my impression is that the differences are greater between Kofyar and neighboring speech communities than within it.

Linguistic variation across "tribal" lines must be viewed as

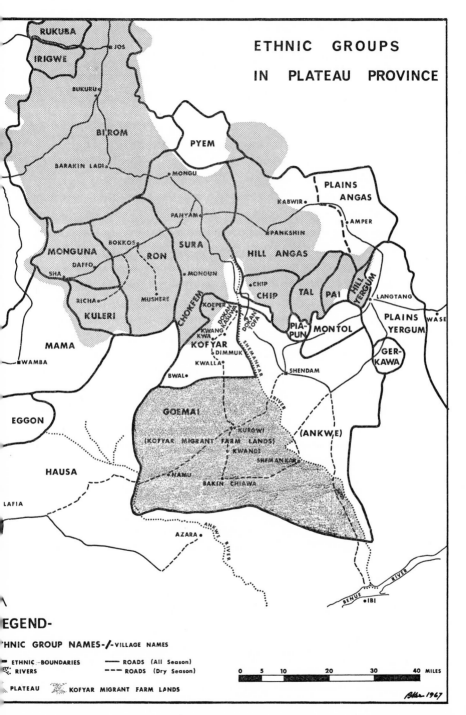

Fig. 3

a matter of dialect in most cases. The languages of the Chip to the north across the Shemankar, of the small Koenoem or Kanam group south of Chip, and of the Goemai (also called Kemai or Ankwe) who live next to the Kofyar along their entire eastern and southern borders, are all mutually intelligible. An inspection of a Goemai dictionary showed that at least 50 per cent of the words were identical with Kofyar and a great many more were easily recognizable cognates. In short, the differences are no more than would be expected from the partial isolation caused by the Shemankar River and by substantial uninhabited bush lands to the south, but they are greater than those found within the contiguous territory of the Kofyar. To the northwest, a deep valley with a tributary of the Dep separates the Kofyar from the Chokfem branch of the Sura people. Still farther to the west in the Dep Valley proper is a village cluster called Teng whose affinities also appear to be to the Sura. Again in both these cases, the differences from Kofyar is dialectal, since a large part of basic vocabulary is shared. A recently published word list of Sura (Jungraithmayr 1964) could with a few alterations serve as a beginning dictionary of Kofyar, and they are not usefully classed as spearate languages (Jungraithmayr, personal communication). The most noticeable distinguishing characteristic is a system of intonation whose exaggerated swings are imitated by the Kofyar when they wish to mimic their neighbors. The Sura are a large high plateau group, and the southern Sura village of Mpoen adjoins the northernmost Kofyar village of Koeper. Though I have never visited this area, reports suggest that this is again a zone of gradual dialect shift with no striking discontinuities. Even the Angas to the northeast, who have no common border with the Kofyar, have a demonstrable ability to understand a fair amount of the language on first exposure. A much more clearly marked linguistic boundary is found in the tier of tribes to the east of Koenoem and Chip and north of Goemai. The Tal, Piapun, and Montol speak languages which bear unmistakable Chadic affinities but are unintelligible to the Kofyar. Farther to the northwest, the Ron languages including Fyer, Daffo, Bokkos, Sha, and Kulere appear radically dissimilar to Kofyar. Their classification in the past was somewhat unclear, but Jungraithmayr (personal communication) now believes that they represent an older stage of the chadohamitic languages on the Plateau than the Angas-Sura group. The picture, then, is one of a gray area of dialectal variation surrounding the Kofyar, followed by a zone of clear-cut language differentiation at a greater distance.

Since the intergrading of dialect areas gives only a general picture of Kofyar boundaries, more specific indicators may be sought in cultural differences. These stand out against a background of shared systems of kin terminology, patrilineal lineage organization, and ceremonial emphasis on a funeral commemoration rite. A sharp alteration in family organization, dress, architecture, and farming methods is apparent between the Kofyar and the Chokfem. Whereas the Kofyar live in nuclear family homesteads and seldom have even two adult married couples in the same homestead, the Chokfem show a decided preference for the large extended family household with brothers and frequently more distant male relatives bringing their wives to live in the paternal compound. The mean household size of nine compounds in one Chokfem village is 14.8 individuals, compared to averages of 3.2, 5.2, and 7.1 in three Kofyar hill villages. Chokfem dress consists of the woven palm leaf penis sheath and a diminutive G string for women, contrasting with the traditional loincloth and leaf covering used in Kofyar. Houses, especially granaries, tend to be higher and narrower in Chokfem than their Kofyar counterparts, and the Chokfem use the lower part of the woman's house as a goat stable. The Chokfem do not pen their animals during the wet season to collect manure and compost for their fields, and they do not prune their oil palm trees. These differences are recognized and frequently form a topic for bantering conversation among members of the two groups.

Cultural contrasts between Kofyar and Chokfem remain clearly defined despite easy communication and a variety of contacts. The raiding that characterized traditional relations was seemingly no greater than that among Kofyar villages themselves, and the same can be said of contemporary acts of thievery. Trade appears to have been continuous, with salt passing to the Chokfem in return for iron. Little pottery is made in hill Chokfem villages, and Kofyar women exchange their wares for vegetables or money. I am not sure of the extent of ceremonial contact, but at least one Kofyar clan claims members in Chokfem and celebrates a hunting ritual there. A few Chokfem males have been adopted as boys into Kofyar villages. The strength of the geographical and ethnic divisions between the two groups is most clearly reflected in an explicit unwillingness on the part of each to intermarry with the other. Kofyar genealogical records indicate very few such marriages even in border communities.

Cultural differences of Kofyar and Goemai are of another order but are also obvious, primarily in settlement pattern, political organization, and ceremonial observance. The typical Goemai settlement is the compact nucleated village with large extended family compounds ranged side by side along a street. Each compound is fenced with *zana* mats or a mud wall in the manner of Hausa households. Fields may be at some distance from the village and are farmed by a system of shifting fallows. The distinctive Kofyar pattern requires that every homestead be surrounded by its own intensively cultivated field which provides a major part of the household's subsistence (Plate IA). Villages tend to be extensive, with homesteads evenly dispersed throughout the arable area (Plate IB). Whereas the Goemai have a complex hierarchy of titled officials, the Kofyar have usually only a chief and his assistant with perhaps a few named lineage heads. Only in those areas such as Dokan Kasuwa, Kwang, and Kwalla, where the Goemai had direct contact with the Kofyar and formerly exercised some form of political domination, have some of the titled offices been instituted. The characteristic

Goemai dance of masked and costumed figures accompanied by a female chorus is not practiced by the Kofyar and has been taken up only recently by Dokan Kasuwa, which contains many people from the Jorto group, a Goemai outlier.

A positive bond shared by the Kofyar is their common myth of origin. The story deals with an ancient cataclysm in which all people of the earth were destroyed except for a man named Kofyar and his sister, who took refuge in a rock shelter on the great Chor promontory. Kofyar's offspring founded the hill village of the same name and from there spread out to populate the rest of the hill range and immediately adjoining plains. All the clans can trace their descent to Kofyar and can give the history of the various movements which brought them to their present location. This relationship continued to be recognized, even though no unified government was ever established, and warfare in precontact times was chiefly between villages.

When the country was being brought under British administration in the early years of the twentieth century, dealings were largely with the chiefs of "tribes" which might more accurately have been termed village areas. Ames's *Gazetteer of Plateau Province* (1934) cites these peoples under the headings Dimmuk, Mirriam (Mernyang), Kwalla, Doka, Koffyer, and Jepal. The first divisional headquarters established in the area was at Kwalla, and the people are sometimes referred to collectively as the Kwall or Kwolla (Fitzpatrick 1910). In fact, the individual plains village areas or districts did have a degree of internal unity, and the hill settlements which were put under their supervision had frequently had a previous relationship of military alliance with them. Though court is now held and taxes are collected only in the larger plains villages, and the chief occupies the position of district head, a considerable degree of local political autonomy remains. Local residents still give only the name of their village when asked what people they are, and they stoutly maintain both to strangers and to neighboring peoples that they have no over-all tribal name such as do the

Hausa, the Fulani, the Tiv, or the Yoruba. No tribute or tax was formerly paid, and beyond the village the only political integration involved occasional voluntary military cooperation.

In recent years, a portion of the Kofyar grouped themselves together at government urging into a Sub-Native Authority known as the Koffiyer Federation. They acknowledged common origin and other cultural ties, but they chose no paramount chief. Because of local rivalries and traditional political relationships to the Goemai, the Kofyar-descended peoples of Dokan Kasuwa, Kwang, and Kwalla preferred to remain under the Shendam Sub-Native Authority. The Koffiyer Federation currently includes the Dimmuk and Kwa districts as well as the plains towns of Namu and Jak, which figure in the origin myth but whose present settlement pattern, language, and political and ceremonial organization are clearly Goemai. For this reason, I have not included the latter towns with the Kofyar.

The Bwal people living in a river valley west of Dimmuk claim descent from Chokfem (Pes) and are not federation members, but their language and customs bear such a close resemblance to Kofyar that I believe they should be grouped together. The Jorto are said to have come down from the Garram Valley in the same migration that took the Goemai to their present territory. Their cultural affinities are not clear, but they appear to be closer to the Goemai and Koenoem than to Kofyar. Perhaps the hardest area to assign is that of Kwalla. It was here that people who came down from the Kofyar hills met Goemai settlers from the south and east. The Kofyar seem to have remained generally north of the present town in the villages of Chim, Yitlar, and Kopfogom, while the Goemai built a nucleated settlement at Mudaa. Continued hostility of the two sections and conflicts over the chiefship reflect the diverse origins. Since I lack information on the proportion of the population that is Goemai and the amount of land they occupy, I have been compelled to include the complete village area and all its people in the

Kofyar group for demographic purposes. The grouping of Kwa, Doka, Kwang, Dimmuk, Kwalla, Bwal, and the hill communities from Koeper to Latok does have a certain validity in the minds of the people. When asked about these villages, they say "we are all one together" (*mun a wu kume koe shak*), but for each neighboring people they have a distinctive collective name.

The Intercultural Environment

Two salient questions present themselves when we consider Kofyar cultural ecology. One concerns how these people subsist in the environment in which they live today. Most of the following chapters will be devoted to answering this. There is, however, the prior question of *why* they live where they do. A satisfactory answer requires some historical knowledge about the contacts of populations and cultures in Northern Nigeria, and such information for this area is almost nonexistent. Let us assume, in the first place, that there is a compelling reason for living in or near hills and that the Kofyar did not just happen to settle in their present territory because of some random whim or chance excursion. Upland areas are the exception rather than the rule north of the Niger and Benue rivers, and the great majority of people live on relatively open, undulating savanna. What was the advantage of perching on the edge of a rugged escarpment or clinging to its base? For an agricultural people, it seems obvious that the loose soils of the level plain are more easily worked than the rocky slopes of hills. The benefits of consistent rainfall, perennial springs, and pockets of fertile soil may have lured some settlers, but recent experience has shown that a man with the same tools and crops can produce more food per unit of labor on the plains than in the hills (see Chapter 8, below). It is true that the Kofyar practice a highly effective system of agriculture, but what were the advantages of their particular environment that made this highly specialized adaptation worthwhile?

Almost everyone who has seen the societies of the North

has decided that the hill dwellers lived there because they had to. This idea is based, whether consciously analyzed or not, on the obvious contrast between the Hausa-Fulani civilization of centralized kingdom states with walled cities, writing, long-distance trade, armies, and Islamic religion and the unclothed "hill pagans" with their "primitive" technology, political fragmentation, and general isolation. Cultural similarities have been noted among many such *Splitterstämme* or remnant tribes existing in the interstices of the developed Sudanic states (Baumann, Westermann, and Thurnwald 1940:50–56). It is obvious that these groups could not hold their own against the technological and organizational superiority of their neighbors. The hills have been called "refuge areas" (Buchanan and Pugh 1955:80), though no one knows when and under what circumstances they were settled. It seems probable that if the ancestors of the Kofyar had not occupied such an inaccessible region, they would have been conquered, perhaps enslaved, and almost certainly absorbed in at least the superficial appearances of some more dominant group. That this never happened is testified both by what we know of recent history and the diffusion—or lack of it—of culture traits.

The Kofyar themselves claim to be autochthonous, but their congeners the Angas say that they were Beri-beri who fled Bornu to escape Kanuri conquest. Though this may be historically meaningless, it does suggest what must have been a frequent response to more powerful neighbors. A nearer threat was possibly that of the Jukun, a pagan state on the Benue which became important during the seventeenth century and extended its raids as far north as Kano (Meek 1931:26). The details of their expansion are still shadowy, but Meek has described the remaining evidences of their typical divine kingship. The Jukun homeland is due south of the Kofyar and marches with Goemai country. The Goemai were admittedly tributary to the Jukun king (Meek 1931:41–42), and their own hierarchy of titled officials follows a Jukun model. The chief, or Long Goemai, affects the topknot and ivory stickpin of the Jukun ruler, and his person is hedged with similar taboos. An attenuated version of the divine monarchy persists in the Chip and Garram Valley tribelets at the base of the Plateau and suggests the high-water mark of Jukun influence. The Kofyar have no signs of direct Jukun contact, and it is probable that the cavalry on which Jukun military advantage depended could not penetrate the hills. In some of the plains villages such as Dokan Kasuwa and Kwang, there is a series of titled offices, but these may be due to intense contact with adjacent Goemai rather than direct subordination by Jukun. The only product of the Jukun that the Kofyar sought was salt from the Awei district, and this trade may well have been mediated by Goemai.

During most of the historic period, hegemony in Northern Nigeria was held by the seven traditional Hausa kingdoms (Hodgkin 1960, Smith 1960). These states and the great Bornu empire received some of their economic and cultural stimulus from trans-Saharan contacts with the Mediterranean Arab world. It was only with the Fulani jihad early in the nineteenth century that decisive inroads were made into the south. From Sokoto, Kano, and Zaria, the mounted Fulani established themselves as a political and spiritual aristocracy. Some areas were conquered and incorporated as fiefdoms for Fulani vassals. Other districts, especially those inhabited by non-Moslem communities in out-of-the-way areas, were kept as slave reserves that could be raided occasionally to supply labor for the estates and for sale. Warrior chieftains from Bauchi emirate formed the state of Wase just southeast of the Jos Plateau and established themselves at Muri and Yola on the Benue (Meek 1931:53). Petty emirates were also established at Keffi, Jema'a, and Nassarawa, and among the Beri-beri at Lafia, all of which acknowledged the overlordship of Zaria (Hogben 1930:142–146). The high plateau was thus bracketed on the east and west by Fulani states, and it is clear that sizable armies passed back and forth on the plain below the southern escarpment (Hogben

1930:147). It is equally obvious that none of the hill tribes were permanently subjugated by these expeditions. Some slaves may have been captured on the plain, and one report mentions Fulani raids from Lafia and Keffi about 1875, but it is highly doubtful that successful operations could have been carried out in the uplands. Paths are so steep and rocky that it is impossible to ride a horse up the escarpment. Narrow defiles and large volcanic boulders provide excellent cover for defenders and make it difficult to marshal a strong force for attack.

The Kofyar recall no Fulani invasion and speak in vague terms of an occasional slave raid on lowland farmers. They paid no tribute, and no Fulani herders brought their cattle to hill pastures. On the other hand, if the Kofyar left the protection of their hills, they risked capture or death. Slave raiders (*shal*) came both from the Goemai, who paid tribute in slaves to Bauchi and Wase, and from the Hausa-Fulani city-states themselves. No pitched battles are mentioned, but captives were taken in forays on people working in the fields and on travelers. The myth of the founding of Namu pits the Kofyar culture hero against daily attacks by slavers whom he finally overcame by thrusting his spear into the ground and magically creating a steep-sided stone hill. The site of Namu may indeed have been determined by the existence of a small inselberg rising from the plain and offering a defensible position.

The need to avoid slaving depredations seems to be reflected in a zone of dense population in the hills and immediately adjoining lowlands, with large areas of fertile plain to the south left empty. Only a few small walled settlements of the Goemai existed on land that could agriculturally have supported many times that number. Hausa, the lingua franca of the North, is still little spoken in the hills, and the recent spread in its usage seems almost entirely due to European administration and education. The limits of Fulani domination are still visible on the map. The orderly succession of Hausa place names is interrupted on a line running north of and parallel to the Niger and Benue rivers. In a few spots on the rivers, local states such as Nupe and Jukun survived, but the major unassimilated territories were those on the Jos Plateau, the Tangale-Waja Hills, and the Mandara Mountains, each with its own mosaic of independent pagan groups. It is safe to infer from an ethnic map (Murdock 1959; Baumann, Westermann, and Thurnwald 1940) that where the tribal areas are small, close together, culturally heterogeneous, and little known, the land is rugged and mountainous. A major concentration of such groups marks the Jos Plateau with a shatter belt of maximum cultural diversity along the precipitous escarpments (Gunn 1953). The Middle Belt designation includes these geographical areas and their inhabitants whose unity is a product only of their common exclusion from the prevailing Hausa-Fulani culture.

The topographic exclusion of outsiders from Kofyar country does not mean that peace was general in the hills. Intervillage feuding and raids by neighboring pagan groups appear to have been common until the British-enforced peace became effective. Kofyar legends describe warfare with peoples from the Chokfem area that decimated the population and forced evacuation of all hill villages except Kofyar and tiny Koenji on the brink of the escarpment. The attackers evidently cultivated parts of the conquered area, because their war leader was finally killed by stealth just after he had finished reaping his acha (hungry rice). More recent fighting that continued into the lives of living informants involved individual villages or alliances. In every case, hostilities followed a murder or unexplained death which was avenged by the mother's brother of the victim and his co-villagers. They were supported by neighboring villages in a more-or-less enduring alliance. In the hills Kofyar, Lardang, Bogalong, and their satellites were known as Gankogom (the side of long grass), and their traditional opponents were Ganguk (the side of hunchbacks), a western tier of villages including Bong, Mangbar, and Zugal.

A serious ten-year feud, still remembered by some of the older men, resulted in the burning and abandonment of smaller villages such as Longsel, Dung, and Koepal lying in less defensible positions between the enemy blocs. Sites of refugee homesteads are still discernible, and present land ownership reflects population movements dating from this period. Today the villages that were abandoned and resettled only after the end of hostilities in the early 1900's show markedly shorter stands of oil palms. Much of the fighting took place in a no man's land and consisted of blowing war horns, waving shields, and rapid spear-throwing forays toward enemy lines. Death or serious injury to either side ended battle for that day. Well-known warriors may have organized the battle lines to some extent, but villages fought as independent units, and allies lacked any formal political unity.

It was only with the coming of the Europeans that the hills no longer provided relative freedom from external attack. Even with the advantages of modern firearms and colonial convictions, it took the British longer to subdue the hill pagans than the populous walled cities of the Moslem North. The Royal Niger Company had established a trading station at Ibi in 1883, and its troops had broken the power of Muri and Wase by 1898 (Meek 1931:60). First recorded European contact with the Kofyar was in 1909, when a Hausa force under British officers fought a sharp engagement with mounted men from Kwalla. The Kwalla were defeated, and the following year a district headquarters was established in their area under an Assistant Resident, Captain Fitzpatrick (Fitzpatrick 1910). An official report of 1912 described the people as "raw pagans," "very superstitious, friendly, and peaceful," who had "taken readily to trade and are progressing very satisfactorily." These statements prefigure the major concerns of British administration: the maintenance of peace and order, and the establishment of trade.

The early reports in the Northern Regional Archives speak mostly of small police patrols which ventured among the Kofyar infrequently to halt cattle thefts (1917) and punish intervilllage feuding (1921, 1926, 1927, 1928). The disturbances culminated in the 1930 killing of Assistant District Officer Barlow by several hundred stone-throwing Kofyar in the hills near Latok. Ten hill villages of the Dimmuk dialect group were destroyed in retaliation, and their inhabitants dispersed or evacuated to the plains. Some twenty-one Kofyar were killed, and approximately four thousand left their homes. The punishment evidently achieved the desired effect in that by 1931 all but forty-four individuals had submitted to government authority and tax was paid in full without a show of force "for the first time in history since British occupation." Until 1937, annual patrols evicted villagers who had returned to the hills to plant crops and rebuild their homes, but there was little violence. The administrative order was rescinded in 1939, and the original communities were all reestablished.

With final pacification of the Kofyar, the administration turned to matters of government, trade, and health. Under the British policy of indirect rule, local government was established by a system of Native Authorities. Some of the plains villages were withdrawn from the jurisdiction of the Goemai chief, and in 1937 a Koffiyer Federation was formed including Dimmuk and the adjoining hills. This Sub-Native Authority was gradually expanded to include Kwa, Bwal, and the Goemai settlement of Namu. Kwalla, Kwang, and Dokan Kasuwa remained part of the Shendam Sub-Native Authority, while Jepal or Koeper was grouped for administrative purposes with Pankshin Native Authority. Reorganization of the districts was based partly on ethnohistorical materials collected by several British officers during the mid-1930's and dealing with origins and intervillage political and religious ties.

Each village area was under the direction of a chief or district head who was traditionally elected but might be removed by the Divisional Officer. In each district a Native Authority Grade D court judged matters of divorce, minor theft, land disputes, and so on, according to customary law. It was made up of village chiefs plus a few lineage notables and representatives of Hausa and Fulani residents. Capital cases were referred to the Provincial Court in Jos. As more responsibility has been given to local governing bodies, a divisional assembly called the Lowland Federated Council has been established in Shendam. It has representatives from each major district with a permanent executive committee and councillors supervising schools and hospitals, finance, police, and so on. Since the late 1950's the Divisional Officer has become increasingly an advisory figure. Under British rule he handled almost all the administration of a district as the immediate subordinate of the Provincial Resident. He was expected to oversee the activities of legislative bodies and councillors, with special attention to financial matters, and to act as magistrate for appeals from lower courts. Every effort is now being made to fill administrative posts with Nigerians, and the first non-European District Officer was posted to Lowlands in 1962.

As early as 1933, divisional reports mention Kofyar trade in salt, palm oil, and yams, especially among the Mirriam, whose own land was insufficient to support the population. At this time markets existed at Kwalla and Dokan Kasuwa, both on the periphery of Kofyar territory. Some minor commercial activity by Hausa immigrants began in Dimmuk shortly after 1930, and an official market was established in 1937. Most indigenous exchange before 1930 seems to have been between trading partners in neighboring villages. Before the Pax Britannica, travel to neighboring ethnic groups and even among Kofyar villages was potentially very dangerous. With guaranteed safety of the roads, local produce could be head-loaded for thirty to forty miles for sale in the mine fields on the high plateau (Findlay 1945). The major link between Lowland Division and the outside world was a one hundred fifty-mile road from Jos through Pankshin and around the edge of the Plateau to Shendam. Roads leading into Kofyar country proper were open to motor vehicles only during the dry season, though a bridge over the Shemankar was begun in 1961 and remains uncompleted. The fact that individual villages were formerly responsible for annual road maintenance resulted in uneven and often-delayed repairs. The completion of an all-weather road from Panyam to Shendam in the late 1950's made possible relatively easy travel from Kwa to Jos and direct lorry connections during the dry months between Kofyar and Jos markets.

In the field of health, major government attention was focused on the eradication of sleeping sickness. From 1935 on efforts were made to cut the brush in stream beds where the tsetse fly sheltered, and to maintain regular examinations of the population. The incidence of the disease was reduced from as high as 25 per cent in some hamlets to practically nil by 1960. In 1951 a dispensary was started in Dimmuk, and a hospital was opened in Shendam in 1955. Some medicines were also distributed by missions at Kwalla and Kwa after their establishment in the late 1940's.

Missionary influence has been felt chiefly in the provision of education. The Roman Catholic fathers of the Société des Missions Africaines (SMA) established a permanent station at Kwa in 1947 and opened a number of elementary schools throughout the surrounding plains and in the hills at Latok and Kofyar. Senior primary schools now operate at Dokan Kasuwa, Kwa, Dimmuk, and Kwalla. A Protestant mission and schools are also maintained by the Sudan United Mission at Kwalla. There was by 1967 a considerable number of literate Kofyar forming a body of native craftsmen, teachers, and government employees.

The Kofyar intercultural environment since European penetration has notably widened. The suppression of local warfare and the establishment of judicial mechanisms for the settling of disputes have enabled individuals to move freely beyond the range of village and kinship networks. Isolation yielded rapidly on the plains and more slowly in less accessible hill areas. The Kofyar may speak glowingly about past military exploits, but they also point out practically that the absence of raids and ambushes allows the planting of more distant fields, resulting in larger harvests and more beer. Markets and roads have made possible the exchange of crops for cash, and this adaptation will be dealt with at greater length in Chapter 8.

The Kofyar are aware that the necessity to avoid intervillage feuding, to settle quarrels in court, and to pay taxes was imposed by conquest. They do not regard these demands as onerous, but merely as the new conditions of daily life. With the exception of the Latok "war" of 1930 and the infrequent arrest and punishment of criminals, the Kofyar have felt little direct governmental coercion. Their subsistence economy has continued without interference. Tin mining has never begun in Kofyar country, so there has been no land alienation. Local resources have also been sufficient to support a growing population, and few men have taken the opportunity to go to the mines as migrant laborers. The acceptance of Christianity or Islam has been voluntary, and a large proportion of the population remain pagan. As education becomes increasingly available, it is accepted as proper for both boys and girls. Schooling is viewed pragmatically as allowing movement into such positions as teacher, policeman, nurse, and government official, which command substantial cash salaries. Disease rates and especially epidemics may have lessened with the partial introduction of Western techniques and medicines, but the overwhelming volume of treatment of illness is still in the hands of native practitioners. Local government dispensaries are poorly supplied and patronized, and hospitalization is considered a radical step.

The social horizon of most Kofyar is still severely limited. The only Europeans they know are missionaries and administrators, each of whom is by local standards rich and powerful but not particularly threatening. In the plains villages live a handful of Moslem Hausa, craftsmen and traders whose behavior and dress are emulated by their Kofyar converts. Though Hausa is frequently the lingua franca of the plains, it is not generally used in domestic situations. Hausamen are not regarded with any noticeable ill will by their neighbors, and the recent arrival of a few Ibo palm wine tappers and bar owners has been met with similar equanimity. (During the disturbances of 1966, Ibo residents fled, and there was fortunately no loss of life in the Kofyar area.)

The pastoral Fulani did not have access to Plateau pastures until after British pacification (Stenning 1957) and the eradication of the tsetse fly. Several households now move up and down the Kofyar escarpment according to season, and some others have settled in the lowlands. Their milk products find little market among the beer-drinking Kofyar, but individuals compete in offering money and services to induce Fulani to camp on and thus manure their fields. With the exception of venturing freely to new farms on the plain and markets within a twenty-mile radius, Kofyar show little change in their tolerant relations with neighboring groups. Few of the strangers in their territory enter into direct competition with the Kofyar, and those who do, such as Tiv filtering north from the Benue, are merely regarded with mild suspicion. To date only schoolboys, chiefs, and a few enterprising traders have ever gotten beyond sight of the Kofyar hills.

Integration into a national society is still minimal. Though there have been indirect elections to Regional governing bodies since 1951, the average illiterate Kofyar farmer has little awareness of political organization and new developments beyond his home district. The chief collecting tax money, the Grade D court with its scribes and messengers, the distant and powerful figure of the District Officer personify government to the villager. He may recognize party symbols, but only the chief, the schoolteacher, and a few other educated young men understand the party platforms and the role of the legislators. The more isolated hill dwellers may know the name of Kaduna, regional capital of the North, but not the name of Nigeria. The mobilization of political power to secure a return of tax money in the form of dispensaries, schools, roads, and bridges is certainly not well understood. Candidates for office make few public appearances, concentrating instead on winning over teachers and chiefs who can be counted on to guide the common people through the confusing steps of voting.

Because of the physical isolation of the Kofyar and the decentralization encourageed by the policy of indirect rule, there is almost no direct contact between the upper levels of government—provincial, regional, and federal—and the people. Independence in 1960 seems to have had little immediate effect in this area. Though school moneys come from the regional government, the payment of teachers, building of schools, and dealing with Education Department inspectors are all mediated by the resident manager, usually a European missionary. Public works such as courthouses, market improvements, and road repairs are authorized by the Lowlands Native Authority and carried out by contractors with local labor. Dispensaries are Native Authority operated and staffed. Tax money is known to be gathered in Shendam, but its further course and allocation are barely imagined. There is no continuing program of agricultural extension or supervised produce marketing in the area. A serious offense such as murder, which goes to the Provincial Court in Jos, passes completely out of the ken of most individuals. Newspapers and magazines are rarely found in the homes of the few literates, but some news of governmental actions may be heard on the radios owned by a few Kofyar. Government as a popularly understood reality is thus limited to the personal and generally traditional forms in the hamlet and village area and to the local bureaucracy of the division.

3

Intensive Hill Agriculture

KOFYAR AGRICULTURE is based on the intensive cultivation of a clearly defined land area adjoining or encircling the residence of the farmer. The Kofyar refer to this plot as *mar koepang*, and I have used the literal translation "homestead field" throughout. Intensive agriculture is a system by which soil fertility is continuously maintained or restored, allowing successive food crops to be produced with little or no intervening fallow period. This may take place naturally as a result of the periodic deposit of nutrient elements by water or wind or through human intervention. Intensive agriculture differs from shifting or swidden cultivation "in which impermanent clearings are cropped for shorter periods in years than they are fallowed" (Conklin 1961:27).[1] The shift-

[1] The distinction between intensive and shifting agriculture applies only to the usual duration of cultivation of particular fields and does not necessarily refer to the amount of labor expended or the premanency of settlement in an area. The same contrast has been made by Hatt between semi-agriculturalists and full agriculturalists without the plow (Curwen and Hatt 1953:246) and by Goldschmidt (1959:193) between horticulturalists and agriculturalists. I have consistently referred to Kofyar intensive agriculture as farming rather than gardening because of its emphasis on cereals rather than root crops or vegetables (cf. Barrau 1958:79).

ing pattern is by far the more usual in Africa, and some of its variations have been described among the Bemba (Richards 1939), the Zande (De Schlippe 1956), and the Tiv (Bohannan 1954). Allan (1965) has provided a detailed survey of several systems in East and Central Africa. The Kofyar also practice a type of shifting cultivation in bush fields, *mar goon,* which must be regularly fallowed, but their primary dependence for staple food crops is on the intensively worked homestead farm.

I suspect that the combination of intensive and extensive or shifting cultivation is a very widespread practice, providing as it does for adjustment to differing soil conditions, plant requirements, and needs for the care and protection of the growing crop. With a variety of crops and field types, the farmer is also protected against total loss due to unpredictable climatic fluctuations. Examples of the combination of cultivation systems include the "house" and "far" farms of the Nuba (Nadel 1947:16), the intensively cultivated *lai lo* and the *zo lo* swidden fields of the Chin (Lehman 1963:54), and the valley gardens and mountain swiddens of the Kapauku (Pospisil 1963:87ff.) The infield-outfield arrangements found in northern Europe may be a continuation of a similar pattern already present in the Neolothic period (Evans 1956:229).

Agricultural Technology

The farming implements of the Kofyar are few and simple. The major tool is a typical Sudanic hoe *(can)* with a spade-shaped iron blade set with a tang into a short crooked wooden handle. Hoes are locally forged and were formerly items of considerable value. The iron was smelted by the Sura on the high plateau in furnaces whose remains still exist. The hoe blade is about one foot in length and longer than it is wide. The cultivator holds the hoe handle in both hands and swings his body from the hips, driving the blade into the soil in front of him and pulling it toward him (Plate VB). By changing the angle of entry it is possible to dig a deep furrow or merely skim off the topsoil, and this latter technique is especially useful in manipulating thin, rocky soil and building ridges. Earth can be lifted and accurately dumped by a slight motion of the wrists. Smaller Hausa-type hoes are sometimes used for weeding on the plain. The only other tools of importance are the ax (*sep*) with a long, narrow, iron blade inserted in a heavy knobbed wood handle, and a small, curved, iron-bladed sickle used for reaping small grain and cutting forage grass. Most cutting of millet and sorghum heads is done with old knife or spear blades. A digging stick is used only to harvest sweet potatoes.

Food-processing equipment consists of tree-trunk mortars and log pestles (*shing*), woven winnowing trays (*koetut*), and grinding stones (*fin*), along with a wide variety of wooden bowls, clay pots, and coiled baskets. Food is stored in jars, cylindrical mud-walled granaries both outside and inside huts, baskets, and calabashes. A heavy wooden drying stage for storing harvested grain is a fixture in most homestead courtyards and provides a shady shelter for many household activities (Plate VIII A). With the exception of some pots, these items are undecorated and purely utilitarian. They differ only in detail from the tool kit of neighboring peoples and indeed of Sudanic agriculturalists in general.

Intensive agriculture is only possible when techniques are available for the conservation and periodic enrichment of the soil. In hill areas especially, erosion can quickly strip the slopes of soil once the natural tree growth and grass have been removed. Perhaps the most impressive feature of the Kofyar countryside is the way in which systems of terraces (*pang*) have been built up the hills to stabilize the soil and provide a series of stepped, level benches suitable for farming (Plates IIIA, IIIB). Retaining walls (*fukoepang*) of rough stone laid without mortar and rising one to six feet anchor the terraces. Smaller walls are used in the bush fields, while high walls are erected close to the homestead to provide wider unobstructed areas for intensive farming. Terraces are almost always at right angles to the slope, and they vary in height and distance apart according to the existing contour. The building of walls serves not only to create surfaces that resist washing but also to secure a greater depth of soil and usefully consolidate the stones that litter the slopes. Oil palm trees planted on the edges of terraces further stabilize the earth.

To questions about the age of terraces, most Kofyar say only that they have been there since before anyone can remember and that no one knows the names of the builders. Stone wall building is still practiced when terraces must be repaired or corrals built, and a few old men once personally engaged in major terracing around their own homesteads. The method was to build up a stone wall leaning slightly in from the vertical toward the hill slope. After the wall had risen a foot or two, earth was hoed down from the slope above to fill in the space behind it. If a higher wall was required, the process could be repeated. The work seems usually to have been done by the owner of the farm and his household with occasional help from near neighbors. Terraces were built or improved, bit by bit, over a period of years. Large groups of people worked together only on one-day repair parties.

Terracing alone is not the final solution to problems of conservation and water control. Since all of the Kofyar rainfall of forty to sixty inches comes within six months and some storms may deposit up to two inches a day for several consecutive days, runoff and potential erosion are a danger even to level land surfaces. Many crops will not flourish if they remain submerged for any length of time, yet they may also require substantial moisture in the soil to tide them over from the last rains in early October until harvest time in December. A characteristic African solution to the problem of keeping crops above the standing water resulting from heavy rains is to create ridges or mounds. This has the added advantage in areas of thin soil such as the Kofyar hills of concentrating top soil in ridges around the roots of the growing crops. By shaping the eight-to sixteen-inch-high ridges (*sagan*) into closed rectangles from four to six feet long, and two to four feet wide, the Kofyar create both high ground for planting and a series of enclosed hollows (*ciil*) which trap water (Plate IIA). The system, called basin listing or tie ridging by agronomists, is used on top of hill terraces and on intensively farmed plains fields. A very similar practice has been noted among the Nuba by Nadel (1947:16). Its utility is demonstrated after a rain when fields appear checkered with pools, divided from each other by earth ridges (Plate IIB). The growing plants on the ridges are not inundated, and water is allowed to sink gradually into the soil both to furnish future moisture and to prevent destructive runoff. Hill streams clear quickly after a rain since they contain little silt. Their beds are U-shaped, often six to eight feet below banks that are perpendicular and uneroded. Gullying is very rare in the cultivated areas of Kofyar. That erosion would take place if unchecked is seen in bush paths descending hills, which frequently form watercourses in the wet season and are scoured down to the bare rock.

Ridging may be adapted to varying topographic conditions and the differing needs of food crops. At the foot of a hill that may be terraced and basin-listed in the usual way, the slope becomes increasingly gentle, and water may have a tendency to collect. Such an area, termed *jagat* by the Kofyar, is sodden or marshy, and the problem is one of drainage rather than retention of moisture. To farm such land, ridges are built parallel to the contour of the slope (Plate IIIC). The ridges are not continuous, and regularly spaced gaps are left which form ditches leading down the hill. The ditch floor is lower than the depressions between the parallel ridges, so that water does not stand. The drainage ditches are spaced closely enough together so that no single one will carry a large volume of water and thus deepen its channel. The height of the ridges depends largely on the dampness of the spot, and where a heavy volume of water is expected, ridges are shortened and built up until they become mounds as high as two and a half feet. Some areas at the foot of the hills are as level as table tops and must cope with a great deal of rain and ground water in the first part of the wet season and a growing scarcity of water toward the end. Farmers of Dimmuk and adjoining Kwalla, where this problem is acute, raise two- to three-foot earth ridges around their homestead fields and plant the staple sorghum (guinea corn), millet, and beans on large mounds or hummocks that keep the roots clear of water when young but allow them to tap the stored ground moisture as they mature.

Some crops require little moisture and can survive on relatively infertile land. Acha, or hungry rice (*Digitaria exilis*), is a very small grain whose seed head resembles that of its relative, the common crab grass. It is sown broadcast rather than being planted only on ridges. Small ridges three to four inches high are made parallel to the direction of the slope, and there are no cross ridges along the edges of the terraces. If basins were made, the acha which grew in the standing water would not do well. Consequently, every effort is made to keep water from being confined. That soil nutrients are thereby lost to runoff is known to the Kofyar. Their usual explanation for exhausted or leached white (*piya*) soil is that *am mang*, "the water took it." But they also realize that acha grows on land that would not support other crops and is well adapted to bush fallowing where long continued production is not expected.

On swampy plots a farmer has the option of employing the ridge and ditch system described above or attempting to retain all rain water and use the resulting paddy for growing wet rice. On the plain at the mouths of narrow, steep-sided valleys cutting back into the hills, Kofyar farmers heap up high continuous ridges around their rice plots. They depend on conserving rainfall that does not sink readily into damp impervious ground rather than irrigating with impoundments and ditches. Some cultivators combine the two systems, growing standard food crops in drained patches and using the ditch bottoms for rice. Road repairs in the Kofyar area must be delayed until after the rice harvest because the ditches on either side of the roads are planted in rice.

The example of practical engineering in the building of terraces and the adaptation of different ridging techniques to varying conditions is striking. One expert, after describing the more modest terraces and ridges of the neighboring Angas people, called them a "perfect demonstration of theoretical anti-erosion measures carried out on a wide and successful scale over a period of centuries" (Fairbairn 1943:190). Professional agriculturalists have told me that the traditional methods of soil conservation practiced by the Kofyar could not be improved upon. It is obvious, however, that such extensive efforts at erosion control and water conservation would be economically feasible only if the land so treated could produce heavily and on a sustained basis. The Kofyar area lacks alluvial plains or any other source of natural soil regeneration. The deficiency is supplied by regular application of organic material. The staple cereals of early millet (*maar*) and sorghum (*swa*) are grown together with cowpeas (*oeroem*) in the homestead farm. All three are interplanted every year on the same plot. Average hill land can support only a year or two of sorghum alone before yields decline markedly. Yet high production has been maintained for generations on the same homestead farms without soil exhaustion. Fertility is sustained at high level by annual applications of compost and animal dung.

In every area where stone is available the Kofyar build sturdy circular enclosures from ten to fifteen feet in diameter and up to eight feet deep. Within such corrals (*bit*), which are a fixture of every homestead, goats are staked out each day for the entire length of the growing season (Plate VIIB). Food for the animals in the form of grass and leafy branches is brought every day by the household members. The forage is always more than the goats can eat. It builds up in layers mixed with goat dung and urine from April, when the crops sprout, through the December harvest. At night, the goats are penned in a hut where dung also collects, so that for nine months of the year every available bit of manure is retained.

When the corral is emptied just before the rains, a substantial quantity of fertilizer (*zuk*) can be returned to the land (Plate IIC). In one case the compost from a filled corral 15 feet 8 inches in diameter and 7 feet 7 inches deep, with a capacity of 1,452 cubic feet, was distributed in 388 basket loads over .4 acre. Even the small corral of a relatively poor household may yield more than 400 cubic feet of compost. Added to this is the manure from the goat hut and from other buildings housing sheep or horses which graze outside the village during the day. Large walled corrals are also built for cows, but they are not stall-fed, and their dung simply washes out through a drain onto nearby fields. People in plains villages where building stone is lacking make low enclosures of logs around pits where goats are tied. Yet the hill dwellers seem generally to collect greater quantities of compost, perhaps because unfarmed slopes around the villages provide a accessible source of fodder. One of the major reasons given for the borrowing of livestock is that this provides manure for fertilizer. Individuals also customarily defecate on the homestead field at some distance from their huts. In Latok where the land is overworked and organic material is at a premium, round stone enclosures (*daan es*) are built for the collection of nightsoil.

With their knowledge of the value of fertilization, the Kofyar have readily adapted to a symbiotic relationship with Fulani herders. These pastoral nomads have only recently appeared in the area, which previously was barred to them by tsetse fly infestation (Stenning 1957). The Fulani are paid in cash and given free labor in carrying loads and erecting shelter in exchange for camping with their cattle on bush fields. This allows plots that were formerly farmed by shifting cultivation to come into intensive use. The Kofyar's acceptance and indeed competition for the benefits of manuring contrasts with the active hostility of the Birom, a tribe on the high plateau, whose people contended that animal dung was injurious to crops (Perham 1946:197–98) .

Fertilization is not confined to the use of the dung-cum-decayed-vegetation compost. When bush fields are being prepared for groundnut cultivation, the first step is the pulling of all grass and brush. This material is given a few days to dry before the field is hoed. Piles of brush are placed here and there on the newly made ridges and fired to provide beds of ashes for the planting. Every bit of wood ash from cooking fires in the homestead is also saved in small huts built for the purpose. Baskets of powdery gray ash are taken to the fields by women when groundnuts are one to two months old and a handful is sprinkled on each plant (Plate VIA) . The same treatment is given to sweet potatoes. Small seedbeds for the sprouting of eleusine are prepared on spots where corn stalks and other agricultural refuse has been burned. The seeds may be mixed with goat dung before being stirred into the soil. Remaining stalks and leaves of plants such as maize, groundnuts, and early millet are carefully returned to the soil after harvest. In acha fields, grass and weeds are not burned but rather uprooted and buried under the small ridge. The Kofyar say that acha benefits from decomposing vegetation rather than ash. They are also aware that acha grown in rich soil or manured land would not do well. Evidently the plant is adapted to rather poor soils, and when it is given extra nutriment it grows too quickly and its weak stalk cannot support the seed head.

In bush fields where only wood ash and turned-under vegetation are used, the productive period of a field is lengthened by crop rotation. This is usually an alternation between groundnuts and acha. Hill practice is to begin with a light sowing of acha the year in which the land is first cleared, followed by a full sowing of acha the next year, and groundnuts alternating with acha from then on. Since groundnuts are harvested early, some farmers may follow them with late millet transplanted from seedbeds (*sunggul*) and thus secure two crops from a field in a single year. People are aware that a field where acha is repeatedly planted is more quickly exhausted (*bes piya*) than one where the leguminous nitrogen-fixing groundnut is cultivated in rotation with other crops. Bush fields in the hills may be used for six to nine years, depending on the length of the preceding fallow period, but the greater pressure on plains land near villages means that fallows are shortened from more than fifteen years to less than ten. Plains fields are said to produce well for only four years at a time. Sorghum may be planted once or twice at the beginning of a cropping cycle, but its greater demands on the soil restrict its use in bush field rotation schemes.

The Farming Calendar: Crops and Techniques

Kofyar calendrical notions are of an approximate nature, and the most frequently mentioned periods of time are the four seasons. The early rains, called *lok,* extend from late March through June and are followed by the later rains, *pas,* from July through September. *Waap* refers to the October to mid-December dry season when the harmattan begins to blow, and the hot, dry period of late December to March, which extends up to the coming of rain, is known as *lugun.* Names exist for the lunar months, but they are little used, and even those older men charged with scheduling ceremonies that fall in a certain moon occasionally make mistakes concerning them.[2]

---

[2] Various Kofyar informants gave either twelve or thirteen names for the lunar months in one year. The names relate to the important activities pursued at that time, and there was general agreement as to the order of the months. The year begins with the first rains, which herald the start of farming.

Month	Kofyar name	Activity
	fungfung	Preparing homestead field, possibly planting,
March		*maap* celebrated
	voevigir	Drinking the sweet juice of locust bean pods
April	*wuplayi*	Big rains, planting

The Kofyar farming year begins its annual cycle in March (see Fig. 4). Four and a half or five months have already passed with very little precipitation, and the first stirring of the soft, rain-bearing south winds has been felt. It is time to clean rubbish from the homestead fields and prepare them for planting. Every household must empty its corral, spreading the compost on the old homestead field and on any extensions of it that are being brought into intensive cultivation. This may be followed by a preliminary working (*pyan*) of the field in which the soil is merely turned over with a hoe or small ridges are made. Though it is well known that this early hoeing encourages quick growth, it is often bypassed on hill farms. There the compost remains in piles until the first cultivation mixes it with the soil. Farmers in the Latok area customarily burn field rubbish in heaps so that the resulting mounds of ash may be used as seedbeds for eleusine. There is usually very little refuse remaining in homestead fields by the end of the dry season. Crop plants are grown so thickly and cultivated so carefully that practically no weed growth can take hold. Sorghum stalks are collected and stacked for use as cooking fuel. With the coming of the dry season, the remaining green plants wither, and there is not enough moisture to allow new growth to get started. Consequently, the farm around the compound is so barren as to constitute an effective firebreak when the long bush grass is being burned.

May	*bangbalang*	First heavy work of hoeing the homestead farm
June	*biyel*	Planting cowpeas
July	*kelele*	Harvesting and drying early millet
August	*moeka*	Hungry time, look for small yams
September	*fwap*	Heavy rains
October	*saa*	Dancing *gala*, transplanting late millet
November	*tarshit*	Moon of cutting roofing grass, paying bride price
December	*kwakwa*	Dancing *kwakwa* on the plains, harvesting acha
January	*tardiip*	Moon of harvest
February	*canyang*	Cutting guinea corn stalks

March	April	May	June	July	August	September	October	November	December	January	February
PRE-HOEING (*piyan*) MANURING	PLANTING		1st HOE-ING	2nd HOEING		3rd HOE-ING					STOR-ING
		Pumpkins..HARVEST LEAVES....H	A	R	V	E	S	T			
		Early millet........HARVEST									
		Sorghum.........		PLANTING Cowpeas........HARVEST			HARVEST				
								HARVEST			
	Yams.........			HARVEST							
	Maize.........			HARVEST							
	Coco yam........					HARVEST					
ASH SEED-BEDS	PLANTING Eleusine	TRANSPLANTING........HARVEST									
		PLANTING-WEEDING									
			Groundnuts..ASH FERTILIZER.......HARVEST								
			Climbing beans...........HARVEST								
			Dwang..........HARVEST							COOK, DRY	
			Sweet potatoes..........HARVEST								
		PLANTING Early acha..WEEDING...HARVEST									THRESH-ING
				Late acha..WEEDING........HARVEST							THRESH-ING
				PLANTING Late millet..TRANSPLANTING-GUARDING........HARVEST							
				Rice..WEEDING.......HARVEST							
				PLANTING Bambara groundnuts.........HARVEST							
				CLEARING AND BREAK-ING NEW FIELDS........							GRASS CUTTING FIRING
	Oil palm fruit	HARVEST.......									
		Locust bean HARVEST			Millet HARVEST						
								Canarium HARVEST			THRESHING
								Sorghum HARVEST..THRESHING			
	MIGRANT FARM PLANTING	1st HOEING...		2nd HOEING..		3rd HOEING				Mound yams	

Planting in the Kofyar area is not geared to any signs in the heavens or the wild vegetation, but to the single fact of rain. The first shower at the close of the dry months sends women out with seeds of pumpkins and other cucurbits for planting in scattered hills ten or twelve feet apart. As their name, *tokmang,* "the bringer of sauce," implies, pumpkins are valued for their quick-sprouting leaves which make a favorite sauce for the staple cereal porridge. (For English names of crops, botanical designations, Kofyar and Hausa names, see Table 2.) If the rain has been a heavy one, early millet, sorghum, and maize may also be planted. A soaking rain is required to sprout these crops, and they may be planted whenever it comes, whether before the middle of March or well into April.

Planting is done with a hoe handle. Its point is used to open a shallow hole, seeds are dribbled in from the left hand, and the hole is covered with an outward push of the hoe handle, all in a series of rapid motions. Small hills are hurriedly hoed up to receive the millet seeds. These may be in the middle of the previous year's rectangular ridge or, where mounds are used, in the place where a bite has been hoed from the side of the old mound to start a new adjoining heap. Ten to fifteen millet grains are put into each hill. This allows for transplanting if some seeds fail to germinate or are burned out as shoots. Only about half of the entire homestead field is seeded with millet. The rest may be filled with transplanted shoots. Enough seed is always saved so that another planting is possible if the first fails through lack of rain. Sorghum, which grows more slowly than millet, is planted in small holes scratched on the sides of old ridges. Six to ten seeds are dropped at a time in holes two to three feet apart.

Maize seeds are sprouted in water for two days before planting. Where maize is a staple, it is planted two grains to a hole about two feet apart. More usually it is a secondary crop, planted sparsely here and there about the field. At about the same time, the tiny seeds of eleusine are mixed

TABLE 2

DOMESTICATED PLANT NAMES*

English Names	Botanical Designations	Kofyar	Hausa
Sorghum, guinea corn, kaffir corn	*Sorghum vulgare*	*Swa*	*Dawa*
Early millet, bulrush millet	*Pennisetum typhoideum*	*Maar*	*Gero*
Late millet, pearl millet (?)	*Pennisetum spicatum*	*Kas*	*Dauro*
Maize, corn	*Zea mays*	*Swapas*	*Masara*
Acha, acha grass, fonio, hungry rice	*Digitaria exilis*	*Goezuk*	*Acha*
Eleusine, finger millet	*Eleusine corocana*	*Koetung*	*Tamba*
Rice	*Oryza sativa*	*Kapa*	*Shinkafa*
Sesame, beniseed	*Sesamum indicum*	*Lem, koedul*	*Ridi*
Coco yam, taro	*Colocasia esculentum* (Also *Xanthosoma sagittifolium*)	*Gwan* *Gwan nassara*	*Gwaza*
Sweet potato	*Ipomoea batatas*	*Doeku*	*Dankali*
Yam	*Dioscorea alata, rotundata*	*Shim*	*Doya*
Rizga	*Coleus dazo*	*Vuu*	*Risga*
Hausa potato	*Coleus dysentericus*	*Dwang*	*Tumuku*
Potato yam, bulbil-bearing yam	*Dioscorea bulbifera*	*Doetwon*	*Doyar bisa*
Groundnut, peanut	*Arachis hypogea*	*Kom*	*Gyada*
Bambara groundnut	*Voandzeia subterranea*	*Komzugut*	*Gurjiya*
Cowpea	*Vigna unguiculata* (?)	*Oeroem*	*Wake*
Lima bean	*Phaseolus lunatus*	*Bala*	*Wake, waken ankwai*
String bean	*Phaseolus vulgaris*	*Chagar*	
Pumpkin	*Cucurbita pepo* (?)	*Tokmang*	*Kabewa*
Okra, gumbo	*Hibiscus esculentus*	*Tokla*	*Kubewa*
Red pepper	*Capsicum frutescens*	*Shita*	*Barkono*
Bitter tomato	*Solanum incanum*	*Kul*	*Gauta*
Gourd, calabash, bottle gourd	*Lagenaria vulgaris*	*Jang*	*Duma, kwarya*
Oil palm	*Elaeis guineensis*	*Mwor bang*	*Kwakwa*
Canarium	*Canarium schweinfurthii*	*Paat*	*Itile*
Locust bean	*Parkia filicoidea*	*Mes*	*Dorowa*
Mango	*Mangifera indica*	*Mangoro*	*Mangoro*
Pawpaw	*Carica papaya*	*Viyap*	*Gwanda*

* For plant names and botanical designations, I am dependent largely on Dalziel (1937). Uncertain attributions are question marked. H. L. Li identified specimen seeds of *Phaseolus lunatus*.

with goat dung and stirred into the ashes of the seedbed mounds. Yams, like eleusine, are a minor crop in the hills and traditional plains villages. Yam ridges may be made shortly after the first planting, and they usually border the manured portion of the homestead field. About six inches of topsoil is taken from a rectangular area perhaps eight by five feet and piled into a surrounding ridge one and a half to two feet high. Yams are not manured, and their plot is usually changed from year to year. The potato yam called *doetwon*, which has edible bodies both under the soil and on climbing vines, is planted on similar ridges that may even be slightly higher and are manured on top. Yams and *doetwon* are both provided with cut tree branches to climb. Coco yams may be planted in conical heaps about two feet high. These are usually a more important source of food than true yams. Each heap is capped with straw and dead grass, both for their fertilizing effect and as a protection against the mound being washed away by heavy rains.

The first hoeing (*ar*, "to bite") takes place from six weeks to two months after planting, when the shoots are eight to twelve inches high. At this time, millet may be thinned and transplanted evenly over the field. The hoe digs six to nine inches deep, turning over the soil, burying the weeds, hilling the infant millet plants, and banking the edges of the terraces. No ridges are built at this time. Along the stony borders of the terraces, eleusine may be transplanted because it can flourish without much depth of soil. The initial hoeing is even more thorough in those villages where maize and coco yams replace millet and sorghum as homestead crops. There the land is dug (*fus*, "to stab") to a depth of one and a half feet, with workers advancing in a line. The coco yams that have remained in the ground from the last season are separated from their clumps, their new leaves cut off, and the corms placed about six inches apart and six to eight inches below the surface. The hoer passes earth between his legs and occasionally turns to plant the coco yams in the earth that piles up behind him. Extra coco yams are piled to one side, a few for eating but most of them sprouted and no longer of any use. Maize plants are carefully skirted or occasionally moved a few feet to a better location. Cucurbits and okra are also noted and preserved in place. It is at this time that climbing lima and string beans are planted on the ridges bounding the field or on terrace edges. The bean vines form an attractive fence bordering the path as they climb the branching tree limbs that are later put in place as supports.

Groundnut planting may begin as soon as the homestead farm has been completed, and work goes on from mid-May into June. The crop requires strong sunlight and seems to thrive in thin soil. Stony unshaded bush land that appears exhausted can still produce sizable crops of groundnuts. Excessive dampness in the soil causes the groundnuts to rot before they are ripe. Unmanured areas near the homesteads may be planted in groundnuts first before the larger bush fields one-half mile or more from the villages are farmed. Where there is sufficient soil, ridges are thrown up averaging one foot in height and one to two feet in width. The basin listing rectangles are about five feet across from the midpoint of one ridge to the midpoint of the parallel one, and six to eight feet long. The long sides of the rectangles are parallel to the slope of the hill and at right angles to the edges of the terraces. As the field is hoed, old ridges are divided in half, part of the earth being pulled to the left and part to the right. The new ridges are thus midway between those of the preceding year. They are formed of the tops of old ridges combined with the topsoil washed into the basin. All grass is turned under in this process, so that almost no greenery is visible after hoeing. The short-bladed Sudanic hoe, which can be used almost parallel to the surface of the ground, is an efficient tool for lifting off the topsoil and concentrating it on ridges.

Once the ridges have been completed, seeds are planted by dropping them two at a time from the left hand into small holes opened and covered by the right hand with a single continuous motion. Holes are made on alternate sides of the ridge top nine to twelve inches apart. All seeds have previously been shelled and inspected, and any shrunken or moldy kernels removed. In some areas acha may be sown in the basins surrounded by groundnut ridges. Even before groundnuts are planted, an early variety of acha called *na-piya* will be put in on different bush fields. Since this type grows in poor soil and is ready for harvest by August or September, it is particularly valued by plains villages. Acha tides over the family for several months until the sorghum is ripe.

In intervals between work on groundnuts in June, minor root crops are often planted. Each woman and child old enough to hoe may have a sweet potato plot consisting of ridges or mounds up to two feet high. These are planted with vine cuttings from tubers that were never dug the preceding year. Pieces of vine are pushed into the soil on the top and sides of the ridge, where they take root. Smaller ridges about the same size as those used for groundnuts are made for a little plant called *vuu,* which has reddish-skinned roots about the size and shape of wrinkled fingers. *Vuu,* like sweet potatoes, does best in a sunny location and is fertilized only with ashes. Broad flat ridges separated by shallow channels hold *dwang,* a black-skinned oval tuber looking and tasting like a very small Irish potato. *Dwang* requires manure or the natural richness of bottom land near a stream.

Among the major homestead crops are a number of kitchen garden varieties grown principally for seasoning. Most hill households grow enough capsicum red peppers for their own use, with perhaps a small surplus for trade. The same is true of the *kul,* a bitter, tomatolike vegetable which gives a viscous quality to sauce. The black seeds of a hibiscus called *gogor,* coming from bright red capsules, are familiar on the plains and are also used for sauce. Leaves, fruit, and seeds of the cucurbits are all eaten, and the okra pod is used both fresh and dried. A small gourdlike plant called *ser* is grown for its seeds, which are collected after the pulp has rotted away in an underground pit. Sesame (called beniseed in Nigeria)—red, white, and black—is a popular seasoning for meat and porridge, and it is frequently interplanted with sorghum. Most homestead farms have a few plants of tall, woody cotton whose fiber is spun by both men and women of the household.

Early millet grows at an astonishing rate, beginning to head toward the end of the second month, with the tallest stalks already ten feet high. With proper rainfall, the bulrushlike heads may be fifteen to twenty-four inches long by early July and ready for reaping. Stalks are pushed over with the foot, and the seed head is severed by being pressed against a knife held in the hand. The millet is collected in a courtyard or on a flat rocky outcropping with a circular stone wall and there dried. It is at this time that the seed for the following year is selected and bound in special bundles. Seed heads of outstanding fullness and uniformity are similarly put aside at the time of maize and sorghum harvests.

In those parts of the Kofyar hills where the late acha is a staple crop, work begins on the bush fields during the latter half of June. The farmers first pull the grass and weeds that have grown on the terraces and in the cracks of the stone walls. The uprooted vegetation is laid in a row between two old ridges and buried under a light cover of earth to form the basis of a new ridge. The low ridges for acha all run in the same direction with no cross-ridging. On an unterraced field the continuous ridges run across the slope. This form of hoeing is called *tal,* and the actual sowing, *fu,* is done broadcast by men (Plate IVA). The tiny acha seed is mixed with condiment seeds such as *gogor* or *koedul* and then scattered with wide sweeping motions of the hand. Sometimes the seed is thrown sharply at the side of a calabash so that it rebounds in various directions onto the field. Following the sowers come women with leafy branches or palm fronds sweeping (*bwur*) the earth haphazardly to cover the seed and hide it from birds. People hope for a rain shortly after planting so that the acha will rapidly sprout and take root.

The second major hoeing (*fus yit*) of the homestead farm may begin in July, but it is sometimes put off until August. The millet stalks and weeds are buried under ridges running at right angles to the edges of the terraces. Transverse ridges are also made to support the growing sorghum and form the rectangular basin which conserves moisture and halts runoff. At the same time cowpeas are planted, and they soon form a dense ground cover.

When new bush fields must be opened in the hills, the heavy work of clearing takes place in late July. Most of the second-growth trees are felled with axes except for an occasional one left to give shade to field guards and workers. Trees are cut off about three feet above the ground, or, if they are very large, the farmer merely climbs them and lops off branches. Felled timber and brush are piled along the edges of terraces to keep the newly uncovered soil from washing away. The soil is rapidly turned over but not ridged, and lightly sown in acha. A significant crop is not expected the first year, which is called *sak gagar*, "farming the fallow." During the next dry season the brush is burned, leaving ash for later working into the soil. The second year, *tal tuk*, should see the field in normal production.

By mid-July the first maize is ready for eating. Maize is hoed twice, the second time in late June. Some is eaten fresh as roasting ears, but most of the crop is allowed to dry and harden in the field. Husked ears are either put by in baskets for immediate use or braided into bundles and hung from house rafters.

On the plains, rice must be planted in late July in paddies, ditches, and flood plains. The hill people from Bong village northward plant their late millet in seedbeds at the same time. The ground is merely turned over, and no ridges are made, but in a particularly wet patch depressions may be hollowed out here and there to collect excess water. The third hoeing (*tanggon*) of the homestead farm comes in September, when the sorghum is already beginning to form seed. It is not as arduous as previous cultivations, seldom requiring more than eight days of work, and its completion marks the end of the heavy work of the agricultural year for many Kofyar.

The last crop to go into the ground is the Bambara groundnuts, which are planted in rectangular ridges during August. Weeding goes on in August and September, with a small hoe used for groundnuts, and coco yams and acha fields weeded by hand. Late millet grown to eight to twelve inches by October is ready for transplanting. New rectangular ridges are made for this purpose even in fields where groundnut ridges already exist. The seedlings are stuck into the ridge on either side and down the center, forming three rows. Each plant is placed at an angle approaching the horizontal because it is said that the leaves of seedlings pointing straight up would quickly wither in the hot sun.

The early varieties of acha and eleusine are mature by August or September. Acha is reaped with a short curved sickle and rubbed between the hands to separate the seeds from the stems. It is threshed in the field rather than being initially stored on the stalk as are most grains. Groundnuts can be pulled in October. The plants are loosened from the soil by a hoe driven in under them. In a shady corner of the field the nuts are plucked from the roots and then carried in baskets to flat rocks where they are dried for storage. The groundnut stems are redistributed around the field to be turned under at the next hoeing. Harvest begins in earnest during November, with the heads of sorghum being cut (Plate IVB) and brought back in bundles to the homestead drying rack (*par*). Cowpeas are collected at approximately the same time. Root crops are ready, and people begin to eat coco yams, sweet potatoes, *dwang, vuu,* yams, and cassava. Most of these are left in the ground, which is by now quite dry, and gathered from day to day according to need. Sweet potatoes are dug first with a stick, getting the tubers near the surface that might otherwise be dug out by goats. Later in the season the entire mound may be destroyed with a hoe to get at all the remaining potatoes. Sweet potatoes do not keep well in the ground, so effective storage for wet season use is only possible by slicing and sun-drying the tubers (cf. Johnston

1958:119). Coco yams are uncovered with a hoe. String beans are picked (*te*) and eaten while still green in August and September, but the larger reddish bean is allowed to dry on the vine before being gathered in December.

Late acha ripens in the latter part of November and is reaped with its associated sesame. The late acha is bundled into headloads and returned to the homestead for drying. Rice is reaped in a similar manner during December. Late millet in bush fields must be guarded from monkeys during its last months. Harvesting of late millet begins in December and may extend until after the first of the year. The seed heads and about twelve inches of stalk are cut off, using an old knife blade, and when a handful is collected it is bound into a sheaf and tossed aside (Plate VA). When the field has been finished, the sheaves are gathered, and thirty-five to forty-five are tied together to make a headload. The late millet is stacked next to the acha on the drying rack, where it remains until shortly before the first rains (Plate VIIIA).

The final activities of the agricultural year are those connected with threshing and storage of cereal grains in February. Early millet and sorghum are usually kept in the seed head and pounded in a wooden mortar just before use. Millet is put away as soon as it is dry, and sorghum is divided and repacked in February. Both are stored in living huts on wooden racks with fires below so that the smoke can help prevent pest damage, or in domed mud granaries. When large amounts of grain are available for sale, it is threshed by being beaten with heavy posts in a cleared courtyard and then winnowed. Late millet is threshed all at one time by being pounded (*tu*) in mortars. The grain is then winnowed and poured into large potlike mud granaries inside houses. The small seeds of acha are loosened from their stems by being rubbed vigorously against a rough stone or a section of hollowed-out log and are then stored in open baskets. Beans are treaded (*dal*) on the homestead floor to separate them from their dried pods. Sesame is beaten (*bwop*) with a stick on a level rocky outcropping and the seed swept up with brooms.

Tree crops are significant both to the diet and to the exchange economy of the Kofyar, but their care does not demand periods of continuous labor. Small fruit trees may be protected from goats, and oil palms are occasionally planted, but most economic trees are self-seeded. A prime marker of Kofyar village settlement is the oil palm that grows on homestead farms. The Kofyar prune dead fronds annually and promote tree growth by cultivating around the base of trees. Oil palms are abundant in hill villages such as Bong, where the water supply is good, and where deep soil exists in stream valleys. The trees are somewhat less abundant on the plains. Palm fruit is harvested as it ripens during the wet season by young men who climb the trees and cut off the bunches with axes. The fruit is mashed and the pulp boiled to recover the yellow-orange oil used in cooking. The palm kernels are dried, cracked, and eaten as nuts. Individual producers sell oil in bottles and four-gallon tins at plains markets. Tapping of oil palms for palm wine is a recent innovation practiced only by immigrant Ibos.

The purple olivelike fruit of large canarium trees is knocked down with long sticks during the period of November to January. It is both cooked for eating and processed into a clear golden oil that is in demand in the market. The pods of the locust bean tree mature between May and August, and brown cakes made from the seeds are sold as condiments. A few mango trees, and pawpaws, or papayas are found near the entrance to most homesteads. Mangoes have been introduced into the area and are most prevalent on the plains, where they are appreciated both for their fruit and for the deep shade they provide. Within most villages, almost the only tree growth apparent is of the above-mentioned economic species, with an occasional *Ficus* used for poles and for goat forage during the dry season. Kofyar livelihood does not depend on their orchards, and the number of economic

Plate I A. Hill homestead, Latok village

Plate I B. Plains settlement, Kwa area,
showing dispersed homesteads, ridging of fields

Plate II A (above). Hoeing of rectangular ridges, Bong village. Plate II B (left). Rain water confined by ridges of a groundnut field

Plate II C. Neighborhood work group removing compost from corral

Plate III A (above). Terraced slope near Pangkurum. Plate III B (middle). Terraced valley with dry stone walls. Plate III C (below). Ridge and ditch farming in a moist area

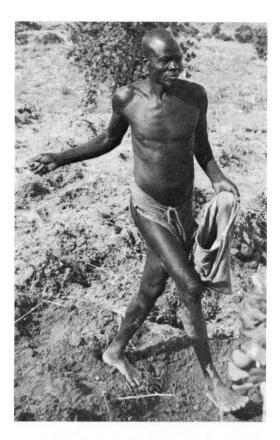

Plate IV A (right).
Sowing acha. Plate
IV B (below).
Harvesting sorghum

Plate V A (left). Harvesting late millet.
Plate V B (below).
Hoeing position

Plate VI A (right).
Applying ash fertilizer
to groundnuts. Plate VI B
(below). Volunteer work
group planting ground-
nuts

Plate VII A (left). Coco yam
with beans and maize, Bong
homestead field. Plate VII B
(below). Goat corral

Plate VIII A. Courtyard drying rack with late millet and acha, Bong village

Plate VIII B. Migrant bush homestead, showing granaries, drying rack, and bagged grain

trees varies considerably on different homesteads. But oil and
fruit are highly valued both for food and exchange, and a
major reason people give for remaining on ancestral land is
often the presence there of tree crops.

The Ecological Balance and Its Conscious Maintenance

The preceding agricultural calendar and survey of farming techniques may give the impression that the Kofyar possess a bewildering multiplicity of crops and grow all of them
extensively. It is true that the entire list of food plants is
familiar to the Kofyar, but only a few of them are basic
staples of the diet. Exactly what is grown and the relative
proportions of the various crops are determined by the striking of an ecological balance. Given factors of rainfall, climate, topography, and soil conditions must be related to
human capabilities in terms of agricultural techniques, organization of labor, physical needs, and practical knowledge.
The basic Kofyar methods of terracing and ridging, manuring, and crop rotation give them a remarkable degree of
control over their environment. Yet, in their territory the
Kofyar must cope with differences of altitude of up to fifteen
hundred feet, terrain that varies from dead level to vertical,
water scarcities and surpluses, and soil that may be deep in
humus, stony, volcanic, or sandy. Because of historical conditions that made physical expansion dangerous, the Kofyar
could not confine themselves to a particular advantageous
type of environment. Instead, they adapted themselves to the
multiple variations of their limited habitat. It is this series of
modifications, of delicate adjustments to varying environments, which most clearly attests to Kofyar agricultural
skill.

Bong village, in which I lived during much of my field
work, was atypical in its homestead crops. The standard
intensive complex on the plains and in many of the Kofyar
hill villages is made up of interplanted early millet,
sorghum, and cowpeas with pumpkin, okra, *ser* gourds,

gogor and a few maize plants.[3] Bong homestead farms feature maize and coco yams with pumpkins and climbing beans (Plate VIIA). Less than half a mile east of Bong, the satellite hamlet of Koepal follows the standard pattern. Coco yams are a subsidiary crop planted in a separate plot. The village of Zugal, three miles north of Bong, also has the standard homestead complex but lacks early millet. When I asked the reason for these variations, answers were invariably in terms of productive efficiency rather than custom or preference for certain foods. Bong people said that they avoided early millet and sorghum because these did not yield well in their village. To further questions, they replied that their special crops were necessitated by the shadiness or windiness of their location. Though I did not at first understand these explanations, they became clear as the agricultural year progressed.

Bong is perched on the edge of a steep valley running north and south and terminating just below the village. The conical volcanic core, Moelaar or Bong Peak, rises on this scarp to a height of 3,400 feet and is the pinnacle of the surrounding country. The rain-bearing winds sweep toward the plateau almost invariably from the southwest. They come up the stream valley from the south and encounter the steep slope leading to Bong. In rising quickly the warm air currents are cooled and precipitation forms. This orographic phenomenon is visible many mornings during the wet season, when Bong is blanketed in fog settling on it from the direction of the peak. The neighboring villages are not so high, and thus they do not have the same incidence of fog. Both the Kofyar themselves and outside observers (Findlay 1945) remark on the cold and damp of Bong. My own crude rainfall collection figures give Bong approximately 27 inches for the 80 days beginning June 1, while Kwa, on the plains, had 18.24 inches. Coco yams are frequently planted in swamps or along stream margins, but the extra precipitation

---

[3] This association parallels almost exactly the crops grown on manured compound gardens by a number of groups in northern Ghana (Allan 1965:242–43.)

in Bong allows them to thrive in ordinary fields. According to Johnston (1958:116), coco yams do best in moist, well-matured soil and shady mountain glades, an environment identical to that of Bong.

The rain and heavy dew in Bong are also favorable for the growth of oil palms, and since these valuable trees are carefully tended wherever they take root, the homestead farms are often well shaded. The amount of moisture and the reduction of direct sun by fog and shade are both injurious to sorghum. Maize, on the contrary, is benefited by increased moisture (Johnston 1958:66). That this is actually the reason for the change in basic crops is proved within Bong village itself. Those homesteads on the high ground to the southwest boast the best coco yams, and the people credit them directly to the moisture in the air around the peak. On the northeast slopes of the village, which are considerably lower and face away from the wind, the land is noticeably dryer and more open. Coco yams and maize are still grown, but a portion of each homestead field is devoted to sorghum. If larger cereals are planted in the bush, it is sorghum that is planted north and east of the village and maize on the west. This is due not only to quantitative differences in sunlight and precipitation but the ravages of a strong south wind (*foefong*) that may blow in September. Exposed sorghum would be flattened before it ripened, while the earlier-maturing maize would already have been harvested. All these factors are taken into conscious account by the farmers.

Sometimes the adaptation to local conditions necessary may result in extra labor. The transplanting of the smaller late millet into extensive ridged fields is recognized as being more arduous than the growing of early millet in the homestead farm. As one goes higher into the hills, early millet ceases to be important, and on the high plateau only the later variety is cultivated. I am not sure of the exact reason for this, but it may have to do with the increased precipitation on the plateau. The late millet requires a moister climate than the early three-month variety and is not found north of Zaria (Irvine 1953:107). Bong farmers claim that early millet turns black instead of ripening properly in their village. This may indeed be the case, because if the weather is wet or even misty the seeds may be attacked by molds that spoil the yield and quality (Irvine 1953:108). I have also heard complaints of birds harming early millet, and it may be that the Bong palms shelter a larger than average population of the particularly destructive finches. Whatever the predisposing factor is, it evidently becomes effective part way through the Kofyar hills. Latok, Kofyar, and Lardang plant only the early millet. The hamlets of Koepal and Kook and the village of Bogalong on a southeast-northwest line plant both. North of this line, in Bong, Zugal, Kwa-Bul, and Koeper, only the late millet grows.

Though crops differ in response to environmental demands, it is possible to substitute one for the other to fulfill the same dietary need. The two kinds of millet are equally useful in making beer. The ground cowpeas, which cannot grow under the thick leaves of Bong coco yams, are replaced by a twining bean that climbs tree-branch arbors to its place in the sun. Not enough maize can be grown in Bong to match the general level of sorghum production. But consumption of cereals is maintained by the planting of acha on the bush fields that Bong has in comparative abundance. The yam does best under the fertile, hot conditions of the lowlands south of Kofyar, and the migrant farmers there eat it in quantity. The poorer soils and the heavier rainfall of the hills seem better suited to the cultivation of sweet potatoes and coco yams. Special household needs may also enter into the determination of what crops to grow. It was said of a Kwa man who put a sizable manured field into eleusine, "He has many small children." Eleusine is used to make a thick nourishing gruel (waar) which is valued as a food for infants and youngsters.

The hill Kofyar differ from many African farmers in that they have no period of the year when food is in very short supply. There is no annual "hungry time" (cf. Richards

1939; Haswell 1953:9) in the hills, and older inhabitants can remember no time of scarcity that approached the severity of famine. This is due not only to the farming techniques but also to the variety of crops and the staggered times of maturation. Figure 5 shows the layout of a Bong intensive homestead farm and village fallow, and it gives some indication of the relative area assigned to each crop.

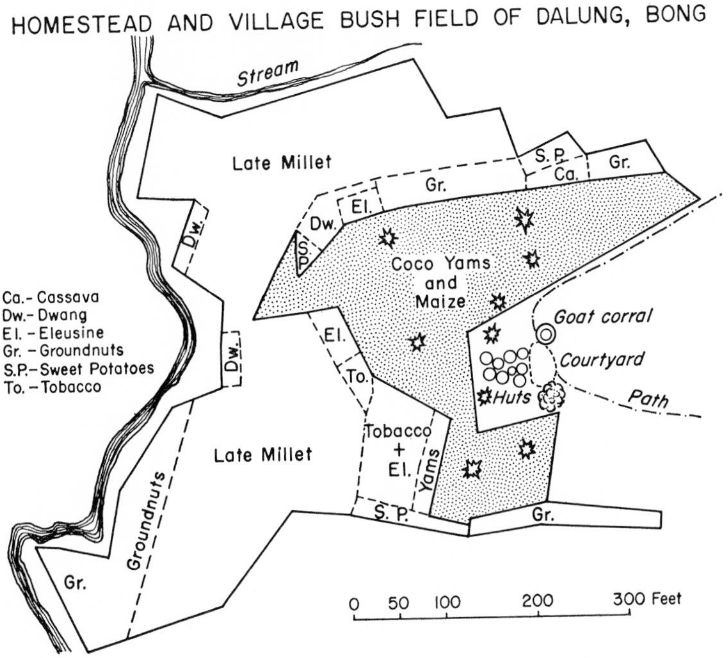

HOMESTEAD AND VILLAGE BUSH FIELD OF DALUNG, BONG

Stream

Late Millet

S. P.
Ca.
Gr.

Gr.

El.

Dw.

S.
P.

Coco Yams
and
Maize

Goat corral

Courtyard

Huts

Path

Ca.- Cassava
Dw.- Dwang
E l. – Eleusine
Gr. – Groundnuts
S.P.– Sweet Potatoes
To. – Tobacco

Dw.

El.

To.

Tobacco
+
E l.

Yams

S. P.

Gr.

Late Millet

Groundnuts

Gr.

0   50   100   200   300 Feet

Fig. 5

Crops are planted at various times from late March to August. In any one year certain crops may fail, but others will almost surely survive. Bong's 1961 groundnut harvest was poor because of erratic rainfall, but the late acha planted a month later gave a bountiful crop. It is also possible that early millet may do very well, while the late maturing sorghum in the same field will be disappointing. During the wet period of July through October, when the new crops of major staples are not yet ripe and old supplies are being

exhausted, the Kofyar garner their early millet and groundnuts along with small harvests of maize, string beans, and
acha. These are the "hunger breakers" that tide them over.
The very early acha (*natagal*) is grown solely for this purpose in the Kwa area. Even with a periodic plague of locusts
eating every green thing, such root crops as coco yams and
sweet potatoes are not destroyed. It is true that in the past
the plains villages sometimes ran low on food and were
forced to beg or extort supplies from their hill neighbors.
This was due both to the limited land available for bush
fields on the plains and to the less dependable rainfall there.
Now, with the opening of Namu vacant lands, plains dwellers can easily fill their needs.

The suitability of soil types and conditions for different
crops is accurately judged by the Kofyar farmer. Sorghum
should have brown soil whose color indicates a fair content
of humus. Groundnuts will grow either on red volcanic or
light-colored leached soils, doing best when there is not too
much organic matter in the field. Kofyar farmers classify soils
by color, texture, and moisture content. Dark brown or black
earth (*yilchip*) is preferred for the demanding crops:
sorghum, yams, and coco yams, but most homestead fields
would be classed as *baan,* light reddish brown. Red volcanic
soil (*jing*), often occurring with black pitted cinders in old
lava flows, is considered inferior. It will grow sorghum, but it
is less satisfactory for millet. It is also more difficult to work,
clinging in a gluey mass to the hoe when wet. Waterlogged
soils such as the swampy *jagat* and the alternately muddy
and hard, cracked *jak* are used for moisture-loving rice and
coco yams. Soils that are leached of organic matter are characterized as *yilpiya,* white land, or *es,* sand. No farming at all
is attempted on seriously degraded plots or on areas of hard,
lateritic material (*sang*) and earth used for building purposes (*wanju*).

As fertility declines, the Kofyar change crops to suit it.
When a Bong homestead is deserted, the field may still be
kept in coco yams for several years though no manure is

applied. When production falls off, it is switched to the groundnut-acha or the late millet–acha rotation. Migrant bush farmers start with sesame on the deep, reddish brown virgin soil of Namu. Yams are planted next, but they grow best on fresh soil, so a new field is cleared for them annually. They are followed by the millet-sorghum-cowpea complex, which may be maintained for seven or eight years. By this time the soil has been visibly depleted, becoming lighter in color and increasingly granular in texture. A sandy field of this type can then support groundnuts or cotton for three or four years before being fallowed.

Wild plants are also indicators of soil fertility. The common wild grass (*togos*) used for thatching grows only three or four feet high on fallowed land that has not yet recovered its fertility. If the grass reaches six feet or more in one season the field is ready for another cropping cycle. The Kofyar say the land is *wam,* that is, "rotten," like decomposing organic material. Grass pulled from such a field will come up with earth tangled in its roots. This shows that the soil is soft and crumbly, in good condition for farming. The failure of tree growth to return to fallowed land is a sign that it has been overworked and will regain its fertility only very slowly.

Of the twenty-four cultivated plants that according to Murdock (1959:68) were domesticated in the Western Sudan, the Kofyar utilize fifteen, which include almost all of their major food crops. Most of the Kofyar staple crops are grown in a number of varieties whose special characteristics are known and utilized. Acha may be off the early *natagal* or the late *napiya* and *koechip* types, which are planted and ripen at successively later periods. The first two varieties do best on poorer, well-sunned fields; the latter gives heavier yields. Subvarieties are classified according to color and taste. Among six varieties of sorghum, *swa kong* thrives in the hills where water is plentiful, while the red *swa bang* likes volcanic soil. Different varieties may be used on home and migrant bush farms. For instance, the Namu bush millet ripens in close to four months rather than three, so that work

on it can be fitted into the slack times when stages of the
home farming operation have been completed. Small early
millets such as *carkum* and *cong* are used for pap, while the
larger types are reserved for beer.

The Kofyar are quick to adopt new strains that have some
readily perceptible advantage. Bong grows a fine yellow ear
of maize that came from the Fulani (and may be of recent
European origin). Though this acquisition supposedly took
place only around 1950, no samples remain of the maize
formerly grown. The old variety, according to informants,
was bigger but not so tasty or uniform. The same process of
adoption is now taking place with a type of groundnut (*kom
nasara,* "the groundnut of the white man"), which has a
thinner hull and a larger seed than those formerly grown. A
number of people spontaneously requested tomato seeds
from my garden, though the plant was formerly unknown in
the area. Other crops, notably yams and cotton, have been
expanded to meet market demands. It is said by the people of
Bong that long ago they did not have the groundnut, and
that late millet came from the north less than one hundred
years ago. Sweet potato cultivation has increased within the
memory of living informants. A 1958 agricultural report
noted "a marked increase in the past four years in the planting of swamp rice" near Dimmuk and Kwa. The Kofyar
farmers who sow rice broadcast and erect sizable earth bunds
to retain water have planted the crop only for the last ten or
fifteen years.

Beliefs held by Kofyar seek to account for the planting of
various varieties. In Kofyar village it is thought that early
and late millet are "not friends" and cannot be cultivated
together. It is pointed out that the few villages where both
types are grown often have inferior early millet harvests. In
Bogalong late millet must be threshed outside the village
before it comes into the presence of the early homestead
crop. Twelve named varieties of acha exist in Bong, and
different ones are said to "like" (*dem*) different farmers. It

may be that a man grows a different one than his father because he did not get good yields from the former strain.

Field Types

Though the observer is most impressed by the permanent cultivation of the Kofyar homestead farms, there are also several other field types that give flexibility to the agricultural system. These form a complete spectrum from plots that grow a single crop and are then abandoned to semipermanent fields that remain in almost continuous production of small grains and peanuts. Kofyar bush fallows differ in several ways from the shifting or swidden cultivation in areas of dense tropical rainfall. The large, dense plant associations which both protect the earth and continually return nutrients to the soil (Geertz 1963:24) are not needed, and Kofyar may sow entire savanna fields in single crops. The soil-conserving function of native trees and grasses is taken over by permanent terraces and ridging. The initial burning of tree growth in a fallowed area seems less important in maintaining fertility than the combination of relatively less demanding crops, regular rotation, careful turning under of organic material, and, in the case of groundnuts, fertilizing with household ash. The efficacy of these techniques is seen in the six- to nine-year productive span of hill fields as distinguished from the one to three years during which rain forest swiddens can give significant yields. The Kofyar do not complain of significant invasions by weeds, but they do attempt to group bush fields together as a partial defense against wild animals. Their preferred fallow periods are fifteen to twenty years, but there are some overworked hill slopes that will not regenerate bush and tree growth within this time. The Kofyar might be said to practice shifting cultivation intensively, a type of land use that Allan calls "recurrent cultivation" (1965:33).

Fields farmed by the Kofyar system of shifting cultivation are of three types, depending on their location and use. I have called them village, bush, and migrant bush fields, though the Kofyar themselves do not make these distinctions. Village fields are those contiguous to the manured homestead farms and lying within the settled area. They may have been intensively cultivated in the past as a homestead site, but with the death or moving away of the occupants, they revert to a rotation of acha, late millet, and groundnuts or assorted tubers and are fallowed irregularly. Parts of such small fields may be manured again if the owner expands his present intensive farm or a new homestead is built there. These conveniently situated plots may be cultivated for longer periods than they are rested, but the more demanding crops (sorghum, early millet) are never planted on them, and yields appear to be low.

The extent of village farms depends on the type of farming and on the pressure of population within the settlement. In Bong, where homestead farms are small, there are not enough households to occupy all the available sites in the village. Most families have approximately an acre devoted to minor grains, tubers, and occasionally tobacco or eleusine, all within the settled area. Kofyar, with the more typical large homestead farms, has correspondingly smaller village fallowed plots. On the plains in Kwa and Dimmuk, homesteads are crowded so close together that virtually no land remains for subsidiary crops.

Bush farms in both hill and plains areas are those lying outside the settled perimeter of the village but seldom more than thirty minutes' to an hour's walk away. They are terraced where necessary, but the walls are often lower and the benches narrower than those inside the village. They are never manured (except when Fulani herders can be persuaded to camp on them), and they must be fallowed to restore fertility. No one spends the night in nearby bush fields, and the only type of structure there is a rough shelter for those who guard the ripening grain from animal pests.

Migrant bush farms require a journey of from several hours to a day. For the most part they occupy vacant plain land south of the Kofyar country. Their distance from the homesteads of the owners prevents commuting and makes necessary the building of a self-contained bush residence. Since migrant bush fields are located on virgin or fully regenerated plots, they can support several years of heavy homestead crops (sorghum, early millet, cowpeas), as well as yams, without fertilization. Unlike the homestead and local bush fields, they are geared largely to producing a surplus that can be sold for cash.

Methods of Studying Agricultural Production

Anthropological studies that focus on agriculture can be expected to deal adequately with peoples' techniques of cultivation, level of scientific knowledge, calendar of seasonal activities, and major crops, as well as with related social factors such as settlement pattern, labor organization, the control of productive resources, and religious and magical observances connected with farming. The important matters of how much, exactly, of the various crops is produced and what yield per acre is obtained are often slighted. Though the significance of such figures in any economic investigation is obvious, there are usually good reasons for their absence. Many farming people conceal the amount of their harvests not only from outsiders but from one another. They may fear higher taxes, increased demands for hospitality, or the magical diminution of food by the very act of counting it. Scattered plots and the jealousies of independently farming co-wives kept Bohannan (1954) from charting Tiv yam yields. Amounts of root crops such as coco yams in Bong, which are left in the ground and gathered as need arises, are difficult to calculate. Yield figures require careful measurements of fields differing in environmental factors. Freeman (1955:30) was forced to make clandestine measurements of Iban rice fields because of local fears that such activity would anger the spirit of the *padi*.

The Kofyar were not outwardly suspicious or uncooperative when I questioned them on the most recent year's harvest of major food crops and on the numbers of their domestic animals. With the help of several literate schoolboy enumerators from the area, I collected this data as part of a standard household census of 542 households in sixteen communities. Interviews were often conducted in the homestead courtyard during the dry season, when the grain crops were exposed on drying racks. The head of the household responded without hesitation to inquiries about the number of bundles or baskets of food he had harvested. For these reasons I felt that the figures provided a reasonable approximation of Kofyar production.

However, an analysis of the figures, combined with further research in 1966–67, convinced me that there were serious shortcomings in this quantitative material, almost always in the direction of underestimating the amount of produce harvested. This was due in part to people's wish to hide the measure of personal wealth from an outsider who might conceivably use his knowledge to bring harm. The Kofyar are both hospitable and cautious, and their welcome to me was always tempered by an imperfect understanding of my motives. It is also obvious that without written records or any cultural emphasis on the accurate remembrance of numbers, the Kofyar household head may not *be able* to give a good accounting of his produce. Sorghum and early millet are both brought to the drying rack in baskets and heaped up there. Only when the grain is taken down to be stored away is it tied into bundles, and then the interest is not in the number of bundles so much as in the equitable division of these among wives and children. The bundles of acha and late millet vary in size acccording both to the strength of the person who was to headload them from the field and to the distance of that field. I therefore offer the following quantitative measures with reservation. I believe that as a relative measure they do show certain meaningful differences among village communities. Experience suggests, however, that the actual number of bundles may be as much as twice that reported by the farmer. Rather than trying to modify my figures to allow for this difference, I have chosen to set down the quantities as given by the Kofyar along with weights of bundles and grain based on my own measurements.[4] The livestock numbers, though considerably more accurate than those given the clerks who make out tax lists, should also be considered as minimum figures somewhat below the true means.

In Kofyar country I was freely allowed to measure more than forty fields, including homestead farms, bush fallows, and plains fields under cash crops. My field measurements were done with a prismatic compass and sixty-six-foot tape, and they usually involved a complete circuit of the field. The boundaries were plotted on graph paper with errors of seldom more than fifteen to twenty feet between beginning and ending points. The rugged nature of the hill country and irregularity of individual fields made mapping a strenuous business involving climbing and descending flights of terraces and taking as many as twenty-five sightings around a single plot. On the other hand, the Kofyar concept of private landownership with marked boundaries and the clear dis-

[4] To convert the Kofyar measure of bundles to a rough average of pounds of grain per bundle, I weighed a number of bundles and then the threshed grain that resulted after the sheaves were pounded in a mortar or beaten with a stick. This was done during my second period of field work. I had earlier used an approximation given to me by a local informant which proved to be seriously in error (Netting 1965c).

AVERAGE WEIGHTS OF KOFYAR CROP UNITS[*]

Crop	Number of Bundles in Sample	Average Dry Weight per Bundle (Pounds)	Average Weight Threshed Grain per Bundle (Pounds)
Sorghum	21	64.7	51.8
Early millet	10	71.5	51.8
Acha	19	45.7	32.4
Late millet	29	60.4	44.1

[*] For comparative data on Hausa agricultural production and equivalent measure see Smith (1955:237–240).

tinction between cultivated land and bush made it possible
to distinguish the limits of fields with considerable accuracy.
Most of the plotting of areas was done in the field, where
discrepancies could be checked.

Agricultural Production and Estimated Land Use

To introduce this summary of Kofyar agricultural output,
it may be useful to contrast the demography and grain production of two villages, Bong and Bogalong. These are adjoining communities in the hills, both of which have populations of about 250 and between fifty and sixty homesteads.

TABLE 3

DEMOGRAPHY OF TWO HILL VILLAGES

Village	Total Popu- lation	Num- ber of Home- steads	Average House- hold Size	Range of House- hold Size	Num- ber of Adult Work- ers	Average Adults per House- hold	Range of Adults per House- hold
Bong	249	58	4.3	1–10	153	2.6	1–7
Bogalong	251	50	5.0	2–8	160	3.2	2–6

Bong has a slightly smaller average household size and number of adult workers per household (Table 3). The villages
are separated by a stream valley and some three miles of
bush land. Bogalong is on a level ridgetop northeast of Bong
and at a somewhat lower elevation. The difference in moisture and exposure to sun that this makes appears in the
different combination of crops grown (Table 4), with Bong
emphasizing acha and late millet while Bogalong depends on
sorghum and early millet. Bong also raises maize, lima beans,
and coco yams, while Bogalong grows cowpeas. Both produce
groundnuts, sesame, palm oil, sweet potatoes, and a variety
of leafy vegetables. Bogalong is a somewhat better endowed
community than its highland neighbor, having more of the
larger field grains and more easily worked soils. Table 5

TABLE 4

GRAIN CROP PRODUCTION OF TWO HILL VILLAGES

Crop	Total Production (Bundles)	Average Production per Homestead (Bundles)	Range of Production per Homestead (Bundles)	Weight of Grain per Bundle (Pounds)	Estimated Weight of Grain per Household (Pounds)
Sorghum:					
Bong	228	3.9	0–30	52	168
Bogalong	613	12.2	0–30	52	634
Early millet:					
Bong	19	.2	0–12 *	52	10
Bogalong	620	22.4	0–50	52	1,165
Acha:					
Bong	436	7.6	0–40	33	251
Bogalong	78	1.5	0–13 †	33	50
Late millet:					
Bong	726	12.6	0–45	44	554
Bogalong	43	0.8	0–40 ‡	44	35

* Three homesteads only.
† Fourteen homesteads only.
‡ Two homesteads only.

TABLE 5

DOMESTIC ANIMALS OF TWO HILL VILLAGES

Animals	BONG			BOGALONG		
	Total	Average per Homestead	Range	Total	Average per Homestead	Range
Goats	288	5.0	0–10	591	11.8	0–50
Sheep	66	1.1	0–15	233	4.6	0–30
Cattle	19 *	.33	0–9			
Horses	9 †	.15	0–1	14 ‡	.28	0–2
Chickens	535	9.2	0–30	967	19.3	0–60

* All in 8 homesteads, includes both dwarf and zebu cattle.
† All in 9 homesteads.
‡ All in 11 homesteads.

indicates that Bogalong is also richer in livestock, though Bong has more dwarf cattle.

Looked at in a wider perspective, hilltop, hillside, and plains villages show certain regular differences in crop production that may reflect both variations in physical environment and relative scarcity of agricultural land (Table 6). Kofyar country lies athwart a transition zone between lowland cultivation of early millet and highland dependence on late millet. An abrupt change occurs in Zugal, Bong, and Koepal, which plant no early millet but replace it with the smaller late variety. The bush farm lands of these villages adjoin one another in the northwestern corner of the sampled area. They appear to be slightly higher, cooler, and wetter than neighboring villages. There is also some tendency to increase average production of acha at successively higher altitudes. From Meer, at the foot of the escarpment, to Bogalong, Buumdagas, and finally Zugal, average acha harvests go from .8 to 7.1 bundles, and a similar progression appears on the northward ascent from Dep through Gonkun and Mangbar to Bong. Since acha has a relatively low yield and is farmed extensively, the production gradient may coincide with the relative availability of land for bush fallow. The more northerly hill villages have rather extensive tracts of bush land surrounding them, some of which has a cover of second-growth tree vegetation almost lacking on the plains and lower slopes. Plains and escarpment villages such as Dunglong, Korom, and Pangkurum may also be shifting their attention from local bush fields where acha is grown to the more rewarding cultivation of cash crops on new migrant farms.

Average total production of cereal crops per homestead appears closely related to the topographical position of the village. An index reached by simply adding average number of bundles of sorghum, early and late millet, and acha (Table 6) groups hilltop and plateau villages together (except for one village) with indexes from 22.9 to 30.0 and separates them from villages on the slopes of the escarpment and in the narrow valleys debouching on the plain (indexes from 13.2 to 19.1). The only exception to this generalization is the hilltop hamlet of Koepal, with the unusually low index of 14.3. The reason for this difference may lie in the availability of level and reasonably open land. Hilltop and plateau sites have a larger arable area than locations on the steep and often rocky hill slopes. They may also receive more sunlight than the narrow valley bottoms. Dunglong, the single village in the open plains for which figures are available, has an index of 21.3, suggesting that here the advantages of level land and adequate exposure to sun are limited by denser population and smaller homestead farms. Regular differences in amount of arable land are also indicated by the fact that five out of eight hilltop villages support populations of 160 and more, while only one out of seven hill slope and valley settlements reaches this size.

The relative importance of various domestic animals remains fairly constant throughout the Kofyar hills. Goats and chickens are kept by almost every household. In ritual contexts, chickens are used for small-scale sacrifices, while goats are reserved for more important ceremonies. Both can be sold for cash, and chickens are frequent gifts during courtship and on the visit of affinal kinsmen. Stall-fed goats are also necessary to provide manure for the compost on which intensive cultivation depends. Sheep, cows, and horses are herded outside the village during the day and thus require special attention. Their possession indicates wealth, and cows and horses are usually owned by only a few people in each village. Though horses are ridden for hunting and formerly were ridden in battle on the plains, the major value of the larger stock is for sacrifice at the *maap* funeral commemoration feast and as a part of bride price payments. For purposes of comparison, an index of domestic animals was computed by assigning a value of 10 to each cow or horse, 2 to each sheep or goat, and 0.2 to each chicken in rough approximation of their relative market values. This index (Table 6) showed no regular relationship between average

TABLE 6

AVERAGE GRAIN PRODUCTION AND DOMESTIC ANIMALS PER HOMESTEAD

Village	Home-steads	Sor-ghum (Bun-dles)	Early Millet (Bun-dles)	Acha (Bun-dles)	Late Millet (Bun-dles)	Cereal Crop Index	Goats	Sheep	Cows	Horses	Chick-ens	Domes-tic Animal Index
Hilltop and plateau:												
Kofyar	48	12.2	11.6	1.1		24.9	9.5	3.7	.02	.29	11.8	25.3
Longsel	28	11.3	8.7	2.5	.4	22.9	8.6	4.5	.10	.32	12.8	26.3
Bogalong	50	12.2	12.4	1.5	.8	25.9	11.8	4.6		.28	19.3	26.0
Buumdagas	14	15.0	10.5	3.6		29.1	14.3	1.4	.14	.14	24.7	40.7
Zugal	42	11.3		7.1	11.6	30.0	8.7	7.7	.35	.35	12.9	18.4
Bong	58	3.9		7.6	12.6	24.1	5.0	1.1	.33	.15	9.2	15.8
Koepal	17	7.3		2.6	4.4	14.3	5.5		.06	.15	9.5	15.1
Mangbar	48	9.3	10.7	5.5		25.5	7.8	1.1	.06	.01	16.3	25.3
Hillside and valley:												
Gonkun	26	5.5	4.7	4.5	3.4	18.1	7.7	1.1			13.8	22.6
Dep	35	7.1	11.2	.8		19.1	9.3	1.2	.20		12.4	23.1
Pangkurum	28	10.8	6.5			17.3	5.2	3.2	.17	.07	4.2	12.8
Korom	14	9.0	6.1	.6		15.7	7.8	1.7	.14		12.6	22.2
Kopfuboem	16	9.5	5.8			15.3	8.1	3.3		.12	9.6	21.1
Wudai	24	8.7	6.2	1.3		16.2	3.1	3.0			7.4	13.5
Meer	32	6.8	5.6	.8		13.2	3.9	.9		.03	10.9	15.6
Plains:												
Dunglong (Kwa)	62	10.2	9.5	1.6	3.4	21.3	4.8	1.2			4.0	10.0
Average per homestead		9.3	9.1 *	3.3 *	7.4 *		7.3	2.6	.10	.16	11.5	

* In those villages where crop is grown.

domestic animal index and village location or crop production. It is probable, however, that other plains villages would
resemble Dunglong in having limited numbers of livestock.
Because of the densely settled nature of the plains, there is
little wasteland where grass may be gathered, and fodder for
goats must be brought from a considerable distance.

The variability in production of different cereal crops
among the homesteads of a single village may relate to their
different uses. The forty-eight homesteads in Kofyar village
grow slightly more sorghum than millet on the average, and
this is true of ten out of thirteen other settlements in the
sample. The range in millet is from one to forty bundles per
homestead as compared to four to twenty-five for sorghum.
Sorghum is a necessity for making the staple porridge that is
the major food of the Kofyar, and every family tries to
provide itself with an adequate supply. Millet, on the other
hand, is converted into beer that is consumed in quantity but
not on a regular daily basis. One who grows little millet can
still obtain beer to drink by buying it, working in communal
labor parties that receive it, or participating in celebrations
at which it is provided. Because beer can be traded for cash,
farm work, and prestige, ambitious individuals may grow
millet in quantities far beyond their immediate needs (Netting 1964). Sorghum enters the market in smaller quantities
and is considered generally less valuable than millet.

To arrive at an estimate of yields, a series of homestead
farms were measured and their crop production tabulated
over a two-year period in the hilltop villages of Kofyar and
Mangbar. An attempt was made to include both large and
small farms with households of varying sizes and composi-
tions. The sample (Table 7) in fact represented households
and homestead farms that were larger than average, the
number of adult workers being 5 rather than 3.4 as in the
more extensive Kofyar survey, (Table 11), and the average
yield of sorghum being 14.8 bundles instead of 9.3 (cf. Table
6). Though I measured the fields in each case, the record of
the number of bundles or baskets harvested depended on the

TABLE 7
Homestead Farm Sample Acreages and Yields

Homestead	Adult Workers	Acreage	Sorghum		Millet		Cowpeas		Total Threshed Weight (Pounds)	Total Threshed Weight per Acre
			Bundles	Threshed Weight	Bundles	Threshed Weight	Baskets	Threshed Weight		
Mangbar 1	6	1.10	9.5	492	5.5	285	2.0	89	866	787
Mangbar 2	3	1.31	6.5	337	14.0	725	1.0	44	1,106	844
Mangbar 3	1	1.36	19.5	1,010	11.5	596	3.5	155	1,761	1,295
Kofyar 1	10	1.80	20.0	1,036	6.5	337	2.5	110	1,483	824
Kofyar 2	2	.99	8.0	414	6.0	311	5.0	222	947	957
Kofyar 3	6	1.97	20.0	1,036	18.0	932	6.0	266	2,234	1,134
Kofyar 4	7	2.28	20.0	1,036	22.0	1,140	4.0	177	2,353	1,032
Average total	5	1.54	14.8	767	11.9	616	3.4	151	1,536	
Average per acre			9.6	497	7.7	399	2.3	102		982

recollection of the informant and is probably somewhat un-
derestimated. Weights of grain are based on sample thresh-
ings summarized in note 4 of this chapter. Using these estimates as a minimum figure, it would appear that hill Kofyar
homesteads produce an average of at least 1,000 pounds of
grain and legumes per acre from their manured farms. This
does not include several baskets of tubers, leafy sauce crops,
condiments, cucurbits, gourds, tubers, and cotton that are
also planted in the fertilized area. High per acre production
seems in general to be closely related to the number of
stall-fed goats. The homesteads with highest yields (Table
7), Mangbar 3 and Kofyar 3 and 4, have from 12 to 15 goats
each. Mangbar 1, with the lowest production, has only 2
goats.

Variation within the sample may be accounted for to some
degree by social factors within the households. Low yields
may result when the energies of the household head are
diverted into nonagricultural channels. Mangbar 1 was
headed by an extremely active native doctor and ritual specialist whose grown sons often accompanied him to other
villages where he was in demand for curing ceremonies. The
village chief who occupied Kofyar 1 had time-consuming
political and judicial duties that often took him away from
the village. In both these cases a portion of the large household labor force helped to maintain cash crop migrant farms
on the plains, and this was true also of Kofyar 3 and 4.

Village and bush fields where shifting cultivation is practiced are even more variable in production than homestead
farms. Differences seem to depend on the relative natural
advantages of particular plots and on climatic conditions. In
the limited sample of fourteen fields belonging to eleven
individuals in Bong, no consistant decline in yield associated
with length of time under cultivation was discernible. Data
on no more than five successive years of any single field's
production were gathered, and these included two or three
different crops planted in rotation (Netting 1963:112–113).
Declining yield may be marked only toward the end of the

cropping cycle, and climatic effects may mask the tendency in intervening years. A disappointing groundnut harvest may be followed in the same year by a bumper crop of late millet as a result of different timing and amount of precipitation. A difference in the per acre yield of acha on neighboring similar fields may result from a few weeks' difference in time of planting. Certain bush farms are considered more valuable because of their soil and topography. Uniformly high yields were recorded from Bong fields located in deep-soiled bottom land or possessing perennial water supplies

TABLE 8

BUSH FARM ACREAGES AND YIELDS

Crop	Fields in Sample	Total Acreage	Average Acreage	Total Yield	Average Units per Acre	Average Weight per Acre (Pounds)
Acha	13	24.28	1.87	173 bundles	7.13	231 *
Late millet	8	16.62	2.11	165 bundles	9.81	433 *
Groundnuts	4	6.11	1.53	20 baskets	3.27	216 †

* Threshed grain.
† Unshelled groundnuts.

from ground-seepage springs. Bush fields tend to be considerably larger than homestead farms and are often worked by several households which share the harvest. A woman and her brother's daughter together administered a 2.8-acre plot, three married brothers worked 2.4 acres in common, and a pair of male lineage relatives together leased and cultivated a 3.6-acre bush farm. Though a single Bong household may have two or more bush fields in any one year (Table 8), their combined areas are still much smaller than the migrant bush fields described in Chapter 8. Bush farm crops are grown for the most part in separate fields, and their yields per acre of 200 to 450 pounds contrast sharply with those of the interplanted homestead fields whose total produce of grains and legumes was two to four times as large.

Given a small sample of measured fields and crop yields, it is possible only to suggest in preliminary fashion what may be average Kofyar land requirements. If we assume that the average combined yield per acre of millet and sorghum is 17.3 bundles (Table 7) and that the average homestead farm produces 18.4 bundles annually (Table 6), average homestead farm size would be on the order of 1.06 acres. Using the same assumption, acha at 7.13 bundles per acre and an average of 3.3 bundles per household would give a field area of .46 acre; late millet at 9.81 bundles per acre and 7.4

TABLE 9

VILLAGE LOCATION AND ESTIMATED LAND USE PER HOUSEHOLD

Village Location	Home- stead (Acres)	Ground- nuts	Acha	Late Millet	Total Acreage under Major Crops
Bong (hilltop)	.43	.89	1.07	1.28	3.67
Kofyar (hill- top)	1.38	1.16	.15	...	2.69
Dunglong (plain)	1.14	.61	.22	...	1.97
Dep (hill slope)	1.06	.46	.11	...	1.63

bundles per household indicates fields of .75 acre; and groundnuts at 3.27 baskets per acre and a Kofyar average of 4 baskets per household suggests the use of fields averaging 1.22 acres.

Because of environmental differences and the resulting variations in relative proportion of crops grown, villages may have significantly different requirements for land (Table 9). In Bong village, where the maize–coco yam association replaces the more usual sorghum-millet-cowpea complex, homesteads are considerably smaller. A measured sample of nine homesteads in various parts of the village averaged only .43 acre each, with a range of .1 to 1.7 acres. On the other hand, Bong bush fields that produce the staple acha and late millet are appreciably larger than those of their neighbors. Though it is impossible with present data to compare accurately land use in several villages, inferences made from the production figures of major crops give a plausible picture of existing differences. In Bong, where the environment discourages homestead grain farming and vacant land permits extensive fallowing, somewhat more land is cultivated. In hill slope villages and those on the plain, land for homestead farms and bush fallow may be scarce, and plots tend to decrease in size.

The average land requirement for a homestead in the four sample villages would be approximately 2.5 acres, including both intensively farmed homestead and bush under shifting cultivation. With the addition of a few small plots for sweet potatoes, Bambara groundnuts, rice, eleusine, tobacco, and so on, perhaps .2 acre, the total land per household devoted to agriculture in any one year, would average about 2.7 acres, or just over half an acre per person.[5] With the requirement of .5 acre per person as a base, and a Kofyar population of 55,000, some 27,500 acres would be needed for farming. This is almost 23 per cent of the entire Kofyar territory, not including land necessarily fallowed, and it represents a notably high proportion of cultivated to unused and unusable land (cf. Allan 1965:26, 28). Definite pressure on land resources is evident in movements since 1930 to establish migrant bush farms in a neighboring sparsely populated area.

Diet

Cereal porridge with a sauce of boiled greens or oil seeds is both the mainstay and the most highly valued dish in the Kofyar diet. Throughout Northern Nigeria this staple diet, known in Hausa as *tuwo da miya,* (porridge with sauce) is

[5] This estimate agrees well with figures for savanna agriculture in northern Ghana and is slightly more than half the average land per person requirements under shifting cultivation in Northern Rhodesia (Allan 1965:65, 57).

found. Only in the south, where savanna gives way to forest country, do grains decline in importance in favor of the root crops: yams, cassava, and coco yams. Though occasional meat feasts are relished by the Kofyar, flesh is thought to make one "fat," and the only food that can sustain the hard work of farming is porridge. The most usual constituent of porridge is sorghum meal, ground fresh and boiled in water to which has been added a little of the bitter leachings from wood ashes. Acha, which has been pounded in a mortar and winnowed until only the tiny white seed remains, is not ground. The seeds are sometimes roasted before boiling to improve the flavor. Porridge (*moen* or *gwom*) is boiled until it is stiff and most of the water has been absorbed. In texture and appearance it is rather like hominy grits, and it is thick enough to be eaten with the fingers. Because the preparation of porridge requires some two hours of work, it is seldom ready until after nightfall, and enough is made to be served cold or warmed over for breakfast. Porridge is ladled with a wooden spoon into calabash or enamelware bowls for eating.

Since the staple changes very little, variety is sought in the sauce or relish (*tok*) poured over the top of the porridge like a gravy. During the rains this is frequently made of green leaves of cucurbits, coco yams, or other cultivated and wild plants. Okra or the seeds of the *gogor* plant are frequently used, and sauce made from them has the preferred viscous quality. The porridge is always liberally salted, and various condiments such as locust bean cakes, dried fish, and capsicum peppers used sparingly may be added to the sauce. Pumpkin flesh and its dried seeds are used in season, and, as fresh greens become rarer, a sauce is often made of pounded groundnuts and sesame. Indeed, a large part of the groundnut crop is consumed in this way. Alternate sauces are of pulverized woody stems called *fuk*, palm or canarium oil, or meat broth. Cereals may also be ground and boiled for a short time to make a thick gruel (*waar*). Some millet is made into gruel instead of beer, and eleusine is particularly valued for this purpose. At markets and beside the roads, women sell a refreshingly cool, thin pap of sorghum to travelers. Uncooked pap, a simple mixture of finely ground grain and water, called *aas,* is also widely consumed. Occasionally sorghum kernels are boiled whole and served when they are tender, with a topping of pounded groundnuts. Dried beans, including cowpeas and, in some hill villages, the red climbing bean, are often prepared as a delicious main dish with palm oil and sesame during the latter part of the dry season and the early rains. Bambara groundnuts are similarly served and, along with beans, are a source of protein.

Though grain porridge is always preferred, the Kofyar consume considerable amounts of root crops. From November to April, coco yams and sweet potatoes are available, and there are also small quantities of *vuu, dwang, doetwon,* yams, and cassava. In Bong village, where tubers are plentiful, they alternate with porridge as dry season daily fare. They are most frequently baked in an overturned pot in a fire pit, but some sweet potatoes are sliced and sun-dried for later eating with palm oil. Yans baked in ashes are widely eaten on plains migrant bush farms, where they grow in abundance and are easy to prepare. Pawpaws, or papayas, are eaten, and the introduced mango trees are widely grown for food and for their fine dense shade, but few other fruits are available. People eat the pulp of ripe palm fruit and later crack and munch the oily kernel. The purple canarium fruit is eaten boiled.

Beer made of millet, or occasionally of sorghum or maize, must be regarded as a food, though it is not an item of daily consumption. Its important place in the culture of the Kofyar has been outlined elsewhere (Netting 1964). When beer is plentiful, no other food is desired, but no one among the Kofyar lives only on beer, as do some central African chieftains. This opaque, yeasty, somewhat sour beverage has a low alcoholic content and considerable body. It is enjoyed by men and women alike and is given to babies still too young to hold a calabash. As in the ancient cereal-based civilizations of the Fertile Crescent, beer furnishes nutritional elements that might otherwise be lacking in the Kofyar diet. The products of germination of malted grain and microbiological growth include ascorbic acid, several B vitamins, and microbial proteins, and brewing also increases the assimilability of complex carbohydrates (Platt 1955).

Beer is regularly obtainable during the later dry season, when it is made for sale in individual homesteads. Throughout the year, brewing precedes religious and magical observances, and beer is the usual reward for cooperative work parties. Where beer is in short supply, singing and dancing are out of the question. Even the smallest bush markets have a collection of beer sellers under a spreading tree. It is difficult to judge the beer consumption of the average Kofyar man because drinking is almost always done in groups and varies with the supply of the beverage and the demand for it. A trial calabash may be sampled at daybreak at the *pe mwos,* "the place of beer," and the last jar may be taken out of hiding and drained late at night. Women and children have neither the opportunity nor the money to wander about the country as men sometimes do in search of beer and probably drink less than adult men, but they may drink quantities of *fis,* the tart unfermented squeezings of the discarded mash. Beer drinking does not usually accompany meals, where water or sometimes pap are the only liquids consumed.

Meat is an infrequent item on most Kofyar menus, and a man who will kill a chicken or a goat "only for eating" is thought to be either rich or thriftless. Most magical ceremonies require the killing of at least a hen, and sometimes a dog or goat, but such meat must often be divided with the native doctor and his helpers as well as lineage members or neighbors who have gathered for the occasion. Chickens are often given to a prospective bride, and presents of meat must be made to her parents. Large animals such as cows and horses are killed only for funeral commemorations, and the meat must be so widely distributed among specified kin that most participants receive no more than a large handful. Large kills on the hunt are rare, but again custom demands the wide distribution of such meat. Men who have received meat usually return with a portion for their wives and are severely censured if they eat it alone in the bush. Every edible bit of the animal is devoured including the smaller bones and the hide. Meat is invariably boiled until tender, then rolled in salt and sesame powder. The broth is saved as a sauce for porridge.

Because grain is stored on the stalk and threshed and ground daily or according to need, it is difficult to judge daily consumption of the important food crops. Records kept by local informants covering twenty-three households over periods of two to five weeks each in May and June give some indication of food intake. Grains and legumes were measured in *mudus* (bowls used for measuring) before grinding. Adults eating the main meal were listed, while children under twelve years old and dogs were arbitrarily counted as one-half an adult. The average weights of uncooked grain refer to the amount used for the main evening meal, which usually also provided a cold morning breakfast, but they do not cover beer, pap, vegetable sauces, and the snacks of groundnuts, root crops, and fruit that people enjoy whenever they are available. An average of 1.57 pounds of sorghum per adult was prepared on those days when sorghum porridge was the main dish. Comparable figures are acha, 1.86 pounds; rice, 1.52 pounds; and beans, 2.24 pounds. In an isolated test of two cooking groups in a single homestead, it was found that approximately 2.2 pounds of root crops were being cooked for each person on those days when cereal porridge was not prepared. A rough estimate of Kofyar daily main mean food intake would thus be from 1.5 to 2 pounds of grain per person or from 2 to 2.5 pounds of root crops. If this level of consumption is projected on an annual basis, food supplies would have to be larger than the estimates by household heads of the amounts of grain harvested. There is no indication that the Kofyar substantially restrict their diet during certain seasons or that they purchase quantities of food. It is probable that actual food production is somewhat in excess of that reported by the Kofyar.

It is obvious that a quantitative study of nutrition is a vital part of any complete discussion of Kofyar ecology. The data now at hand are fragmentary, but they bear out the general impression that the Kofyar are adequately fed in terms of calories, proteins, minerals, and vitamins. Outward signs of malnutrition are rare, and persistent complaints of hunger were never heard. The results of a survey of nutrition among the non-Moslem Sura living directly north of the Kofyar on the high plateau showed a total calorie intake per person per day of 2,704, and an average protein intake of 103 per cent of the daily requirement.[6] These nutritive values, as well as the height and weight curves of local children, are markedly superior to those reported for the forest belt of Western Nigeria (Collis, Dema, and Lesi 1962).[7] The Kofyar diets based on intensive farming in an area of somewhat higher rainfall are, if anything, larger and more varied than those of the Sura. The concentration on cereals probably provides all the savanna groups with a more satisfactory protein intake than that of forest dwelling root crop producers (Clark and Haswell 1964:7). Additional protein is provided by groundnuts, beans, and occasional meat. Though milk and milk products are periodically available from Fulani herdsmen, they have found little favor with the Kofyar.

Some idea of the relative contributions of various foodstuffs to the Kofyar diet can be gained from records of house-

[6] The average calorie intake for Nigeria is 2,680, which in turn is the highest in tropical Africa (Clark and Haswell 1964:17.)

[7] Though the Sura diets sampled were limited in both number and duration, they were collected during a season of comparative scarcity and probably represent somewhat less than average values (Collis, Dema, and Lesi 1962:145).

hold, or in some cases personal, consumption kept by local informants and schoolboys. In traditional hill and plain villages where sorghum is the dominant crop, porridge made from it will be eaten at 60 to 75 per cent of all meals. Sorghum kernals boiled with cowpeas appear in about 13 per cent of all menus, and root crops including yams, sweet potatoes, coco yams, and cassava are boiled or baked for another 14 per cent. Yams are important chiefly in the months of January through March, when they can be brought from migrant bush fields. With the coming of the rains, the more effectively stored cereals again become mainstays. Bong village households have a more varied diet, with acha porridge 41 per cent of the time; other grains including sorghum, rice, and maize, 12 per cent; beans, 22 per cent; coco yams, 16 per cent; and sweet potatoes, 7 per cent. Variety in foods is appreciated, and the main dish of one day is seldom repeated on the next. Groundnuts, sesame, palm oil, cucurbits, and leafy vegetables are the principal sauce ingredients, but groundnuts are eaten alone in about 2 per cent of main meals. As might be expected, the plains migrant farmers devote a larger proportion of their menus to yams, using especially those tubers too small for sale. Yams also have the advantage of easy preparation, requiring only to be baked in ashes. They may also be boiled, cooked and mashed, or sun-dried and ground to flour. Yams form about 26 per cent of the diet in the Namu area as compared to cowpeas, 15 per cent; rice, 10 per cent; and sorghum, 49 per cent.

Individuals vary in their access to different kinds of food. Schoolboys who go back and forth to market towns daily may have fruit, bits of meat, and Hausa-style prepared foods (bean flour balls, fried groundnut flour loops) that are offered for sale more frequently than do other Kofyar. Older men, especially chiefs and well-to-do diviners, may drink beer in quantity, and during periods of intense cooperative farming activity, both men and women may often have enough beer to go without dinner. An adult male teacher with a regular cash income and access to a market was able to drink beer at least once a day and sometimes more often, while his consumption of oil, meat, and fruit also increased. These luxury foods, however, did not affect his continued dependence on cereal porridge and yams as the mainstay of his diet.

4

Population Characteristics and Settlement Pattern

IT IS an anthropological commonplace that "the nature and effectiveness of exploitative patterns are a prime factor in population size, density, and distribution," but as Helm (1962:634) also points out, it is only in recent years that attempts have been made to connect population characteristics with cultural patterns and social organization. Too often, ethnological monographs offer merely a few estimates in place of precise demographic data. This lack of concern may have historical roots:

Anthropologists, reacting to the claim by some anthropogeographers that extreme environmental determinism was operative on man, soon demonstrated that details of culture were not controlled directly by the environment. This broad denial overlooked man's nutritive dependence upon the environment, and long inhibited quantitative investigation of the relationship between man's population density and environmental factors. . . . Most ecologists agree that no data are more crucial than those bearing upon population size, structure, and density. (Bartholomew and Birdsell 1953:496).

More sophisticated studies such as that by Baumhoff (1963) on the relation of California Indian populations to specific food resources are beginning to appear. Forde (1947) has linked an increase in the size and stability of local groups with the development of unilineal kin affiliation.

Certainly it is necessary to examine population in any consideration of the relation between effective environment, productive technology, and sociocultural patterns. I have included demography as a social instrumentality, though perhaps it would be better to consider population size and density as an intervening variable that is ecologically conditioned and in turn creates problems requiring social solutions. The way in which people group themselves in terms of local aggregation and dispersion is more clearly a social fact. The regularities seen in density of local group and spatial distribution of habitation are usually dealt with as settlement pattern, and it is the ecological relevance of such data that I will consider. A similar viewpoint is evident in the comments of Gray (Gray and Gulliver: 1964:7) :

Settlement patterns are too often taken for granted as basic, irreducible data which are of scientific interest mainly as determinants of kinship systems or "rules of residence," whereas a more realistic understanding should result from considering in detail the ecological processes by which a people adjusts itself to the environment in establishing its pattern of settlement.

Population Size and Density

The available information on Kofyar population comes almost entirely from government statistics. One of the first tasks of the Assistant Resident who first entered Kofyar country in 1909 was to take a census and begin tax collections. I suspect that until recent years, tax counts continued to provide the basis for censuses and that therefore the available figures consistently underestimate actual population. After 1930, tax collections became more systematic, and the numbers of adult males were probably recorded with reasonable accuracy. Though the annual compilation of the tax list contains questions on women and children also, a truthful answer is often not given in these categories. My own figures on total population gathered by a house-to-house census and revised during a period of observation differed by from 12 to 50 per cent from tax lists for several hill villages. The government census of 1952 did not depend on pre-existing records and is probably the most accurate count to date (the official results of the November, 1963, census were not available at the time of writing). The 1952 totals consistently exceed those contained in tax lists. It is almost impossible to check the official figures, however, because enumeration districts did not correspond with tax districts, and no maps are available to indicate exactly what hamlets were included in each district. Since settlement of some areas is almost continuous, border hamlets may be grouped with any one of two or three villages, and it is impossible to tell from the census how the district boundaries were drawn.

Table 10 summarizes the population data available in 1967, and it gives a 1952 total of 55,174 in the Kofyar area. The traditional Kofyar territory is quite limited, a total of only 190 square miles.[1] Its population density reaches an average of 290.4 per square mile, a rather impressive concentration for nonurban, nonirrigating subsistence farmers. Even if the area is doubled to include the bush farms opened since 1930, there would still be an average density of 145.2 per square mile. Findlay (1945), by eliminating uninhabited areas and wastelands, arrives at a density of 250 per square mile in the hills and 1,200 in the two-mile-wide plain belt encircling the hills. The Kofyar density contrasts with a figure of 40.46 people per square mile in Lowland Division as a whole and an estimated density in the Northern Region of 50 (Buchanan and Pugh 1955:58).[2]

---

[1] This figure was arrived at by plotting the Kofyar area on 1953 Federal Survey 1:100,000 maps made from aerial photographs and computing the area. It is somewhat less than the 233 square miles given as the area of the four component tribal districts by Ames (1934).

[2] A similar pagan area in the Mandara Mountains had an estimated density of 170 per square mile (White 1941). Grove has estimated that under the Hausa system of mixed permanent and shifting cultivation, maximum population in the Anchau area would be 160 per square mile (1961). For comparison with other parts of Nigeria, it may be noted that

TABLE 10
KOFYAR POPULATION

Population Unit	1913 (Temple)	1921 Census	1931 Census	1952 Census	1963 Census *	Area (Ames 1934)
Kofyar Population (from published sources): †						
Mirriam	8,644	8,490	14,081	13,031	16,739	51 square miles
Dimmuk		9,250	13,399	17,447	21,145	86 square miles
Kwalla		5,750	14,652	16,496	25,403	71 square miles
Bwol (Bwal)		1,260	1,674	1,171	3,853	25 square miles
Jepal (Koeper)				3,055		
Doka (Dokan Kasuwa)				3,974	5,806	
Total Kofyar population		24,750	43,796	55,174	72,946	233 square miles
Provincial and Divisional Populations: ‡						
Muri Province:						
Area		19,696				
Population		261,735				
Density (per square mile)		13.3				
Shendam or Lowland Division:						
Area			2,812	4,800		
Population			118,302	194,208		
Density			42.07	40.46		

* These unofficial figures were furnished to me through the kindness of M. C. Oyeyipo, D. O. Lowland, and Simon Bala.
† The 1921 and 1931 censuses do not have separate categories for Jepal and Doka, and it is now impossible to determine with which group the population of these areas was grouped.
‡ Muri Province was broken up in 1926, with Shendam Division becoming a part of the newly created Plateau Province. Shendam Division was enlarged in 1931, and its name changed to Lowland Division in 1952.

It is obvious that the combination of favorable climate, good soils, and effective agricultural techniques allows the maintenance of substantial density of population among the Kofyar. Under intensive farming a relatively small amount of land per capita is required for subsistence, and since the same fertilized homestead field is kept in use indefinitely, large reserves of fallow are not necessary. A predictably adequate rainfall plus the protection from marauders offered by the hills provide what Porter (1965) calls a low "subsistence risk." The manner of past population expansion is still visible in the hills. There a young man leaves his father's house shortly after marriage and occupies an old homestead or builds new huts on fallow land. In either case he brings the land to higher production by applications of manure, improvement of terraces, and more painstaking cultivation. Where considerable bush fallow is available, this type of conversion to intensive use will accommodate a sizable increase in numbers. On the plains this process seems to have resulted in the solid band of settlement at the base of the hills and along watercourses. All available land is filled with homestead farms, and the supply of drinking water must sometimes be policed during the dry season to insure its maintenance. It is possible, though not yet demonstrated, that the limits of plains settlement are defined by the joint requirements for perennial sources of water and shelter from enemies.[3] When the latter of these conditions was removed by the Pax Britannica, an almost immediate exodus of migrants to bush farm land began, indicating areas of significant population pressure. Kwa, Miket, and Dimmuk all

---

Kano Emirate, with its highly developed patterns of cash cropping, commerce, and urbanism, has 210 per square mile, and Ibadan Division, with the largest native city in Sub-Saharan Africa, has a density of 220 (Buchanan and Pugh 1955). Portions of Iboland go up to 1,000 per square mile, and half the Eastern Region has average densities over 300, but this is regarded as one of the most densely populated areas in all tropical Africa (Prothero 1961).

[3] This exactly parallels the situation in the Nuba hills (Nadel 1947:5).

show signs of overfarming, and I have been told that before the new bush lands provided a safety valve, some men were unable to get farms. District officers referred frequently to trading activities and extensive thievery in the Kwa area during the 1920's and 1930's. The Kofyar report that hill villages have rarely suffered any food shortage, but that formerly plains residents were regularly forced to beg or buy grain during the wet season when the new crops had not yet reached maturity.

On the basis of current information it is impossible to account fully for the difference in population pressure between the plains and certain hill villages. Hill terrain certainly provides more marginal agricultural land that may be more difficult to convert to intensive uses than land in the plains. It is possible that sleeping sickness was more serious near the fly-infested wooded sections of the hills than elsewhere. Even these possible limiting factors are not uniformly effective because the homestead and bush lands of villages on the scarp and its summit are farmed at close to capacity, and reserves of vacant land exist only near Bong, Zugal, and Koeper. Hill villages have joined the migration to bush lands in direct proportion to their proximity to the plain.

The Kofyar population is obviously growing. Census returns indicate a trebling of the population in the forty-two years from 1921 to 1963, an impressive increase even if the figures are somewhat in error. There may, however, have been an equally dramatic decline in population in the first decades after European contact. In an attempt to reconstruct the population of forty to fifty years ago, older informants were asked to name all household heads living at that time. The homesteads mentioned could be located at particular sites, many of which are still visible. Lardang declined from an estimated 225 homesteads in 1910 to 105 in 1967, Bong dropped from 85 in 1920 to 44 in 1967, and a part of Latok that in 1920 had an estimated 93 homesteads showed only 33 in 1967. Only a few of these cases can be accounted for by recent permanent moves to plains settlements. If we can assume that homestead households were much as they are today (informants claimed they were if anything somewhat larger), it appears that total population in the hills fell by more than one-half. The drop was not credited to warfare, either intervillage or with Europeans. Rather, the old men referred to epidemics, particularly of meningitis, which killed its victims with great speed, and of sleeping sickness, which remained a serious threat in the area up through the 1940's. Before these diseases swept the Kofyar hills there were pressing shortages of land, and informants told of some families having experienced regular food scarcities.

Judging solely on the basis of extensive linguistic similarities, the Kofyar have not been long separated from their congeners, the Sura to the north and the Goemai to the south and east. With no lexicostatistic analysis or archaeological evidence, it is not possible to give even approximate dates for the Kofyar occupancy of their current habitat. Yet it may well be that population growth and the present adaptation to the environment both took place in a relatively short span of time. Terraced hillsides and close adjustment to microenvironmental differences need not suggest a long history, and the recent readiness of the Kofyar to seize new opportunities points to adaptive capacities far superior to those postulated by the myth of primitive conservatism.

Though population growth and agricultural intensification are obviously correlated, the manner of their interaction is far from clear. Carneiro (1961) has suggested on the basis of South American evidence that an increase of population in regions where the area of cultivable land is distinctly circumscribed gives the impetus required to turn shifting into intensive cultivation. Using a wide range of economic data, Boserup (1965:28) has convincingly supported her contention that "the transition to more intensive systems of land use took place in response to the increase of population within a given area." The Kofyar population was traditionally both protected by its hills and limited by them in the land area it could exploit. We may infer that the most

effective way to maintain expanding population was by increasing reliance on existing intensive techniques (such as
terracing and the application of house sweepings to the
fields) and the development of new methods (perhaps the
stall-feeding of goats and the basin-listing system of ridging).
These practices would have given an immediate and obvious
selective advantage to their possessors, supporting larger
numbers and reinforcing continued populating growth. The
process involved need not be revolutionary. A gradual extension of techniques for maintaining soil fertility coupled with
a progressive shortening of the fallow period could accomplish the necessary transition without radical dislocation of
existing patterns. Other groups have adapted to land shortages and decreasing soil fertility by the development of manuring and permanent agriculture (cf. Barrau 1958:18).

Mere knowledge of intensive techniques is not enough to
secure their adoption. The Chokfem Sura, sharing the same
physical environment and crop repertoire with the hill Kofyar and living near enough to allow the easy diffusion of
ideas, have remained primarily shifting cultivators. If intensive methods are a response to land scarcity, we might expect
the Chokfem to have a lower population density. This indeed seems to be the case. The most recent tax list (1965–66)
for the Chokfem district lists a total population of 4,909.
They inhabit an area of between 60 and 70 square miles, giving a maximum density of 82 persons per square mile. Only a
few miles away, the hill Kofyar have average densities almost
twice as high, 162 per square mile, and this may represent a
decline from past peaks. The Chokfem are not forced by
pressure on the land to apply the extra effort demanded by
intensive, permanent agriculture, and like pragmatic farmers everywhere, they do not do so (Boserup 1965:53–55,
62–63).

Population growth and associated land shortage may also
lead to military expansion (Sahlins 1961, Vayda 1961) allowing extension of existing agricultural patterns without
change. The Kofyar intercultural environment with techno-

logically superior groups controlling the plains may have discouraged this course. The extent to which intervillage feuding was generated by land scarcity is not clear (see above, p. 47). We might speculate that the legendary Chokfem invasion resulted from greater pressure of population on the land under shifting cultivation. The more recent local conflicts of the Kofyar may have involved some pillaging of grain stores and domestic animals, but there are no accounts of land being permanently annexed. The short-range effects may well have been to take disputed areas out of cultivation, and the combination of decreased food supplies and violence may have limited population. When more is known of the conditions surrounding Kofyar warfare, it might profitably be compared with the endemic fighting of highland New Guinea.

Population Distribution

Within the Kofyar country population density varies, and the heaviest concentrations are found on the plains. About 36 per cent of the land area is in the hills, but only 11,090 persons, or 20 per cent of the population, live there. Along the base of the hills, settlement is almost continuous, and contiguous homestead farms keep practically every square foot of arable land under cultivation. The level land is broken only by occasional small streams or ridges of volcanic stone, and village boundaries can be discerned only by those familiar with the area. In the hills, level land and deep soil are scarce, and villages on the flat tops of ridges and in a few broad well-watered valleys are easily distinguishable. The steep slopes of the escarpment and of the deep stream valleys which seam it often make even terrace farming impractical. Hill populations are thus more fragmented and divided into generally smaller units. Isolated clusters of three to six homesteads may be thought of as hamlets of some larger village, while a group of 15 to 20 homesteads may consider itself an independent village. Other villages on more favorable locations may have as many as 80 homesteads. In 16 hill and hill-foot villages ranging in size from 14 to 62 homesteads, the average number of homesteads was 33.9 (see Table 11). Homestead number gives only a rough approximation of population, however. In Kofyar village, where individual households are larger, there was an average of 7.1 persons in each of the 48 homesteads, while Gonkun numbered only 3.2 occupants in each of its 26 homesteads. The average total population of 16 villages was 174.1.

All the settlements mentioned in Table 11 were covered by a 100 per cent sample, with the exception of Zugal, where only some two-thirds of the total number of homesteads were censused. Each community forms a named group of co-

TABLE 11
VILLAGE AND HOMESTEAD POPULATIONS

Village Name	Total Population	Home-steads	Average Population per Homestead	Total Adult Workers	Adult Workers per House-hold
Kofyar	345	48	7.1	215	4.5
Longsel	139	28	4.9	96	3.4
Bogalong	251	50	5.0	160	3.2
Buumdagas	89	14	6.4	54	3.9
Zugal	219	42	5.2	160	3.8
Bong	249	58	4.3	153	2.6
Koepal	71	17	4.2	48	2.8
Mangbar	160	48	3.3	111	2.3
Gonkun	84	26	3.2	62	2.3
Dep	113	35	3.2	95	2.7
Pangkurum	145	28	5.2	92	3.3
Korom	86	14	6.1	59	4.2
Kopfuboem	82	16	5.1	50	3.1
Wudai	162	24	6.8	102	4.3
Meer	154	32	4.8	100	3.1
Dunglong	436	62	7.0	280	4.5
Total	2,785	542		1,837	
Average	174.1	33.9	5.3	114.8	3.4

residents in a single territory. Some, such as Buumdagas and Koepal, might better be called hamlets because they adjoin Bogalong and Bong, respectively, and function as part of the larger villages in many political matters. It is not possible, however, to separate hamlets from villages on the basis of size alone. Meer, Wudai, Korom, and Dunglong are all contiguous hamlets or wards of Kwa and acknowledge a single chief.

The settlements listed fall into certain geographical groups (see map, Fig. 2). The first consists of villages stretching from the rim of the escarpment (Kofyar) to the western border of the Kofyar Hills (Bong and Zugal). Mangbar, Gonkun, and Dep lie along the more gradual southerly descent from the hills and are culturally affiliated with Dimmuk. The last group includes villages below Kofyar on the escarpment itself (Pangkurum, Kopfuboem), on the foothills and valleys at the base of the plateau (Korom, Wudai, Meer), and on the open plain proper (Dunglong). Populations appear to vary with the availability of arable land as determined by local topography. Differences are evident, however, in the size of homestead households. Mangbar and its neighboring settlements, along with Bong and Koepal, have households averaging fewer than 4.5 members and homestead work groups of fewer than 3 members. In both categories, they are consistently smaller than other communities. The settlements with small families may have poorer soil and scarcer land than their neighbors, but this cannot be demonstrated with available data. Certainly more obvious is the fact that the larger household size is found in villages such as Kofyar, Wudai, and Dunglong, which are heavily involved in migrant bush farming.

Settlement Pattern

Given the Kofyar emphasis on intensive and permanent exploitation of land, their characteristic dispersed settlement pattern appears to have adaptive significance. It is both enjoined by agricultural considerations and permitted by relative freedom from outside attack. The earliest observers noted that Kofyar homesteads were separated from one another, with each household situated on its own intensive farm. A network of paths connects each independent cluster of huts and often forms the boundaries of its unfenced fields (Plate IB). Until quite recently there was no example of a nucleated town with abutting compounds in Kofyar country. This contrasts sharply with the densely populated cities of the Yoruba and Hausa and the nucleated settlements of some Ibo. Even with the growth of schools and markets among the Kofyar, it is only the few Moslem traders and craftsmen, Christian artisans and teachers, and government employees who occupy town houses. For the rest, it is assumed that the family living on a clearly demarcated homestead is cultivating it and that the produce of this land will belong to the family members.

On arable land each homestead farm is bounded by several others. Streams, steep declivities, sacred groves, and stony hillocks interrupt this regular pattern and often set off the group of homesteads that form a Kofyar village or hamlet.[4] The reasons for this immediate propinquity of residence and farm seem to revolve around the method of cultivation and the value of crops produced. Intensive agriculture implies a degree of attention, both in actual work and close observation, that is not necessary in extensive plantings. Crops must be sown, transplanted, weeded, and harvested according to their particular requirements. Because of the variety of food plants at different stages of growth in the Kofyar homestead field, the farmer must check their progress frequently. He can mend a break in a terrace or prop up a sagging sorghum stalk before any damage is done. His wife harvests leaves and vegetables for sauce daily as they ripen. The use of

[4] A very similar pattern of "straggling settlements . . . loosely scattered over valleys or hillsides" has been reported in the Nuba hills (Nadel 1947:24), again in a situation of intensive "house farm" cultivation. In New Guinea, where bottom lands are farmed intensively for sweet potatoes, the Kapauku try to have gardens as close to their homes as possible (Pospisil 1963).

manure in dressing the soil makes it advisable to keep animals as close to the field as possible. Carrying the compost a long distance without carts or draft animals would be an arduous and time-consuming task. The bringing of fodder for the stall-fed goats is also easier if farms are scattered over the landscape near various bush fallows and overgrown stream beds.[5]

The concentration of crops into a small, high-yielding, labor-intensive plot also enjoins constant vigilance on the part of the household against pests and thieves. Large antelope and domestic cattle can do great damage to such a field if unchecked. The constant presence of humans discourages birds from molesting ripening grain. Because each homestead has several near neighbors as well as at least one dog, guarding against thieves is quite effective. Without this protection both domestic animals and valuable tree crops might be stolen.

Though a dispersed settlement may have certain agricultural advantages for intensive cultivators, it forms a less defensible unit from a military viewpoint. Kofyar homesteads, with their single entrances and huts connected by stone walls, form individual fortresses, but a determined attacker could destroy them one by one. It is obvious from informants' statements that most Kofyar fighting went on in open fields between villages with an accepted code of limited hostilities. The rocky hills with their steep paths, defiles, and lookout points provided such admirable defenses against outsiders that no further village defenses were required. Only the village of Bong had more elaborate arrangements, a wall at the base of a volcanic cone that sheltered the entire village

[5] Geographers have developed a sophisticated theory of the relation between field location and land use expressed in terms of marginal return on labor. As the cost in time and energy for travel to cultivate, manure, and transport produce increases, the total output per unit of labor expended by the farmer goes down. This results in a noticeable decline in the intensity of agriculture on successively more distant fields (Chisholm 1962:49ff.). The spatial relation of Kofyar intensive homestead farms, village shifting fields, and bush fallows in roughly concentric rings conforms neatly to this model of maximization.

when it was besieged by neighbors. Dispersed settlement ends abruptly on the southern boundary of Kofyar country. There, on the exposed plain, it is replaced by the walled, nucleated towns of the Goemai. This appears to be directly related to the increased danger of armed attack and the need for cooperative defensive measures.[6]

The integral association of dispersed settlement, intensive agriculture, and defensive requirements is borne out by a recent study of changes in Eastern Ibo communities (Udo 1965). This shows a correlation between population density of more than five hundred per square mile and dispersed continuous settlement in contrast to the more traditional nucleated street villages and compact settlements of many Ibo groups. As population increased, land became too scarce to allow shifting cultivation, and a pattern of intensive compound gardening took its place. The abolition of the slave trade and halting of tribal wars permitted the disintegration of defensive village groupings. Udo points out that an unsatisfied demand for farmland leads inevitably to disputes, and a more effective claim to ownership could be entered by the individual actually living on the land. Though the Kofyar lack a history of recent settlement fission, it seems evident that the same factors of population pressure on a limited land base, agricultural intensification, and the absence of military reasons for consolidation are functionally related to their pattern of dispersed homesteads.

[6] For examples of defensive requirements contributing to the agglomeration of population, see Demangeon (1962:511).

5

Mobilization of Labor

PERHAPS ALL human social groups serve multiple functions. A complete analysis of a social system would require a detailed consideration of the structural composition and form of the group, as well as the ways in which it operates to maintain the total society. It may be more useful here to limit our discussion to the instrumental values of certain enduring groups in relation to subsistence. Thus we will stress, for instance, the utility of a certain type of family for production, leaving aside its role in socialization, sexual regulation, and reproduction. We will examine in this way the ecological relevance and function of various Kofyar institutions including the division of labor, households, voluntary labor groups, lineages, neighborhoods, and villages.

The Division of Labor

The division of labor in Kofyar society is influenced by two major factors: (1) a subsistence adaptation to the environment in which techniques for securing food, clothing, and shelter are relatively simple and generally known, and (2) household organization based on the nuclear or independent polygynous family. It is expected that every adult will understand and practice farming. Until very recently, every able adult actually worked the soil and contributed directly to his own nourishment. Even today, the few full-time specialists such as teachers or carpenters get most of their food from a close relative who is an active farmer. One's daily food, as distinct from beer and snacks, is not something on which money is willingly spent. There are part-time craft specialists in Kofyar. Most villages have a smith, but his work is confined largely to the early days of the rainy season, when tools must be repaired. Weavers set up their narrow looms only occasionally during the dry season. Expert housebuilders are known and employed, but again their occupation is strictly subsidiary to farming. A respected medicine man may come closest to specialization, but he always cultivates a plot of some nature. Full-time craftworkers such as tailors, butchers, barbers, and leather makers have appeared only with the advent of markets, and they are usually Moslem. A pagan who wishes to learn such a skill or engage in trade must apprentice himself to a Moslem, and this usually entails the acceptance of Islamic religion along with Hausa language and culture. A handful of Kofyar in each market center have taken this course.

The nature of traditional subsistence farming in an isolated area allowed the development of a population of self-sufficient homogeneous farmers. Until 1909, their hills protected the Kofyar from conquest and insulated them from major trade. The only necessities they did not themselves produce were iron and salt, which they bartered for with trading partners in adjoining tribes to the north and south, respectively. The prevailing lack of specialization extended even to jobs limited in other African societies on the basis of sex, and this was due to the organization of the household unit. I shall suggest below that the nuclear family is peculiarly adapted to the practice of homestead agriculture. A corollary of the establishment of a small independent household as the major productive unit is that its few members must be to a certain extent interchangeable, since it is sometimes necessary for a household member to be absent for an extended period. Kofyar leave their homes to live in the homestead of a native doctor during the course of a serious illness, in the event of a difficult pregnancy, and, often, when labor starts. The native doctor aids in childbirth and watches over the health of mother and infant, who often remain in the homestead for the period of the postpartum sexual taboo lasting one and a half to two years, during which a wife may visit her husband's homestead only during the day.

A man who has only one wife cannot leave his homestead because the woman falls sick or divorces him, and he cannot be sure of help from female relatives who have their own households to manage. The least disruption results if he is willing to accept female tasks himself. Among the Kofyar every man can use the mortar or the grinding stone, the winnowing tray, and the cooking pot with skill. Men can and do prepare food for themselves for extended periods of time. A young man may live alone until a runaway wife returns or a new marriage is arranged. Elderly widowers often continue as the sole occupants of homesteads. A married man whose only wife has given birth may have to cook for himself and his remaining children for over a year while his wife lives in a native doctor's homestead. Ceremonial food is often prepared by men in the sacred grove where women may not enter. On the other hand, if a man is absent from his home, either when ill or in prison, his wife or wives carry on adequately. They tend the animals, make decisions about farming, and cut down the low-growing palm fruit. A widow may choose to live alone and rear her children in the homestead of her dead husband. In such a case she is nominally under the protection of a neighboring male, but he may make few direct contributions to the household economy. There is little changing about of residence except in the case of marriage and divorce, and every effort is made to preserve the integrity and self-sufficiency of a household once it has been established.

In many important tasks, roles are not rigidly assigned by sex. In farming operations, men and women work side by side. Hoeing, transplanting, weeding, and harvesting are all cooperative. Occasionally functions are complementary, especially when considerable strength is required. Thus men work together to wrest free the tangled mats of compost and heave them over the corral wall, while women distribute the fertilizer about the field in baskets. The heavy stones of the goat corral are put in place by men. In groundnut cultivation, young mothers and older women may leave their hoes and begin the lighter job of planting while men continue to make ridges (Plate VIB). Likewise, women have the longer but easier task of transplanting late millet in the prepared field. If the work party is small, women may hoe an equal share and men may help in the planting. Older men often do the broadcast sowing of acha, perhaps because of their special skill in evenly distributing the seed. Women do much of the small crop cultivation, but men, especially the heads of small households, may help to heap the sweet potato ridges or the beds of other tubers. Bush clearing is a male task, but it forms a rather insignificant part of total farming operations.

In joint operations no strict hierarchy is apparent. The male head of the household organizes work on the homestead and major bush fields, deciding when the necessary tasks must be done and arranging for volunteer help when required. He cannot, however, give peremptory orders or assert his authority to any significant degree. If either a husband or wife fails to participate in major agricultural activities without cause, stormy public arguments follow. In most major farming activities men and women work side by side. The amount of subsidiary root crops, vegetables, beans, and peanuts that a woman grows is her own affair, and these crops are tended according to her own schedule.

Housebuilding, roofing, and thatching are men's work, though women mix mud for the walls and weave the grass thatch. Women, however, know all the techniques and may with no assistance build small houses for storing ash fertilizer and cooking pots. Thatching grass is cut and headloaded home by both sexes. Women perform the major work of brewing, the grinding, straining, and boiling; but men are expected to bring water for malting the grain, to decant the beer, and sometimes to supply part of the firewood. A single man can always buy grain and arrange with women to brew for him, while a lone woman calls on the neighborhood work group for aid in major building and thatching.

Selling in the markets of the plains is usually done directly by the producer. A woman sells her own beer, pap, baskets, and pots. A man sells hoe blades, salt containers, bags, or loincloths that he has made. Both men and women dispose of their own livestock and crops. A woman's earnings from her products and crops grown in the field given her by her husband are her own. Her husband is entitled to a share only if she leaves him for another man. This fact, together with women's freedom from taxes, means that they often have more ready cash than their husbands.

A few activities are so strongly identified with one sex that any suggestion of their performance by the other is laughable. Men hunt and women do not. Women alone make baskets and clay pots. Though both sexes spin, weaving is done only by those males who have learned the craft. Blacksmithing is exclusively male. Only men perform magicoreligious rites. The complicated knowledge of divination is limited to males. One old chief even protested the shift of women from the wearing of leaves to cloth on the grounds that a skirt resembled the skin apron worn by diviners. Perhaps the sharp sex distinctions in the realm of the supernatural may compensate for the relatively undifferentiated common pursuits of men and women and the economic self-sufficiency of women. This is further borne out by the periodic visitations of a spirit (*kum or*), which warns the women of a village to desist from such unwifely conduct as staying late at beer parties and slacking on household duties. The guttural voice of the spirit is provided by men who ascend the hills at night and in secret. Only in the issuing of magical commands and prohibitions do men have an unassailable monopoly and the expectation of unquestioning obedience.

The lack of rigid sexual division of labor except in craft and magico-religious activities may reflect both the relatively unspecialized nature of Kofyar subsistence production and the economic independence of households, even those with limited personnel. Though physical strength is not a crucial determinant of most tasks, it is apparent that intensive agriculture requires a larger expenditure of effort per unit returned than shifting cultivation (Clark and Haswell 1964:33, 47). Productivity in terms of output per man-hour actually declines as land use becomes more intensive (Boserup 1965:41). More efficient mobilization of labor results when both male and female members of the group engage fully in subsistence production and when individuals, regardless of sex, may freely substitute for one another in many household duties.[1]

Household Cooperation

The major cooperating group in Kofyar subsistence production and consumption is the household occupying a single homestead and structured along kinship lines. The household typically consists of a nuclear or independent polygynous family. Observers of tribal societies have recognized the central importance of the family in patterns of exploitation. In the words of Gray:

The labour and skills necessary for exploiting the natural resources are funnelled through the family in actual application while the goods consumed are distributed through family channels. Individuals obtain their vital sustenance largely through the mediation of the family

[1] As agriculture becomes more intensive in other parts of Africa such as Uganda and Gambia, there is some evidence that old distinctions of work between the sexes are breaking down. Men may cultivate, weed, and harvest, though these were formerly female tasks (Clark and Haswell, 1964:42, 46).

structure. Thus the family is a principal locus of ecological process (Gray and Gulliver 1964:5).

The members of a Kofyar household work the homestead farm as a group. When the family is very small or temporarily diminished by illness, neighbors may lend a hand, but in most cases all the work from planting through harvest is handled by the resident household. Women and adolescents may have small individual plots of root crops, beans, or condiments, but the major millet-sorghum-cowpea or maize–coco yam crops are cultivated by the entire group and the produce divided among the adult women according to the number for whom each is cooking. Village plots of groundnuts or acha are farmed in the same way, and if the household is a large one it may handle most of the work on bush fields by itself. No one absents himself from such family labor without a good excuse, and children are incorporated into the work group to the full extent of their capabilities. Though a man may have several wives, he seldom leaves them to work alone. A former chief once expressed pleased surprise to me after finding that his three wives continued their labor while he was away for two hours. As long as a son and his wife remain in the parental household they work together with the other occupants. Once they set up their own household, their attention and labor are absorbed by their own homestead farm, though they may continue to cooperate with the parental household on the bush fields. Anyone living in the household, whether a relative, a visiting friend, or a patient, takes part in all family work as far as he is able. A native doctor whose homestead shelters several pregnant women or recent mothers may benefit substantially by this arrangement.

Family members may all take part in the cutting of grass for the goats, while the herding of horses, cows, and sheep is usually children's work. Threshing of late millet and the making of palm or canarium oil require the joint endeavors of the entire group. Though the master of the homestead often does the building of new huts, women and children assist in bringing water and stone, mixing mud, and acting as hod carriers. Seldom does an entire family go to market or even to a village beer drink. Someone, perhaps a child or an aged relative, must stay behind to guard the homestead.

The size and composition of Kofyar households show characteristics that appear directly related to their functions as productive groups. This is not to say that the familiar family responsibilities of sexuality, reproduction, and socialization are not important, but merely that these functions can be fulfilled by variously constituted groups, and that the regularities observable in Kofyar households are traceable to economic or ecological factors.

The standard household includes a head (*wupinlu*), his wife or wives, their unmarried children, and perhaps a few dependents such as younger siblings of the head, a mother or a father's wife of the head, a child of a wife's sister, or a grandchild. From census data collected on 588 households in sixteen villages and hamlets covering a total of 2,999 persons, the average number of individuals per household is 5.10 and the proportion of extended families is 8.5 per cent.[2] The extended families are usually those of a father and his adult married son but are occasionally formed by two brothers or two friends. They are based on the partial dependence of one of the nuclear families, either an elderly couple or a newly married pair, and are thus often transitional stages in the creation of a new independent family household. Only four cases of households containing more than two married couples were found. Some households are made up of incomplete families, usually a single divorced or aged man or a widowed woman with her children, but these comprise only 8 per cent of the total. It is possible to say with some cer-

[2] This is a larger sample than that used in Table 6 and its composition differs slightly. Corresponding figures for Table 6 are 2,785 persons in 542 households, with an average size of 5.3 members and the proportion of extended families of 10.8 per cent.

tainty that Kofyar households, especially those in the hills from which most of the census data come, tend to be small and based on nuclear or independent polygynous families.

The characteristic structure of the household results from fission that occurs shortly after marriage. As a man's sons marry and begin to have children, they move out of the parental home onto fields that either belong to their father or are leased by a son from someone else. If a household is small or the head is aged, a married son may remain to help his father, but he is under no obligation to do so. It frequently happens that after a man's death his homestead remains vacant, his sons having in the meantime established themselves elsewhere. Households occasionally divide even earlier when a man installs one of his immature sons and the boy's mother in an empty homestead belonging to him.

I have dealt elsewhere (Netting 1965c) with the relation of intensive agriculture and household composition, but it may be useful to recapitulate the evidence here. The hypothesis that the small household is peculiarly adapted to the labor needs of intensive homestead cultivation is supported by comparative data, functional analysis, and the covarying factors observable in a situation of change.

Though showing a great many similarities in culture and strong linguistic unity, the Kofyar differ decisively from their neighbors, the Chokfem Sura and the Angas, in agricultural practices and household type. The physical environment of the Chokfem villages appears to parallel in every significant respect that of the Kofyar hills from which it is separated by a single stream valley. The Angas have some terracing but farm their land almost entirely by shifting cultivation. Neither has the systematic development of stall-feeding animals and manuring homestead fields that is basic to Kofyar agriculture. Crops of sorghum, acha, and late millet are grown on bush fields that must be fallowed after one to four years of use. Chokfem and Angas households are absolutely larger in average number than their Kofyar counterparts, and they show a markedly higher proportion of extension. Table 12 illustrates this contrast. Covariance, however, does not prove that the variables are functionally related.[3]

Informants in both Chokfem and Kofyar groups explained household composition in terms of labor needs. In Kofyar it is thought that a young couple with an independent homestead will work more conscientiously because they must provide directly for their own subsistence. They will not be tempted to let others support them. The Kofyar are convinced that extended family households are prone to exploitation by lazy and parasitic relatives. On the other hand, the

TABLE 12

HILL TRIBES HOUSEHOLD COMPOSITION

Ethnic Group	Number of Villages or Hamlets	Total Population	Number of Households	Size of Household	Extended Family Households (Per cent)
Kofyar	16	2,999	588	5.10	8.5
Chokfem Sura	1	133	9	14.8	89.0
Hill Angas * (Ampam area)	?	3,043	294	10.3	70.0
Plain Angas * (Kabwir area)	?	2,522	187	13.7	81.0

* Angas census figures from Father Donnelly, S.M.A. (MS, n.d.).

majority of tasks connected with homestead farming and small stock raising can be managed successfully with only a few hands. Chokfem people justify their large households by citing the need to complete work on the extensive bush fields with dispatch. To grow a given amount of crops they must cultivate a larger area, and the need to shift fields often implies a more distant location. An increased number of household members allows prompt mobilization of labor for work at the optimum point of the growing season. It also

[3] Gross correlations between types of family and types of economy viewed cross-culturally have been offered by Nimkoff and Middleton (1960).

permits the work force to be split, with some members tending nearby plots while others cultivate widely dispersed fields. Central direction promotes cooperation in the performance of complementary tasks and the pooling of the produce for common consumption.[4]

The Kofyar themselves use exchange labor or volunteers paid in beer for bush fallow farming, but the crops so raised are not crucial staples in most cases. The Kofyar household head can enlist outside help only at the convenience of his friends and neighbors, and thus the planting or weeding they do may not be effectively timed.

Observation suggests that widespread cooperation is not necessary to maintain a homestead field. Annual organic enrichment of the soil means that the field can be small and yet highly productive. Its permanent use allows residence to be maintained in the immediate vicinity. The farm work is not heavy, but only by careful and frequent hoeing, transplanting, weeding, and selective harvesting can high yields of the closely interplanted grains and vegetables be maintained. Fresh fodder must be brought for the goats at least every other day, and they must be watered regularly. The hut cluster in the middle of the homestead field is ideally situated for the occupants to protect their crops from damage by animals or birds, as well as human intruders. The fact that single adults or incomplete families of the very young and the elderly maintain independent homesteads suggests that this type of exploitation depends on small amounts of labor consistently applied by individuals continuously resident on or near their fields.

On extensive bush fields the soil is usually less fertile. Yields appear lower, subject to rapid declines, and less predictable. The fine-comb methods of intensive agriculture are not economical in terms of returns attainable. Thus shifting cultivation is characterized by the extent of the area farmed and an economy of labor but not by the quality of the work

[4] The advantages of the extended family as a productive unit are enumerated by Sahlins (1962:120–23).

(cf. Pospisil 1963:99). If one or two individuals had to hoe several acres alone their progress would be slow, and the operations of planting, weeding, and harvesting would each be spread over several weeks. At any one time the crop would be at various stages of growth with varying climatic requirements. It seems more advantageous to do the major cultivation all at one time with a party of people who can stimulate one another's efforts by competition, jokes, and songs. The difference in agricultural strategy is the same one prevailing between the high labor input with low area coverage of truck farming and the low labor input with high area coverage of dry wheat farming. Lacking mechanization, the Nigerian hoe cultivators can farm larger areas only by increasing the labor force and sacrificing painstaking methods for speed.

Labor input has not yet been measured with any degree of certainty in most operations of Kofyar agriculture. Some fragmentary figures do, however, suggest the substantial differences between the requirements of intensive and shifting cultivation. A single hoeing of the homestead field requires some 70 to 80 man-hours per acre. This is repeated three times during the growing season, bringing total man-hours per acre to approximately 225. This does not include time spent in sowing or harvesting. A bush acha field may require an initial hoeing of 80 to 90 hours per acre, but the only further labor of cultivation is a single weeding, bringing total time expended to about 120 hours. Thus, close to twice as much labor time per acre is devoted to the homestead field. Since this plot is small, the average homestead of 3.4 adult workers must put in 90 man-hours on each hoeing of their 1.2-acre homestead. Kofyar work six to seven hours a day at this demanding task, and a single cultivation may therefore require from three to five days. Even a single person working alone can do the job in less than two weeks. Whereas a bush acha field of 2.8 acres (approximately 250 man-hours) can be an easy day's work for 40 or 50 people, it would require 18 days of uninterrupted toil for a man and his wife to do the same job.

A regular relationship of agricultural system to space, labor, and production might be stated as follows:

Agricultural System	Field Size	Yield per Unit Land	Work Force	Total Labor per Unit Land
Intensive	Small	High	Small	High
Shifting	Large	Low	Large	Low

Such a correlation appears to apply generally to Kofyar agriculture, but it does not tell us which of the two systems is more efficient in terms of production per man-hour. Cross-cultural studies have recently given strong support to the idea that shifting cultivation generally gives higher rewards per unit of labor expended. Intensive systems may require less initial clearing of the land, but their demands for preliminary cultivation, more frequent weeding, manuring, water conservation, and irrigation are extremely high (Boserup 1965:35–42). To compute accurately the time needed for the practice of intensive homestead farming among the Kofyar, we would have to include day-by-day care, staking of beans, construction and repair of terraces, tending economic trees, and the substantial extra labor of stall-feeding and watering manure-producing livestock. It is above all the scarcity of land that makes this additional effort mandatory. If total dependence were placed on shifting cultivation, the Kofyar population could not support itself in the same location for more than a few years. If new land becomes available in quantity, time-consuming intensive practices will rapidly give way, as they have in the Kofyar migrant bush area, to the more labor-efficient shifting methods.

If it is true that a small resident labor force is sufficient to work the average homestead farm, then it would follow that additional labor would not bring a corresponding increase in production. Data from a sample of seven homesteads in two villages bear out this interpretation. In Figure 6, the index of homestead crops (total bundles of sorghum and millet) varies in direct proportion to the size of the homestead field. The number of adult workers on each homestead appears to

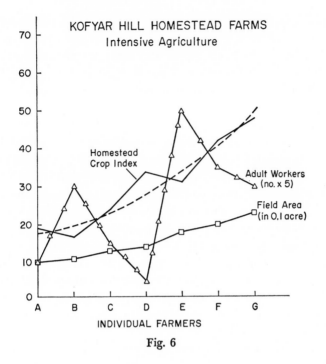

Fig. 6

vary independently. Total production is kept close to its maximum by customary intensive methods and can be expanded only by the addition of manured land. Extra workers do not increase yields, and it is probable that their efforts are felt mainly in more extensive bush fallow cultivation. In Kofyar village, those households that grow sizable quantities of groundnuts and acha on bush fallow fields have a somewhat higher average number of adult workers (4.8) than those which depend more heavily on homestead crops (3.7).

An alternative to periodic fission of the household is obviously the expansion of land area in the homestead. This course is sometimes taken if some bush fallow land adjoins the intensive cultivation. Usually, within a village, however, each homestead is bounded by other homesteads that are in use. A vacant plot at some distance from the home farm cannot easily be brought into intensive use unless residence is established on it. Moving to the outskirts of a village where space is available exposes the farmer to increased hazards from pests and thieves, as well as the necessity of gradually building up the fertility of bush land and foregoing the benefits of economic trees. Consequently, most homesteads in use are those with a long history of occupation and definitely limited land area.

Perhaps the most convincing evidence that household composition is indeed a social instrumentality is the recent tendency toward alteration of its characteristic form in response to the changed labor needs of shifting cultivation of cash crops. This subject will be considered at length in Chapter 8. Suffice it to say that with the adoption of migrant farming on newly opened plains fields, Kofyar households show a statistically significant trend toward increased polygyny and extended family organization. In the larger fields, production increases proportionately with additions to the labor force and is not directly related to the area of the field.

Exchange Labor

Exchange labor among the Kofyar is of two kinds: the simple informal assistance given and received on a variety of projects and the neighborhood group that performs certain specific annual tasks. *Mar wuk* is the term used for a plot worked with the help of others, who ask in return only similar aid in their own farming. It is used particularly for agricultural labor that is beyond the ability of one household to accomplish in a few days but does not demand a large number of workers. An elderly couple may invite a few people to help them prepare a village groundnut field. Weeding bush acha, a time-consuming but not too difficult task, is often done by exchange. The average membership of 16 mutual assistance groups in Bong was 16.4, but many of these were large harvesting parties. Inclusion of the smaller exchanges on village fields would certainly lower this average. The late millet harvest, however, demands larger parties, and, because grain is in short supply at that time of the year, labor must be reciprocal and not rewarded by beer. Morale among the harvesters is maintained by singing traditional songs in which men and women comically abuse each other's sexual prowess.

The neighborhood of seven or eight adjoining homesteads is mobilized for cooperative work at the time of thatching and again when compost is to be spread on the homestead fields. If neighborhoods are very small, two adjacent ones may go together. Though each household procures its own grass, it takes the combined efforts of all households in the neighborhood to thatch the huts of one homestead in a day. The women bind swatches of grass in parallel to form a mat that is unrolled round and round the conical roof. Men renew the rafters of houses where necessary and fix in place the timbers between the huts that form a covered entranceway. The grass is put in place, tightened, and lashed down by the men. Excavating the corral and spreading the compost on the field is done by neighborhood men and women going to each homestead in turn at the end of the dry season. On the plains a neighborhood may act jointly to fence water holes at a time of scarcity in the dry season.

If someone absents himself from neighborhood work without excellent reason he may be berated and made to pay a fine in beer to his neighbors. The virilocally married women resident in a neighborhood often have no kin ties with one another, but they are organized for certain internal judicial functions. In the event of some woman's failing to appear for cooperative work, the circumstances are discussed by the group and the consensus then voiced by the chief of the women (*long surap*). This female chief must be living in a specified homestead, but she is elected from among the adult women of that homestead by all the women of the neighborhood. Marital problems such as quarrels between a man and his wife may be referred to an older male neighbor for advice. Though men living in the same neighborhood tend to be patrilineal relatives, it is the geographical unit, rather than kin ties, that is important here. If the household heads come from three different lineages or two opposing clans, they observe the demands for neighborhood work with the same conscientiousness as do near kin. Both exchange labor and neighborhood groups are given token refreshment, perhaps a milky drink of pounded acha (aas) by the owner of the field or homestead where they work.

Voluntary Work Parties

The group of workers who voluntarily assemble to help a particular person and receive drink or food as a reward is a familiar type of labor organization throughout Northern Nigeria. It is known in Hausa as gayya and in Nupe as egbe (Nadel 1942:248). To the Kofyar it is simply mar mwos, the "field of beer," which suggests both its generally agricultural character and the invariable payment for services rendered. The principle of collective labor is familiar to all the Kofyar, but it is most frequently utilized in those areas where bush farms are extensive. Around Kwa, where bush land is limited, cooperative work parties are correspondingly few. But in practicing shifting cultivation for cash crops on migrant farms near Namu, the Kwa people depended on large groups for the bulk of their cultivation. Bong village, with its bush tracts in acha, groundnuts, and late millet, has a high development of cooperative labor. During the farming season there are continual discussions of what farm is to be worked on which day. At beer parties or clan meetings, household heads announce what days they wish to have. These must be scheduled so as not to conflict with one another and far enough ahead to allow the brewing of beer.

Occasionally a man may invite a particular neighborhood to work for him, but usually the invitation is an open one, and anyone in the village who is not otherwise occupied may come. In Bong, twenty-two work parties that I counted ranged from thirteen to eighty-two participants and averaged thirty-eight. In a few of the smallest groups the male members came from the same clan and were joined by their own wives and the wives of other clan relatives. In these cases all the workers tended to come from adjoining neighborhoods. In no single instance, however, was the party limited to a single lineage or neighborhood. Obviously the purpose of the cooperative work group is to mobilize labor beyond the bounds of kinship or immediate locality. There is a noticeable bias in that a higher proportion of a man's near neighbors, who are usually also his close kin, are on hand than members of a distant ward who belong to a different clan. This is natural because it is the physically and genealogically closest people who are most aware of the brewing and other preparations for the party and who have most to gain by cooperation.

As an example, a small party for transplanting millet sponsored by the widow Naden included twenty-two persons: ten men and twelve women. Seventeen of these were members of Naden's dead husband's clan or wives of clan members. Five came from the other clan in the village, and a total of five lineages were represented. Twelve persons were from Naden's neighborhood; five came from immediately adjoining neighborhoods; and three from a nearby hamlet. In another case, Danok's farming group of fifty-seven included thirty-four men and twenty-three women, thirty-one from his own clan and twenty-six from the other. Of these, thirteen were from his own neighborhood, while the two adjoining wards had nine persons each. Five other neighborhoods and one hamlet were represented by from two to eight workers.

In organizing a work party the kinship or neighborhood link is never publicly invoked. The date is communicated by word of mouth, with the understanding that anyone is welcome to help and equally entitled to reward. Visitors from other villages commonly join in. It may be that the owner of the field lacks brewing grain at the time of his farming. In this case he may call his workers back for their drink at a later time. A rash of drinking parties in April is payment for work done in the preceding July or August. Some beer drinks may come more than a year after the labor they recompense. The only sanction forcing reciprocity is the threat that without it no one will work for the owner a second time. Once the work has been completed and the beer consumed, there is no further obligation on either side. The crop belongs entirely to the owner, and he is entitled to no more labor from the participants.

The season when cooperative work parties are in full swing from June through October is a busy and exciting time. The villagers make their way out to the bush fields after morning chores, calling to one another along the paths. Men take their spears and clubs in case game should be sighted, and perhaps also as a carry-over from warring days when the bush fields bordered enemy territory. Women nest two or three hoes together and balance them on their heads. Early arrivals may gossip in the shade while the owner of the field and his wives clear away trash or sort seeds. Between 9:00 and 10:00 A.M. the work begins in earnest, with the workers swinging their hoes vigorously and moving up the terraces in a line. Everyone has a definite share, his personal "field" to complete, which is often three ridges wide. Several household heads may count the ridges and assign tasks to the other members. As the work proceeds, loud arguments may break out as to who has left the occasional untilled patch in the field. People pause for breath as they become winded or weary, but there is seldom a general rest until the field is completed. Older men or women may halt after a time to smoke a quiet pipe and prepare for the easier work of seeding. An acha field of 2.8 acres was hoed and planted by about forty-five persons in between five and six hours. The higher and more elaborate ridges for groundnuts or late millet take longer. Toward the end of a work period the young men who have finished first rest or help out some of the slower workers.

The workers return together to the village, stopping to bathe and put on a blanket or a colored cloth, and then going to the owner's homestead for beer. No beer is taken to the field, and there is never any drinking while the work is in progress, as is the custom with some African groups (Platt 1955). The crowd as it gathers sits quietly on logs or stones in the courtyard. The owner of the field at last gives the signal, and the young men rush into the huts to hoist the beer jars on their shoulders and distribute them. The stirring, pouring into calabashes, and drinking takes only a minute. Immediately, as if transformed, the people begin to talk and laugh, the young people joking with their lovers, everyone remarking on the quality of the beer, and repeating stories from market or the hunt. After another round, people begin to think of rounding up their animals or preparing the evening meal. If beer is plentiful, some may stay drinking and chatting until after dark.[5]

Collective labor is also organized in named groups of men. In Bong village, there are four such *doegap* ranging from ten to thirteen members each and roughly age graded. Men older than perhaps forty-five and beyond their prime as active farmers do not participate. The eldest group has members aged thirty to forty-five, while two others range in age from approximately twenty to thirty-five. A yet unnamed group includes the unmarried boys from twelve to twenty. Each *doegap* chooses its name and maintains its identity as the members grow older. Each cuts across lineage, clan, and neighborhood lines. Leadership is provided by members holding offices named after the Hausa fashion (*sarki, madaiki,* and so on) or the European ("DO," soldier, messenger, cook) . The *doegap* accepts invitations from any fellow villager to farm a bush field. Since the members of a *doegap* group are peers, there is a strong element of competition in their work. The party is summoned to the field by horn blasts in the early morning, and they fall to with a will. As men hoe they call, and, as one finishes his three rows, he shouts triumphantly and runs brandishing his hoe to the next plot. When I asked why a man did not finish a larger area before straightening up and running on, I was told that the abrupt change of position was in itself a release and a rest. Certainly the fact that the workers are close to each

[5] For a discussion of the place of beer in Kofyar culture, see Netting, 1964.

other means an increase both in competition and in high spirits. In a 2.5-acre level acha field, a party of twelve young men worked at high speed, each hoeing three ridges in a section twelve feet by thirty. The *doegap* is sometimes given a dog or goat to eat along with beer. If beer alone is given, it may be as much as twelve jars, equal to more than a gallon for each participant. The younger boys are not yet considered fully competent workers, and their group sometimes receives cooked beans in lieu of beer. The adult *doegap* in Bong celebrates the *yang fu can* (washing of the hoes) festival at the end of the farming season, when each makes beer by a subscription of grain and buys an animal for feasting.

Not all the hill villages have the *doegap* organization. Named drinking groups (*shar mwos*) whose members entertain one another and go together to beer parties are quite common, but only in Bong and a few neighboring villages is the aspect of joint agricultural labor emphasized. This may be connected with the fact that Bong differs from the standard pattern in obtaining an important part of its subsistence from bush fallow fields where a larger labor force is a positive advantage. Another type of organization for young men, known as *jebswal,* is probably copied from the Hausa *samari* association. In the plains and in some hill villages, these young men under their elected chief can be mobilized for community labor, road and bridge building, path clearing, and so on. They may also act as a political and judicial body. As far as I know, the whole group does not function together in agricultural efforts.

The advantages of collective labor under conditions of shifting cultivation are obvious. As compared to homestead intensive farms, the bush fields are both larger and less productive per unit of area. The emphasis must be on extensive tilling, but very careful hoeing is not necessary. Group effort allows the job to be done, as the Kofyar say, "in time." A work party not only enables the entire cultivating and planting or harvesting operations to be completed on a single day, but perhaps most importantly it furnishes the social stimulus of excitement and competition along with the expectation of a pleasurable reward. The social conditions of speedy, highly motivated work are thus met in the same ways as the demands of agricultural efficiency. Lacking machines, the Kofyar cultivate their larger, less productive fields by voluntarily mobilizing human resources.

Localization and Kinship

It would appear that the effect of the Kofyar exploitation pattern has been to limit the spatial extension of effective descent groups and tie their operation closely to a locality. Kofyar patrilineal lineages and lineage segments show strong concentration of residence in particular neighborhoods. Clan segments, the largest unilineal kin groups that act corporately, are localized within villages. Clans with a membership spread through several villages are little more than name groups. I suggest that the permanency and intensive nature of agriculture have something to do with the characteristic structure of descent groups.

Kofyar descent groups are composed of individuals tracing patrilineal descent putatively or demonstrably to a common male ancestor. Precise distinctions of genealogical depth and contemporary range are not clearly established. One could analyze the system in terms of minimal-minor-major-maximal levels corresponding to groups of brothers and their sons, lineages, localized clan segments, and clans. The Kofyar themselves give distinctive names to two categories, that of the lineage in which members ideally may trace common descent to a known ancestor two to five generations removed, and that of the localized clan segment in which several lineages claim common descent from a single progenitor though they lack genealogical evidence of relationship. Both lineage and localized clan segment form the basis for periodic assemblages of male members and carry out jural, political, and religious functions. The descent group is important in hunting organization and in settling economic disputes, but it does not act directly in agricultural or other productive pursuits. Large lineages may have lineage segments, unnamed groups that show a marked genealogical and geographical separation from one another and whose limits describe the lines on which lineage segmentation may occur. Lineages may also be allied for political purposes in intraclan debates, and this is justified on grounds of spatial contiguity or friendship rather than genealogical closeness.

The generic terms used for lineage and clan segment are not mutually exclusive. Groups at the lineage level are called *jebfup* (sons of a father) or *mwol*, but *jebfup* is also synonymous with *pan* and *was*, which usually refer to a clan segment or nonlocalized clan. Individual lineages, however, bear the names of their founding ancestor with a prefix indicating "we are the sons of" (*Moela-Paya*) or "the original place of" (Kop-Dakung). Clans and localized clan segments are designated simply by the ancestor's name, for example, Mutper, Jidong, and this is the answer most frequently given to the question, "What is your descent group?"

Exogamy is not a major indication of lineage membership. Only when biological relationship to a common ancestor can be demonstrated is marriage prohibited. A man may freely marry the daughters of members adopted into the lineage, slaves, or those to whom connections cannot be traced. In certain highly ramified lineages, marriage is still prohibited between individuals four and five generations from the eponymous ancestor, but the elder men expect marriages to take place among the most distantly related members in the next generation. A clearly related exogamous lineage core comprising at least 70 per cent of member males is evident in 11 of 15 native lineages in two villages. In nine of these lineages, all members are directly descended from a common ancestor. Kofyar village lineages range from two to 14 and average 5.1 adult male household heads, while in Bong the range is three to 15 and the average is 7.6. Though women retain membership in the paternal lineage throughout their lives, they do not attend lineage meetings and they take little active part in group affairs.

Kofyar lineage membership is substantially reflected in residential contiguity. The residence of a lineage in one neighborhood or adjoining neighborhoods is plainly evident irrespective of the way in which the members are related. A neighborhood is an individual territorial section of a village containing from 3 to 20 homesteads. A sample of 27 hill neighborhoods in 4 villages gives an average figure of 7.22 homesteads per neighborhood. Comparable data are lacking for the plains, but my impression is that neighborhoods there average approximately 15 homesteads. Neighborhoods are often set off from one another by the natural barrier of a stream, a hill, or a barren patch of ground, but sometimes the boundaries appear quite arbitrary. A man may establish a homestead wherever he chooses, provided he has the permission of the owner of the land, but the natural process of budding off from a parental homestead, the desire to make maximum use of family land, and the effort to maintain agricultural cooperation with kin are all effective factors in preventing wide spatial dispersion of the lineage.

The Kofyar term for ward or neighborhood, *toeng lu,* "the tree of houses," suggests the branching lineage that relates most of the neighbors to one another. As a lineage grows it may well overflow its original neighborhood, but its members tend to settle in adjacent neighborhoods, and the center of gravity of the lineage remains in the same general area of the village (see maps, Figs. 7, 8). Twelve out of fifteen lineages in two villages have at least two-thirds of their members in two adjoining neighborhoods. The large Moelapaya lineage of Kofyar village has twelve out of its seventeen constituent homesteads in four adjoining neighborhoods, all on the northern side of the village. Moeladakoen lineage of seven households has residents in five different Bong neighborhoods, but the homesteads are still almost contiguous, forming a narrow band along the southern border of the village. Strangers settling permanently in a neighborhood may be easily assimilated into the dominant resident lineage. Where a lineage appears to inhabit nonadjoining neighbor-

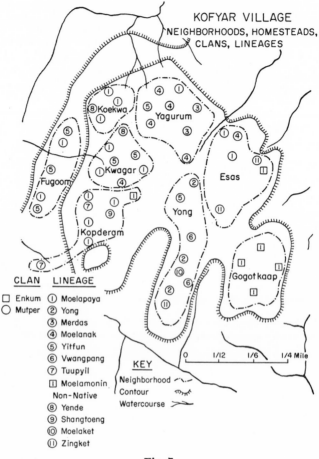

KOFYAR VILLAGE
NEIGHBORHOODS, HOMESTEADS,
CLANS, LINEAGES

CLAN   LINEAGE

☐ Enkum ① Moelapaya
○ Mutper ② Yong
         ③ Merdas
         ④ Moelanak
         ⑤ Yitfun
         ⑥ Vwangpang
         ⑦ Tuupyil
         ☐ Moelamonin
         Non-Native
         ⑧ Yende
         ⑨ Shangtoeng
         ⑩ Moelaket
         ⑪ Zingket

KEY
Neighborhood ⌐⌐⌐
Contour   ⌐⌐⌐
Watercourse ⌐⌐⌐

0   1/12   1/6   1/4 Mile

Fig. 7

hoods, the split is usually a reflection of genealogical distance. Thus Moelalatoeng of Bong divides into a lineage segment of seven members in Goedang neighborhood and another of six households inhabiting the adjoining neighborhoods of Goebong and Moelaar in a separate section of the village. The two lineage segments cannot prove common ancestry and may intermarry. As Kopjidong lineage has expanded, three core members have moved to take up residence in farms bordering the original neighborhood, while

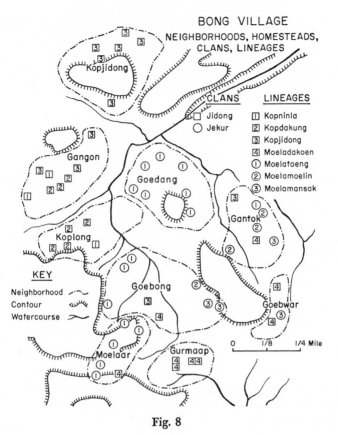

Fig. 8

the descendants of several men adopted into the lineage have established a satellite hamlet on the side of the village that is associated with their lineage.

A Kofyar lineage is strongly anchored to a particular place: its group unity has a marked spatial dimension. This does not seem to be the result of stated principle so much as a concomitant of sedentary, permanent residence and intensive land use. If a man lives apart from his lineage, it may well be a temporary matter due to scarcity of land. All things being equal, a young man would probably choose to live near his brothers and other lineage mates. They can be expected to make land available to him most readily and protect his interests most assiduously. He can trust them to aid him in the fields, to support him in most disputes and fights, and to consult with him on political matters. These advantages are enhanced by nearness of residence. A new-comer tends to be identified with the dominant lineage in the neighborhood where he settles. He may join their meet-ings and moots. If he takes up permanent residence he may be given land by a lineage member. The final step to full lineage membership is made when the adopted person or his descendants begin to take part in lineage religious observ-ances.

The identity of the lineage is associated with a sacred ancestral homestead called the *pe wuyon* ("the big place") in the neighborhood from which the lineage originated. The eponymous ancestor may be buried there, and it is in this place that his descendants meet for discussion, prayer, and the butchering and sharing of big game. Lineage fission is traditionally marked by the establishment of a new location where meat is cut up. Such a homestead, which must not be left unoccupied, is the haunt of beneficent spirits (*moe-wang*) resembling fairies. The graves at the entrances of homesteads recall lineage members who lived there in the past and who may be honored from time to time with liba-tions of beer. Each lineage or lineage segment may also have a sacred grove where magical ceremonies are conducted. Thus a certain neighborhood or an area of several neighbor-hoods is not only the physical but also the spiritual home of the lineage. It is obviously not possible to separate the prima-rily adaptive qualities of lineage localization from the impor-tant mystical association and emotional attachment of line-age members to their natal neighborhoods. The Kofyar are reluctant to abandon their traditional homesteads, though they may migrate to distant bush fields for the major part of their farming. When asked why he does not move away, the Kofyar typically replies: *"Goe fut n kop fup goe a?"* ("Do you leave the place of your fathers?"). Burial and funeral celebrations must still be held at the ancestral homestead (cf.

Rowling 1952:14). The sentiment is reinforced by strict lineage sanctions against any member who by departing from the community leaves an ancestral homestead vacant.

The localized character of Kofyar descent groups is most apparent on the level of clan segments and clans. Unlike the classic segmentary lineage systems of Africa, the Kofyar do not mobilize manpower on kinship lines beyond the village. Tradition traces the descent of all Kofyar from a single ancestor and charts the dispersion of named clan founders. The same clan with the same history may be found in several villages, and it may even occupy adjacent sections of the various settlements. Thus, on the triangle formed by the three neighboring villages of Bogalong, Bong, and Zugal the nearest border of each is occupied by the Jidong-Enkum clan, and the story is told that related founders of the sections went in three directions from the central river valley and settled the nearest available lands. Each localized clan segment, however, maintains its own sacred spots, conducts its own business, and feels no special obligation to defend or support its congeners. Jural proceedings, ceremonies, and the sharing of funeral meats are all confined to the local group. Members of spatially separate clan segments may steal each others' wives, and this contrasts sharply with the general prohibition on wife stealing within a village. In war, the combatants tried to avoid fellow clansmen from other areas, but they were certainly considered enemies. Dispersed segments of a clan make no decisions in common and share no rights in an estate.

A clan segment may be further subdivided, with members both in a central village and in subsidiary hamlets. In this case some clan activities are pursued jointly while others are independent. The larger the hamlet, the more opportunity there is for constituent lineages to consult apart from the parent segment, and this undoubtedly reflects a general tendency toward fission along village lines. This progressive isolation and the lack of pyramiding of kinship groups in complementary opposition is possibly characteristic of stable populations and movement into an uncontested domain. The Kofyar have no tradition of conquering their territory from its original inhabitants. As Sahlins (1961:342) suggests:

> Expansions into an open environment may well be accompanied by segmentation, the normal process of tribal growth and spread. But in the absence of competition small segments tend to become discrete and autonomous, linked together primarily through mechanical solidarity. These circumstances, in other words, favor fission but select against complementary opposition or fusion and long term occupation will eventually fix this structure, make it comparatively inflexible.

In the hill villages there are usually two major clan segments, so that a dual division is approximated. Even when there are three or more clans represented, they are grouped as followers or "friends" of either Mutper or Enkum, the original clans of the parent village, Kofyar. The dual division furnishes a line along which political conflict and rivalry may develop. In the hill region, the chiefs of those villages nearest to the plain (Gankogom) come from Mutper or related clans, while the next tier of villages to the west (Ganguk) draws its chiefs from the Enkum offshoot clan called Jidong. Because of the mixture of various villages, probably due to forced relocation, it is impossible to discern a regular division among the fragmented clans of the Latok villages. Throughout Kofyar, the chief comes from a particular lineage of the dominant clan, while certain magico-religious powers reside in related lineages. The chiefly clan claims first occupation of village land and possession of the earth ceremony (*ya fu yil*). The subsidiary clan may be said to be strangers or returned slaves.

A marked territorial division of village lands follows clan lines. A line drawn through Bong village following the course of the River of Palm Trees (*Kong Mwor Bang*) and one of its tributaries separates the major clans of Jidong and Jekur, with only two Jidong men remaining in Jekur territory. The conical volcanic core rising behind the village is also divided evenly between the two clans.

Kofyar descent groups become nonfunctional to the extent they are nonlocalized. In the household, the lineage, and the clan segment, they have a territorial base. In the clan and genealogically related clans they have no role in production, exchange, jural relations, or warfare. Without the stimulus of a common land area to defend and the frequent association of agricultural cooperation and intravillage politics, there is no longer a basis for corporate sentiment and activity. The characteristic self-sufficiency of the Kofyar and their reliance on permanent agriculture suggest that there is little to be gained by maintaining ties of clanship with other communities.

For the sorts of help that only outsiders can give, especially certain kinds of magical assistance, sanctuary from punishment by the descent group, and economic aid in time of disaster, the Kofyar rely on ego-centered groups of maternal kin, the mother's brothers or *koen*. Sickness is always reported to the mother's brothers, and they are expected to witness the divinations and inquire into the cause of the illness. When the patient shows no signs of recovery, the attendant mother's brothers may accuse his paternal kin of bewitching him and exhort them to stop. Death is also reported to the mother's brother, and he may demand an explanation in cases where he suspects foul play. A man's *koen* do not form a permanent corporate group, but come together only on matters directly connected with his personal well being. In the past it was the *koen* who would avenge a homicide of his sister's son by killing the murderer or raiding his village.

Today a close personal relationship of affection and mutual respect is maintained between mother's brother and sister's child. It is exemplified by licensed stealing, help in odd jobs, gifts at marriage, presentation of some of the meat from game killed, and the giving of a specific portion of the sacrificial animal at funeral commemoration ceremonies. The Kofyar use kin terms infrequently in addressing relatives. Father and mother are usually called by kin terms, and anyone who stands in the mother's brother relationship is always addressed as *koeni*. The terminological system of Crow type [6] reflects the special relationship with a distinctive reciprocal kinship designation. It appears that these institutionalized personal ties in the absence of dispersed kin groups or more inclusive political organization are the only counterweight for the individual Kofyar's heavy dependence on localized units.[7]

[6] Kofyar kinship terminology corresponds most closely in pattern to the Crow Reductions, Type II outlined by Lounsbury (1964:371). It differs, however in separating the MB/Ss term (*koen*) from that used for siblings (*emnoegoen*). In generations above ego's, only male relatives, the MB and the MMB, are referred to as *koen*. In generations below that of ego, sister's children, MSd children and FBd children are all *koen*, regardless of sex. Offspring of male *koen* are always designated as siblings, while those of female *koen* are themselves *koen*.

Among the Kofyar peoples, there are at least two variations in terminology. It is not my purpose to analyze these at this time, but a minimal description is appended for the use of others. Differences in terminology are confined to the descendants of the FS. The system used in Bong and Latok villages labels FSs as father and FSd as mother. In succeeding generations, the children of anyone termed father are siblings, while those of mother are themselves father and mother. The Lardang variant puts FSs and FSd into the MB (*koen*) classification, and their offspring follow the general rule given above for descendants of *koen*. Both systems set apart a series of uterine relatives whose rights and obligations to ego are clearly defined. Though some of them may live in ego's village, the statistical preference for marriage of women outside their natal communities means that most individuals have *koen* scattered in a number of the surrounding settlements.

Kofyar kin terms and their applications are illustrated in the table in the appendix (pp. 234–235), using Lounsbury's abbreviations for kin types (1964:358) followed by an abbreviation in parentheses referring to the Kofyar kin term.

[7] Though we lack any knowledge of historical development among Kofyar descent groups, it is interesting to note that similar ecological conditions have lessened the inclusiveness of wide-ranging associations. Winans (1965b) refers to Gulliver's findings that Arusha age sets have diverged from the general Masai pattern by identifying groups of initiates with the small geographical area of coresidence: "This appears to be a response to the Arusha intensive and fixed pattern of agriculture and is marked by the lessening of the significance of the age set as it occurs in Masai society and a heavy emphasis on location as a determinant of jural, ritual, and economic conditions" (174).

The Village

The village, a discrete, named collection of homesteads in neighborhoods, is the most inclusive unit of continuing social importance among the Kofyar. Though many of the members of the community have consanguineal or affinal ties with one another, it is common residence rather than kinship that most significantly binds them together. The village has definite boundaries within which its members have specific rights to land. The inhabitants form a consistent group for pooling productive labor, preserving order, providing recreation, and defending their territory. The deciding of questions involving the whole community requires a village council meeting of all adult males. Though only the chief of the village and a specific lineage head from the dominant lineage can conduct the rites for restoring fertility or overcoming misfortune, the sacrifice is given to the earth (*yil*) rather than to particular clan ancestors, and again the entire male population is present. Wars, insofar as I can determine, were always fought by village groups as a whole, though this meant that members of the same clan in different villages were opposed to one another. In the blood feud, the grievance of one member became an incentive to all those coresident in the village, whatever their relationship, to support him with arms. All the men in a village may be called *koen*, "mother's brother," by an outsider, though the avuncular relation may in reality only hold with a single individual. In every case of large-scale cooperation, whether in hunting, farming, or celebrating one of the great seasonal dances, the bounds of participation are identical with those of the village. In all but a few large villages it is not permitted to steal the wife of a coresident, and village members unite in trying to persuade dissatisfied wives not to run away. Recognized extramarital relations are carried on always between lovers in the same village.

Hill villages are clearly demarcated geographical entities. The settled area is often hedged by precipitous ravines, and village boundaries are most frequently marked by a perennial stream. In former times a high position commanding open treeless areas allowed quick spotting of enemy movements. Frequently the only approaches to a village are through narrow valleys or along rock-strewn paths that can be easily defended. In time of war the smaller hamlets, which frequently lacked both manpower and a naturally defensible position, took refuge with their larger neighbors. Boundaries were exactly drawn, and trespassing by people from another village, even if only to cut thatching grass, was sufficient cause for killing the offenders. War among the Kofyar seems never to have been conducted for conquest and the appropriation of territory. The object was to overrun and loot the enemy village, and perhaps destroy the houses. Under the system of subsistence farming with negligible trade, there was little economic advantage in seizing more territory, and political techniques by which a captive people could be effectively exploited were lacking. Thus each sizable hilltop site held an independent village, a self-governing, stable unit with lands made up of fields held by individual village members. The only time when the village did not appear as an entirely independent political entity was during a war, when there was a system of traditional military alliances. An *ad hoc* war leader might be recognized, but there was no further political integration.

Villages were never insulated from their neighbors, and there has always been a flow of population from one to another. Women may be married within the village, but the greater number of wives come from surrounding settlements. Of 852 married women in 12 villages, 657, or 77 per cent, come from outside their husband's village. Since residence is virilocal (I did not meet with a single case of a man's going to live with a male relative of his wife), it is women who most frequently change villages. Remarriage of a woman is almost always effected by her running away to another village. The hill and plain villages, however, form separate marriage groups with little passage of females between them.

Male population tends to remain relatively more stable, but it is not unusual to find several men in each village who were not locally born. Boys sent to other villages for treatment of sickness may remain after they have been cured and eventually take up farms. The network of intervillage affinal ties is important to those wishing to change their residences. A confessed witch was formerly threatened with execution unless he went to live with his mother's brother, where his safety was assured. A child who felt he was being poorly treated at home could go to live with his maternal uncle. People driven out of their homes by war might stay for years in a neighboring village. Some of these cases result in the owning of village lands by people not now resident there. Because such land is readily available at token rent, such absentee ownership does not restrict village sovereignty or local land use.

Plains villages seem to have been similar to those of the hills except for certain mechanisms adapting the structure to a denser population and more continuous settled area. People are concentrated in a band from one to three miles broad along the base of the hills and reaching up river valleys as far as there is level land. Streams and occasional areas of poor, rocky soil cut the inhabited strip transversely, but these do not hamper movement or furnish any measure of military protection. Named villages continue to exist with their constituent neighborhoods, but now they are amalgamated in a village area or district under a single chief. These districts were the groups referred to by the Europeans as "tribes," and they now form the basic units of local government. Each component village in the district has a *naa yer,* chief or headman, now often called *mengwa* after the Hausa *mai ungwa,* "master of the ward." The chief's council may be made up of these *mengwa,* and through them, community activities are coordinated. In Dimmuk, there is also a series of titled officials, each elected from among its members by a lineage with rights to a title. These men, all from the chiefly clan, sit in council with the chief, act as judges, and are each responsible for a set of villages where they act in a liaison role and oversee the gathering of tax. The power given to some of these officials to supervise affairs in hill communities is entirely a product of colonial government.

Because of the emphasis on localization, modern political devices such as voting districts and census tracts which have a territorial basis are easily assimilated into Kofyar social organization. Though the units may be larger than traditional ones, affiliation by residence is the same. Kofyar migrants have staked out farms in the new lands around Namu without reference to lineage, clan, or native village. Bush neighborhoods have grown up with a mixed bag of residents from hill and plain. Households have moved individually to claim available lands, and relatives seldom emerge with adjoining tracts. Those who find themselves in the same area unite for agricultural purposes and recognize as representative leaders the first settlers of that particular tract. In this they follow customary usage, which assigned political precedence to the first occupants of the land. There is no sign that, in the more fluid situation of shifting cash cropping, the traditional alignments of kin or village are significant. Coresidence in the locality is the basis for cooperative activities, the settlement of disputes, and whatever embryonic government exists.

6

Rights to the Means of Production

Any study of the social organization of subsistence activities must consider the social rules for the use of resources and tools. As techniques improve and property takes on value these rules must grow in complexity and inclusiveness; they must explicitly cover a wider range of situations. The common understandings about use, ownership, and transfer of productive goods among the Kofyar reflect the scarcity of available land and the permanence and high returns of their intensive agricultural adaptation.

Rights in Tools

Kofyar technology requires a relatively small and simple tool kit. The average household can provide materials for its own shelter and storage facilities by collecting building mud, stones, timber rafters, and grass for thatching. These are freely available, and the major expense involved is the labor of individuals expended during the dry season, when demands for agricultural labor are minimal. The skills of house-building, the erection of granaries and drying platforms, and the manufacture of pottery are possessed by most adults, and experts are seldom employed. Portable items belong to their maker and may be sold. Permanent structures are improvements on the land, and their ownership follows from possession of the ground on which they are built. Iron tools, though often forged locally, require the importation of iron and the services of a specialist smith. The hoe is the major farming implement and was formerly an item of considerable value. Hoes often formed part of a bride price payment along with salt and domestic animals. Individuals obtain hoe blades by purchase or barter, and the tool is held as personal property by every household head and most adult males. Women rely on their fathers or husbands for such equipment, and it is said that a wife turns over some of her store of crops to her husband at divorce "because she has used his hoe." Spears belong to individual men, and both sexes may possess knives. Today all these items are easily purchasable and may be given away or passed on to children at the death of their parents. Much more important than the possession of tools in Kofyar society are rights to the major productive resource, land. The relation of individuals to arable land underlies many of the institutions and associations of a society, and land tenure has often been used as a diagnostic criterion of social organization (Fried 1952).

Rights in Land

If we can imagine various possible systems of land tenure, ranging from a communal form with all rights vested in a social group to freehold in which individuals exercise unrestricted control over land, the Kofyar tenure would occupy a position toward the latter end of the spectrum.

Table 13 suggests that though no permanent alienation is possible without permission of the owner's lineage, most other important rights to land inhere in individuals rather than kinship groups or official personages. In this the Kofyar differ significantly from most traditional African societies, which assign land to the collective ownership of kin groups or to a chief acting as representative of a village (Biebuyck

TABLE 13

RIGHTS TO LAND OF INDIVIDUALS AND GROUPS

Rights to Land	Owner	Tenant	Lineage Head	Lineage
Unrestricted usufruct	x			
Usufruct with conditions		x		
Occupation and dwelling	x	x		
Rights to lease, loan, share	x			
Inheritance of all rights	x			
Conditional inheritance of tenancy		x		
Reversion			x	
Permanent alienation				x

1963:54; Allan 1965:361). Typically, the individual farmer has rights of usufruct only (Grove 1961; Meek 1957). Such a system is a realistic and flexible adaptation to shifting cultivation, setting up as it does a pool of land from which individuals may draw according to their need and in which fallow land is held for future exploitation. Labor put into farming produces food, but it results in at least temporary loss of value in the land per se. A member of the community has rights to the products of his labor and to the necessary land on which to farm. Rights to a particular plot, however, are often lost by abandonment or terminated by death (C. M. N. White 1963:364).

The Kofyar insist that every square inch of arable soil, both village and bush, has an owner, a single person to whom the land belongs and who alone may decide on its use. This is probably a direct outgrowth of intensive farming. Wherever land can be made to produce heavily and continuously over a long period of time, it increases in value to both the occupant and his heirs. Terracing, annual manuring, and the care of economic trees demand a sizable investment of time and labor. Unlike the return of worked-out land to the village pool, good developed homestead farmland cannot be turned over to others or to collective ownership without economic loss by the current user and windfall gain to the new possessor.[1]

Wherever there has been a shift from subsistence farming to agricultural production with a high initial investment and long-term rewards, the transition has been accompanied by pressure for individual tenure replacing communal property. In West Africa this process has been most apparent in the adoption of certain cash crops, such as cocoa. Individual land ownership seems also to be a concomitant of intensive agriculture among the Hausa with regard to manured fields and swamp rice *fadamas* (Grove 1961). Where land is at a premium in the most densely populated Ibo areas, communal village or extended family control of land has been largely replaced by nuclear family tenure (Morgan 1953; Udo 1965). Monica Wilson has actually witnessed such a transition among the Nyakyusa (1963:384) :

A redistribution in each generation operated without much friction so long as land was plentiful and there were few permanent improvements or long-term crops, but as land became more scarce and men built more lasting houses and planted coffee, then it became impossible. Owners were neither prepared to lose the improvements they had made nor, having secured fertile land, to vacate it.

The Kofyar traditionally grew a limited amount of products for barter such as palm oil on their homestead farms, but even more important were the improvements they made which often *created* an intensive subsistence farm where only bush land had been before. Considerable preparatory labor in the form of terracing, annual manuring, and tree

[1] Rowling, in his report on Plateau land tenure (1952), claims that extended family or collective ownership is the rule in the area, though he recognizes that the hill-foot Dimmuk, Mirriam, and Kwalla show tendencies toward individual tenure (11, 14) : "It is nonetheless true that the individualist aspects of all Plateau tenure are as it were orchestral variations over a collective ground bass." Rowling seems unaware of the important difference between the intensive homestead farming of the Kofyar and the shifting cultivation of neighboring groups. He contends that personal land ownership is an innovation connected with a movement to new areas, whereas the exact opposite may in fact be true.

tending were required to build up and maintain high fertility in the soil. This extra work may well have been a response to the shortage of land that developed as population grew within a confined area. The rewards for such an investment of labor were dependable long-term production of staple crops and annual yields of edible palm and canarium oils to supplement the diet and allow trade. Economic trees provide a good example of the value generated by sustained yield coupled with scarcity. Oil palm trees are long in maturing, must be protected and pruned for maximum production, and do not grow well apart from the well-watered areas of the hills. In support of their wish to maintain residence on ancestral homesteads, the Kofyar often speak of their trees and the fact that their loss would be difficult to replace. It is a plausible speculation that among agriculturalists "the tree . . . gradually evokes the first feelings of property and of home soil" (Febvre 1932:294). Perhaps individualized rights tend to appear wherever a resource affords continuing dependable returns of a scarce and desirable good.[2]

Though communal and individual tenure are often seen as opposed principles, the difference between them is actually one of degree rather than kind. Where abundant land exists, fallow land is of little value until it has naturally regenerated its fertility. The important right is not that to a plot formerly farmed but to the usufruct of sufficient suitable land allocated from the village or kin group pool. As intensive cultivation increases and the fallow is progressively shortened, the period of usufruct gradually changes from temporary to permanent. Under conditions of increasing population and correlated land scarcity, individuals or families will recultivate their old plots because they cannot find more desirable land elsewhere (Boserup 1965:80). Though the tenure system appears to change, the principle may re-

[2] Even without economic trees, increasing intensity of cultivation and dispersed permanent settlement on homestead farms stimulated by population pressure are regularly associated with individualized land tenure (cf. Udo 1965).

main that of individual rights to the fruits of the land as long as it continues to produce.[3] As land becomes concurrently less available and potentially more productive, its increased value is seen in boundary marking, litigation, and considerations in return for temporary or long-term transfers of rights to its use. Pledging, leasing, and payments for improvements may all occur, though outright sale is still prohibited (Allan 1965:369).

Though Kofyar rights in land are mainly individual, not everyone has them to the same degree. Women are not entitled to land. Many adult males have no inherited land, either because their fathers possessed none or because the patrimony has gone to another brother. Moreover, land is not necessarily held by a single person. In Bong, two young brothers, Dayil and Dakop, lived together with their wives in a single homestead, working their father's land together and sharing all crops produced. They told me that if they ever quarreled seriously, they would divide (gap) their shared land and cease to work cooperatively, but they regarded this as a remote possibility. However, it was obvious that with a growing family each would soon require a full-sized homestead field, and the younger brother began talking of reclaiming for intensive use some nearby village farmland belonging to his father's brother or moving into a recently vacated site in another neighborhood. When the father's brother, who was also a lineage head, suddenly died, the elder brother moved onto his farm while the younger stayed in the father's homestead.

In the case of homestead farms, the occupant, if he is a rightful heir, is the owner. Other heirs by moving away from the homestead give up their immediate rights in the land, though not their right to inherit it. Age is not a meaningful criterion, and it often happens that older sons may move away from the parental homestead to leased plots while a remaining younger brother may succeed to ownership. Only

[3] Manners (1964) illustrates this process in the recent shift to individualized tenure among the Kipsigis of Kenya.

if the father's house is left vacant may another son move back to it, but even this is not mandatory.

Perhaps the key to understanding Kofyar land policy is the concept that land is only to a limited degree a commodity. Rights of ownership are not alienable by sale or gift, but a rights of use are easily transferable. Land cannot be viewed as a really valuable resource unless it is being kept in production by its owner. If the owner has no need to work it himself, he is prohibited from profiting by the sale of it, and he exacts only token payments by way of rent. If a homestead is vacant, the owner may either use it himself or lease it to another occupant rather than let it stand idle. The residual interest of the lineage appears only when the land of a member is threatened with permanent alienation or neglect. The lineage may ostracize *(fet shi)* any member found guilty of selling his land. The accused must confess before the assembled lineage or clan segment. He gives nine goats which are killed at the lineage sacred place; blood is poured into a hole in the earth, and a formula is repeated which breaks all ties of relationship and exiles the offender. This punishment was recently threatened by a Kwa lineage to prevent a rumored sale, and the guilty party had to give up his plans to sell and pay a fine to the lineage in order to be reinstated. Merely to leave land with no provision for its use or future assignment is also punishable by the lineage. These rules have contributed to making the Kofyar into migrant farmers rather than permanent settlers of new land.

It seems relatively easy today for the Kofyar hill farmer to secure the use of land, at least enough to make a homestead farm. Though farming techniques and attitudes toward land seem to reflect its scarcity, there is some evidence (p. 113, above) that the demographic pressures have substantially lessened in the last fifty years. Not only was the hill Kofyar population apparently much higher in the past, but bush fallows in the vicinity of the village were strictly limited because of the possibility of raids and ambushes. With many homestead sites now vacant, a prospective tenant can merely ask the owner's permission to use one. He must make some sort of payment and remain under certain obligations to the owner, but the terms are seldom onerous. A plot that is giving the owner only small irregular harvests as a village fallow can be converted into heavy annual production by a tenant's careful manuring. Even land outside the village can be brought under intensive cultivation. Palm trees indicate the now deserted sites of old homesteads set up outside Bong by wartime refugees. In other words, there is a large amount of land available for development by resident tenants, so that landowners cannot profit much by farming it themselves or by trying to exact a high rent for its use. Tenants are entitled to occupation and usufruct as long as certain rental conditions are met. Though tenancy may be inherited, the tenant cannot independently reassign his rights to some third party.

In Kofyar village, ten out of forty-eight homesteads are occupied by tenants, with rent ranging from nothing or a single chicken to one pound and a cock. There is no standard rent, but a large amount, such as a goat or one pound or more, is usually a single payment which secures a lifetime lease for the tenant. This may be equivalent to what is often called "pledging" land. Smaller sums, such as seven shillings or a bundle of sorghum, are paid on a regular basis, usually once every seven years. Perhaps more important than these payments in money or kind are the rights of the owner to all tree crops produced on the property and to a free jar of beer whenever the tenant brews. In Bong, where palms are plentiful, the owner receives the palm oil from fruit the tenant has gathered and crushed, while the tenant is allowed to keep only the kernels. The same rule applies to canarium trees. The owner can also approach his tenant from time to time for small informal presents of *aas* (pounded grain), chickens, and beer.

Bogalong village has a large proportion of renters—thirty-four out of a total of fifty homesteads. Twelve of these homesteads are leased from men in neighboring villages. Lease payments range from nine shillings to three pounds and one goat, and periodic rents are as high as a sheep and a hen every seven years.[4] Pressure on the land may be greater in Bogalong than elsewhere, but I have no direct evidence of this. In some cases, men acknowledge that the land they farm is not their own but say that their father or grandfather leased it and no further payment is necessary. If an owner wishes to remove a tenant and reclaim his land, it may be very difficult in situations in which several generations of tenants have lived there. As the people say, "No one knows how much his father or grandfather received from the tenants long ago." One informant also gave the opinion that a land-owner could not dispossess a tenant who was in the same clan (and thus a distant patrilineal relative). In one case a tenant died who had previously paid regular rent in palm oil to the owner of the land, a lineage relative. The tenant was succeeded by a matrilateral kinsman who refused to pay the rent. The owner was indignant and claimed he had the right to evict the tenant because he was not a patrilineal lineage member. The only grounds for driving off (*cen*) a tenant who is a patrilineal kinsman is his connivance at the divorce of one of the owner's wives, stealing from the owner, or practicing witchcraft.

One of the very rare instances of sale was recorded in Bogalong. Wubang bought a homestead field from Dawam for eight pounds, the transaction occurring when Dawam wished to take the field back and could only be persuaded to drop his claim by a sizable cash settlement. Dawam himself lived on a leased field as did several other men who owned property. The sale undoubtedly had the approval of Dawam's lineage. A 1950 land sale in Kwa for three pounds, three shillings was deemed so important that the terms (a three-year waiting period during which the purchase price

[4] For comparison, the annual tax rate per adult male is currently two pounds.

could be refunded and final witness of the transaction by the chief and elders) were included in the divisional officer's touring notes.

Permanent transfer of land was effected in the past by means of pledges that went unredeemed. If a man died without heirs or wealth, his local clan segment might still feel it necessary to celebrate a *maap* funeral commemoration for him. If they did not possess a large animal for the sacrifice, they might be willing to pledge a plot of land to anyone who would provide them with a horse or a cow. If an equivalent animal (*bi teget,* the thing withdrawn) was not returned to the donor within a seven-year period, the land became his permanent property. If the clan does not wish the land to be lost (*kyem*), they must return the pledge, and the Kofyar can point to examples of both such situations. Pledging could only be entered into for the purpose of making a *maap* ceremony, and even then it was expected that the clan would try to redeem the land rather than alienating part of their patrimony.

Where bush land is important, as in Bong, there may also be considerable leasing. A single payment entitles the lessee to work the land for a cropping cycle of anything from four to ten years. When the field is left fallow, full rights over it return to the owner. Payments depend somewhat on the size and fertility of the field. A three-acre long-fallow field that may produce well for 10 to 14 years costs two pounds. A tin of palm oil worth £1 5s. was given in 1960 for a 2.8-acre field with an expected useful life of 10 years. Hoes and goats sometimes serve as partial payment, but I have never heard of a share cropping arrangement. Rents given to fellow villagers may be smaller, as little as 3s. or merely occasional beer. Eight bush fields averaged 16s. 6d. in rent including both cash and kind. It is said that land cannot be reclaimed from a lessee who is actively cultivating it unless he has committed some offense against the owner.

Land around and inside a village is not necessarily owned

by current residents of the village. Some homesteads and bush plots were taken up in Bong by refugees during the feuds that made certain villages and hamlets untenable in the early years of the century. The land continued to be held by these men and their heirs though they had not lived on or near it for close to forty years. Members of a lineage may also leave the ancestral homestead to settle in another hamlet or village, and whether they return to cultivate their land or not, their rights in it remain unimpaired. If a man sees a field in the bush that he would like to cultivate, he should seek out the owner and ask (*dang*, to beg) for its use. Mutually acceptable terms must then be arranged. If the owner is unknown, the man may start work, safe in the knowledge that someone will appear to claim rent. If payments are refused, the owner has the right to cut all of the grain and take it for his own use.

Rent is not always exacted for the use of land. A man with extensive holdings gave the use of a field and its trees to a father's brother's son who had insufficient palm oil to meet his needs. Older women who have been widowed may be allowed to use their husband's homestead field for as long as they desire, or they may be given bush farms by a brother. Such a loan applies only to the usufruct and does not give the woman title to the land or affect the usual rules of inheritance. On a smaller scale, every wife has some land given by her husband on a year-to-year basis. Groundnuts or late millet are preferred crops in such fields. A woman may use some of the groundnuts she grows in preparing meals for the family, but husbands say they cannot interfere with a wife's decision over disposition of such produce. A man who without asking his wife appropriates the foodstuffs grown in her own plot is subject to native court action and fine. Women may independently make beer and gather large work parties to farm land to which they have access.

The multiplicity of arrangements for sharing, renting, and loaning land insures that an existing land base can be periodically redistributed according to need while preserving the principle fundamental to Kofyar intensive agriculture, that land is an individual possession.

Inheritance

Land and other property pass at a man's death to his sons. If there are no sons, the man's brothers are his heirs, followed in line of succession by brother's sons, father, father's brother, and father's brother's son. I know of one case in which a man inherited from his father's father's son's son, a patrilineal descendent of his grandfather. If there is no person in any of these classifications, property goes to the head of the lineage. I could discover no strict rules indicating which relative should inherit if there is more than one of the same degree of eligibility. One informant said that if a man were survived only by the sons of two different brothers, the elder of these would be his heir. During the father's lifetime he may divide his bush lands and homestead sites among his sons in order to prevent quarrels. If an odd parcel remains after the land has been equally divided, the sons should continue to own and use it in common. In Bong there were instances of two sons in separate homesteads who still farmed bush fields jointly with their father and others who had been given specific fields as their own. When a father apportions his lands he may retain some for himself that his sons cultivate for him.

A man's homestead farm and house go to the son who lives with him. This may be either a younger or an older offspring, but often, when there are several sons, the older ones have married and moved away by the time of the father's death. A clan head in Bong died, leaving his farm to the youngest of six sons. Several of the older brothers had moved many years before to new homesteads on their father's village land or to leaseholds. A man may let it be known which son he wants to remain on his homestead, and this is believed to be a mark of personal affection, indicating the father's love for his child or appreciation of the kindness shown to him by his son. Technically an heir does not succeed to ownership of a homestead until the clan segment gathers for the *koecer* ceremony involving the reburial of his father's skull and the erection of a grave cairn. This may be a number of years after the actual death. The clan formally decides which son should inherit and awards him the skin of one of the goats killed at the preceding *maap* funeral commemoration. I know of no case in which the clan removed an occupant, and indeed the whole custom may be more honored in the breach. On the plains where land is in shorter supply than in the hills, succession is more rigid. There the oldest son inherits on the death of his father. If the senior son is not considered a responsible man, the lineage may decide to give the land to one of his brothers. Moveable property goes to the son who is to make the *maap* (funeral feast) for the deceased. This is usually the same son who succeeds to the homestead farm. Household implements such as hoes, spears, and pots may stay with the major heir or be divided equally among sons. All of the dead man's wealth including money, domestic animals, and cloth should be reserved for use at *maap,* and anything that remains can be divided among his heirs. The sons often prefer to retain the inheritance undivided for future bride price payments. In any event, the surviving brothers would be cooperating to secure wives, and it is regarded as proper to use their inherited wealth for such purposes. If one of the deceased's daughters marries, the bride price received for her should also be saved for the *maap.* If no one is left in the paternal homestead after a death, a son may choose either to return to it or not. Homesteads that are inconveniently located at the bottom or a ravine or in an isolated neighborhood may be simply abandoned in this manner.

A man who has no sons may adopt a boy to become his heir. This may be the child of a friend who has a large family or a wife's sister's child. The boy may inherit the farm of his foster father, but he retains his own name and lineage affiliation. In former times a rich man could increase his family by buying boys as slaves. Such youngsters were assigned to one of the wives of the purchaser and reared as his own sons with rights to receive a bride and land. Though members of his lineage, they could not succeed to the position of lineage head. In Bong, four of these slaves are now household heads, but there are no overt social signs of their origin.

Where a man owns a vacant homestead not contiguous to his own, he may often install one of his young sons there along with the boy's mother. This is obviously an economically sound move, because food production is increased by opening up new intensive farms rather than by expanding the labor force on existing land. Continuing to cultivate the land will also prevent it from growing up in long grass that might catch fire during the dry season and ruin valuable tree crops. It is interesting to note that many stories of the founding of new Kofyar hamlets or neighborhoods emphasize that a certain man built a homestead and put his immature son in the place, thus increasing the number of household units even before the son was ready to be independent. While the child is still young, the second homestead is managed by his mother who is herself past childbearing. Such a homestead is complete in its own right, with attached goat corral, domestic animals, huts, and farm, so that the boy continues to live there with his mother even after he is married and has children. The homestead of the father, where he lived with his remaining wives, will then descend to another son.

When a man dies without heirs, a relatively frequent occurrence in Bong, his land goes to the hereditary head of his lineage whose rights in it are solely reversionary. The farm does not become common property of the lineage. It can be either used, loaned, or leased by the lineage head on his own initiative and for his own benefit. The interest of the lineage in instituting sanctions against those who desert their patrimony has already been mentioned. There is also substantial evidence for a traditional practice (found in Bong but not in Kwa) by which a nonkinsman could inherit property from a man who died without heirs. If no lineage (*mwol*) made the *maap* funeral ceremony and sacrificed the required animal, the dead man's land went to any member of his clan (*pan*) who accepted this obligation. It is said that Tuganmaap, a powerful Bong chief living two generations ago acquired seven homesteads by giving cows or horses with which to *maap* their deceased owners. All of these properties are either worked or leased out to other members of the same clan by Tuganmaap's descendents today. This practice, depending as it did on wealth rather than any direct genealogical connection, made possible some peculiar successions. Although women are not supposed to inherit land, a woman of Dung named Noekat *maaped* her childless brother, Swaret, and came into considerable property in Bong village. Noekat organized large voluntary work parties to farm in return for beer and was known as a wealthy woman. She passed the land to her son, Dadwak, and it is now under the absentee ownership of her grandson, Jongyong.

Perhaps the most interesting aspect of this trading land for funeral rites is the statement that if the *maap* was not made by anyone, the property reverted automatically to the *koen*, that is the mother's brother of the dead owner. This actually took place in the case of the childless Leklat. He died in Bong, and his patrilineal relatives in Dung refused to make the *maap*. His land went therefore to Datal, his *koen* and *kukmi*, or leader of the maternal relatives, and has since passed to another maternal relative, Chom. Chom claims that sometimes a patrilineal relative was forced to make *maap* on threat of losing the land to another lineage. The *koen* and his descendents were by custom bound to an important reciprocal relationship with ego, but only in this single instance did they exercise any claim over ego's land. A central feature of *maap* is the giving of a substantial portion of meat and beer to the mother's brother and by extension to *mi*, the maternal relatives. We may speculate that the rendering of sacrificial meats is the last obligation in a series beginning with the bride price (*shagal namat*), which a man must give to the woman's father and brothers in return for her services as wife and legal paternity of her offspring. If this obligation is not rendered, the woman's lineage may take the land of the deceased in lieu of it. The practice is now in abeyance, said to have been forbidden by European administration, which supposedly declared that land should not be alienated from the patrilineage.

Land Disputes

With land scarcity and individual tenure, and lacking any sort of survey or written records, it is obvious that the Kofyar should have land disputes. For the most part, field boundaries are well marked either by natural streams and valleys or by paths and marker stones. Narrow rocks are often upended along the edges of terraces, and by sighting from the top of the hill it is possible to follow the edges of the field with considerable accuracy. When a boundary is unclear, the man who suspects trespass will summon the owner of the adjoining field along with the chief and some of the older men of the village. After viewing the alleged incursion and listening to the disputants, the elders will give their opinion. They cannot compel acceptance of their verdict, and if the quarrel continues, it is usually decided that no one should have the use of the contested area. A sliver of overgrown land, six feet by twenty, between two large bush fields in Bong was pointed out to me as the result of just such a *kwal,* or dispute. On the plains the chief, the *kbou* or vice-chief, and the *mengwa* or headman, accompanied by many of those who live near the scene of disturbance, all visit the field when the dispute cannot be settled within the neighborhood.

Relatively few disputes concerning land come before the courts, whether clan or village moots or the Native Authority courts officially administering customary law. In comparison with arguments over women, divorce, and the repayment of bride price, land cases make up less than 5 per cent of the disputes heard before NA courts. My impression is that a good many of the disputes over land ownership may be settled by informal hearings in a local clan segment or a village. Witnesses, both men and women, who know the property lines in a particular area are called, and if their testimony agrees, it is accepted as authoritative. In a recent case in Bong, controversy broke out when Doesogot and his wife moved onto a previously vacant homestead site. At issue were the ownership of the land and the right to collect rent in palm oil from the trees growing there. One contestant, Daliap, claimed that his late father's brother had lived there. Another, Dayil, insisted that his late father's brother had told him the land belonged to him. Since the disputants were members of the same clan, Jekur, the case was brought to a clan moot. Witnesses were called, and an old man from Chokfem and a woman born in Bong but married in Male both professed ignorance of the matter. Finally an older Bong man from a different clan segment, Jidong, testified that Daliap's father's brother had originally tried to secure a homestead site from the head of a Jidong lineage. He had been refused because the man wanted to settle one of his own sons there. He had then gone to the father's brother of Dayil and been granted the use of an adjacent site. This statement settled the quarrel and confirmed Dayil in his claim of ownership. Dayil did not ask for return of the chicken given by the tenant to Daliap because, after all, "we are in one clan."

A more frequent source of dissension, but one which is often difficult to detect, is that which arises between a father and a married son living on the same homestead. This is not directly over land but rather concerns the allocation of crops produced on that land. The household head has rights to the first harvest of the early millet and to three or four bundles of sorghum. The remainder is shared equally among all adult members of the household, with smaller shares for each child. The portion belonging to the head may be used partly for seed, with the rest going onto beer for voluntary field labor parties or funeral celebrations. Cash or tax money may also be raised by selling some of this grain or the palm oil, locust beans, and canarium fruit to which the head also has prior claim. In effect, the surplus above immediate consumption needs is controlled by the household head. When surplus production is strictly limited by the amount of land in the homestead farm, the son may feel that he is not receiving a fair share of the crop. The power of allocation, and with it the major authority in household matters, remains with the father.

On one occasion a young man divided the household's bundles of late millet when his father was not present and, when reprimanded, angrily denied the older man's authority. The lineage members did little more than shake their heads over the matter, and shortly thereafter the son built his own homestead on land leased from an unrelated person. The issue of control over the produce of land may well be a major cause of the household fission so characteristic of traditional Kofyar society. In conversation, the Kofyar try to minimize such sources of friction, but it is perhaps significant that witchcraft is thought to be practiced *only* by a close patrilineal relative, and that when a man is sick, his father, brothers, and sons are the first ones called on to deny publicly that they are witching him.

Disputes are frequent in the newly opened migrant bush area where each man has marked out his own farm. A man who wishes to expand his farm will sometimes cultivate across the rear corner of his neighbor's land so that his field is wider at the back than where it borders the road. The chiefs take into consideration not only the defendant's actual offense but whether he has need of the extra land. A judgment I witnessed outside Namu stated that a man was obviously encroaching on his neighbor's land and that he could not use more land because his brother was too lazy to work it and his original tract was already larger than his neighbor's. Sticks were then put into the ground at intervals to mark the revised boundary.

Other disputes over land have to do with destruction of crops. A man can demand reparation if a neighbor's livestock damage his standing grain. Datugun once barred all paths through his Bong village acha field because people were trampling the crop as they went to collect firewood from a fallen tree. A neighbor, in reply, threatened angrily to cut off all access to Datugun's house on the path that led through his homestead. Evidently even the public ways through a man's property are his, and he may restrict their use at will.

Arguments over inheritance occasionally come before the courts. One long-standing quarrel in Bong concerned a man whose grandfather had allegedly given a goat for the *maap* of a landowner and thereby claimed a particular farm. Though the family lived on the land for two generations, another man appeared after the occupant's death and claimed that

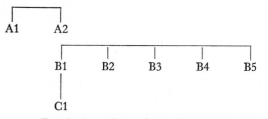

Fig. 9. Genealogy of Land Case Disputants

his grandfather had given five tubes of salt at the *maap* and the land should be his. When his claim was denied he put a charm on the field to harm anyone who worked it. Since all those originally involved were dead, the case could not be decided, and the village chief ruled that no one should use the tract.

Kwa Native Authority court heard two cases involving a man, C1, from Kofyar, who was trying to get possession of some land leased by his family (Fig. 9). C1 first asked for sole rights to a farm being occupied by his paternal grandfather's brother, A1, and was told that he could not have the land until A1 died. Another leased homestead site passed from C1's grandfather, A2, to his father, B1. C1 lived there for a time with his uncle B2 and then moved away. When C1 returned after B2's death to occupy this homestead, he found that it had been taken over by another paternal uncle, B5.

The judges asked the surviving uncles, B3 and B4, to decide who was to get possession. The uncles agreed that the present occupant, B5, should remain and that their nephew should not be admitted. In this case the rights of a brother of the deceased took precedence over those of his own son, but this would probably not have happened if C1 had not weakened his claim by moving away. It is interesting to note that the owner of the field was called in on the case. He made no effort to get possession of the field himself but said his sole interest was in seeing that the land was used by a legitimate heir of the original tenant. Litigation in Kofyar village may well be more prevalent than in other less crowded hill communities.

Other court decisions confirmed the right of the owner to receive one pot of beer every time his tenant brewed, thus upholding the local custom. Though it is said to be difficult for an owner to dispossess a tenant, a 1938 case in Dimmuk and a 1949 trial in Kwa both upheld the owner. The earlier judgment concerned a Bong farm loaned by the father of the plaintiff to the father of the defendant. Since neither party had witnesses, the matter was referred to ordeal, which "proved" that the defendant was lying. The land was promptly restored to the plaintiff though the defendant claimed that his father had paid for the land. It may be that if proved payments have been made for lease, the tenant may not be dispossessed. In the Kwa case, it was only necessary for the plaintiff to show that he had loaned the farm to the defendant and now wanted it back. One Kwa informant said that a tenant could only be dispossessed if the land was required by a son of the owner.

The modern Native Authority courts have the power to punish by fine and, at the higher levels, by imprisonment. It is probable that all land cases are first discussed at the village level. A clan group or a village meeting under the chief attempts to arbitrate the dispute. When no decision is acceptable to both sides, the contested land may be removed from use or the case taken to the NA court. Neither lineage head nor the chief has the power to enforce a settlement. It is said that formerly old chiefs might be called in to settle boundary disputes in neighboring villages, but their influence depended on their knowledge and prestige rather than any sanctions they could bring to bear.

Older men remember land disputes between villages, mostly in regard to trespass when members of one group cut thatching grass on the land of its neighbors. This might lead to an attack and some small-scale raids, but it is never mentioned as the cause of a long-continued feud or war. Even when, in prosecuting a blood feud, one village succeeded in routing their opponents and looting their settlement, they did not try to appropriate the fields or homesites of the conquered. Hamlets in no man's land between warring alliances might be deserted for years, but when peace returned the farms were taken up again by the original owners or their descendants. Evidently refugee populations could be absorbed in remaining communities, suggesting that the pressure for land resources in the hills was not great. Attachment to a native place where land is owned and ancestral graves remain is, however, strong. Eight years of armed patrolling by the British administration was insufficient to keep a forcibly relocated group of Latok people from returning to their ancestral homesteads in the hills.

Kofyar intensive agriculture, with its reliance on high continuous yields from small patches of land, gives a considerable measure of stability and resistance to change to the settlement pattern. There is little evidence for territorial expansion by conquest or by rapid budding off. The farming system was sufficiently effective that hill population could grow to some extent by bringing ordinary fallowed land into intensive cultivation rather than by spreading out into new areas. The level well-watered lands at the foot of the hills had no accompanying marginal land into which a population overflow could go. Leaving the shelter of the hills exposed the group to predatory slave raiders, so that any population increase merely raised the density, bringing it closer to the maximum that could be supported on the land. During bad crop years there was the possibility of fighting as plains people tried to secure food from their hill neighbors, but this was merely an emergency measure and never to my knowledge resulted in the occupation of hill lands. We may speculate that intensive farmers are much less likely to go to war for territorial gains than shifting cultivators or pastorialists who need both more land per person and a supply that increases directly with every expansion of population.[5] The only mention among the Kofyar of conquest followed by appropriation of land concerns a legendary war with the Chokfem branch of the Sura. In this case a large area in the hills was taken over to the accompaniment of cannibalistic slaughter by the Chokfem and used for the shifting cultivation of acha. Even today the Chokfem rely mostly on bush fallows for subsistence and must seek migratory mine and farm labor to avoid hunger.

In more recent times there is evidence that even boundary disputes between different tribal groups could be adjudicated without recourse to war. It is said that the chief of Bong and the chief of a Chokfem village settled a contested boundary by resort to a public ordeal in a neutral village area. The test was concerned with which party was lying when he claimed that a certain piece of land was "owned" by his village.

Permanency and Flexibility in Land Tenure

Kofyar rules of land tenure and inheritance provide permanent, individuated rights in land along with subsidiary, conditional rights. They obviously reflect the imperatives of intensive agriculture in terms of (1) the need to protect the permanent high production of staple crops and economic trees achieved through heavy investment of labor and continuous attention, and (2) the need for flexibility in distribu-

---

[5] If this is indeed the case we could also expect a higher proportion of segmentary lineage structures among shifting cultivators and pastoralists than among intensive agriculturalists (cf. Sahlins 1961).

tion to accommodate changes in population in situations of actual or potential scarcity of land. Competition for land resources with increasing population density and its concomitant intensification of cultivation encourages permanent residence on the farm and a strong claim to exclusive, heritable rights in the land. A household that subsists over a period of time as an independent, self-sufficient unit on an improved homestead would certainly resist any efforts to deprive it of this vital possession. Individual rights are subordinate only in cases in which final title is to pass permanently out of the control of the owner and his heirs. An individual may loan or lease land without hindrance, but the permanent alienation of land by sale, gift, or desertion deprives his lineage of its residual rights. The kin group which first occupied and developed the land in the course of budding from an ancestral homestead sees its integrity and continuity threatened by the loss of its localized land base. Only with lineage permission in the event of a rare sale or tacit consent in failing to celebrate the funeral commemoration of a successorless member can the land pass finally into other hands. This happens most frequently when the land concerned is outside the area of lineage residential concentration where it can neither be properly defended or effectively exploited.

Yet with all the emphasis on inalienable rights in land, the unequal reproduction in number and sex in various families, the limited size of homesteads, and the advantages of each family's having a separate residence make it necessary to redistribute land in each generation. Except when an heir is resident on the premises, the death of a household head always requires decisions as to future occupation of the homestead. In large families, sons may lease the land of others or intensify the farming on a portion of their father's bush fallow. Owners of excess land in turn benefit by the small payments of tenants and their services in guarding and harvesting fruit trees. Vagueness and disagreement among informants emphasize the problems in maintaining vested interest in land that has been occupied by tenants for several generations. It is possible that prior rights may lapse or be forgotten in such cases. But as land becomes scarcer there is evidently greater pressure to keep the lines of ownership clear so that in an emergency the original possessor could reclaim his patrimony. Though land disputes seem to increase in proportion to population pressure, few of them (in comparison to marriage cases) reach the courts. This may be interpreted as showing a close functional fit between land use and the rules governing landholding and reallocation.

7

Attitudes and Ideology

ONE OF THE OLDEST and still the most fascinating areas of cultural ecology for many students is the influence of environment and technology on the group personality and prevailing ideology of particular peoples. Numerous investigators have noted peasant characteristics of concern with security, high valuation of procreation, and desire for wealth (Redfield 1953:39) and the emphasis of herding peoples on warfare, masculine sexuality, and personal arrogance (Goldschmidt 1959:160). Impressive techniques are now being developed for separating factors of age, sex, and tribal culture from the effects of ecological differentiation (Edgerton 1965). I did not make an intensive study in this area because I lacked the special skills necessary and because empirical connections to the ecosystem were so difficult to demonstrate. In dealing with personality traits or types of religious observance, several alternative lines of functional explanation are available, and any single-cause formulation is probably inadequate. Therefore I offer some notes that are frankly impressionistic.

If I were forced to characterize the Kofyar, I would call them hardheaded hillbillies. They combine a practical and utilitarian attitude toward nature with a positive valuation of work. Their manners are independent and assured. They do not take kindly to commands and react negatively to assertions of personal authority. Marks of status and gross social inequality are rare among them. Their attitudes toward productive labor accord with their adaptation as self-sufficient intensive agriculturalists, and their paucity of farming ritual suggests a confident mastery of subsistence problems.

To Work Is to Eat

The Kofyar are an industrious people, whether more or less so than other primitive or peasant farmers I cannot say, but idleness is rare among them. They have their daily chores, a necessary activity of those people who keep domestic animals but probably lacking among simple gardeners or swidden cultivators. The goats must be staked in their corral and the sheep and cows herded beyond the village fields. There are loads of fresh grass to bring the goats and water for the basin stones from which they drink. Hens may scratch for themselves, but they need an occasional ration of corn. Even the dogs are entitled to pot scrapings and specially cooked pumpkin if they have whelped. The man who roves about to beer parties is warned to look to his livestock or risk their loss to thieves. Though the Kofyar are keen hunters, they never go so far afield that they must camp out for the night. When I suggested going some miles into bush in order to get larger game, they replied with peasant caution that they could not leave their homesteads unguarded overnight.

Among subsistence agriculturalists the farming cycle is a round of annual necessities. Only the prompt and efficient fulfillment of these seasonal demands stands between the individual and hunger. The rains bring planting, weeding, guarding, and harvesting in inexorable succession. If a terrace goes unrepaired the topsoil washes down to sterile stone. Poorly stored sorghum rots on the rack. When the sun of the dry season shines, thatching grass must be cut, or it is lost forever to advancing bush fires. The new house that is not roofed before the first storm dissolves into a lumpy heap. I remember only one case of refusal to work. A lad from Chokfem living temporarily with a Bong family did not perform his assigned tasks. The remedy was simple and drastic. The women of the household denied him food. A schoolboy told me that his portion of the farming was left for him to do after classes and that he was not fed until he completed it. It was hard for the hill people to conceive of habitual laziness, but the only solution for such behavior was clear to them: "We work for our food. If one does not farm, he cannot eat."

In an effort to elicit values connected with agricultural work I showed several Kofyar men and women a drawing of a boy standing and watching some people occupied in hoeing. Of ten respondents, two said that the boy was about to work, one, that he was showing the others where to farm, one, that he was waiting to take the place of anyone who got tired, and three, that he was on the road, a messenger or a stranger (that is, not expected to work). Only when I suggested it did they consider the fact that the boy might refuse to take part in labor without a good reason. The responses to this were that one must work to get food, that it was bad to be lazy, that no one would help the boy when he needed assistance, and that people would scold him. The social sanction of being publicly referred to as lazy was most frequently mentioned. This sanction was actually exercised in the case of a young stranger who lived in one hill village as a hunter. Though he was thought to steal, cheat, and chase women, the accusation most frequently leveled against him was that he was the only one in the village who did no farm work at all. It is plain that the Kofyar attach a moral value to agricultural labor.

A child is not told when to begin work. He merely follows his elders and imitates their motions. He is rewarded with indulgence for his awkwardness and praise for his energy. By the age of ten he can use a hoe with skill and endurance. He will farm with it until he is physically incapable. Wealth does not free a man from work. I have seen the brother of a chief who possessed eight wives, several grown sons, and cash-crop farms put aside his robes and begin the hard work of breaking a new field. It is possible, however, to work too hard. One young man was supposedly having difficulty in remarrying because he had demanded of a former wife that she match his own exceptionally long hours in the field.

Farming, with all its insistent calls on time and energy, does not demand the same toil every day. The task varies according to season, but there are always other things to be done. Even if the mind is occupied, there are jobs that the hand can do almost of itself. The discussions at a clan meeting are accompanied by the twisting of rope or the cracking of palm kernels. Both men and women clean raw cotton and spin as they sit at a beer party. The pots shaped, the baskets woven, the loincloth hemmed, and the cloth loomed in spare time, are useful additions to the household economy or an opportunity for profit at the next market day. Kofyar attitudes toward work are seldom expressed. Their direct relation to the environment and its imperatives is too clear to require emphasis.

If the Kofyar exhibit typical peasant virtues of industry, thrift, and frugality, they may also display what civilization considers the vices of the hillbilly. It is difficult to assert power over another man whose livelihood is secure, whose land, houses, and flocks are his own. Real, though largely covert, conflict may center around the household head's control of the allocation of food and more especially the surplus of crops and livestock that can be converted into cash, consumer goods, labor, and wives. The solution to tensions of this kind between fathers and sons or coresident brothers is for one nuclear family to move away to its own homestead. The Kofyar consider it right and natural for a young man to found an autonomous homestead, though they justify this in terms of economic utility rather than an internal struggle for power. Once independent, a man may continue to cooperate with kin in certain farming activities, but this is wholly voluntary, and his control over his own homestead enterprise and its fruits is unquestioned.

The limited life of households due to fission and the restriction of the size of homestead farms enforces a rough equality among residents of the same village. No one is economically dependent on his neighbor, but neither is it easy to become markedly richer than one's fellows. There are differences in number of wives, size of bush fields, and possession of livestock, but these are not directly reflected in patterns of deference or political influence. When social offenses are committed within the village, judgment is not by any single man, but by a group of lineage peers or neighbors. Chiefly authority appears negligible in terms of swaying group opinion or enforcing the wishes of the headman. A chief relies on persuasion and consensus to lead, plus others' respect deriving from his role as intermediary with the local earth spirits. It is only with governmental encouragement and physical support that he had begun to exercise executive functions such as tax collection and the apprehension of criminals.

If the Kofyar pay little attention to their own constituted authorities they also have a merely grudging acceptance of external political forces. They have by turns fought, fled from, and evaded the more galling strictures of the conquerors. In this they resemble mountain dwellers everywhere. No ruling power likes hillbillies. People who are both poor and occupants of a natural fortress can scarcely help being robbers or engaging in some other activity which the administration considers illegal or subversive. They are habitually casual taxpayers, infrequent school attenders, and unfaithful churchmen. They have firmly fixed in mind the unsettling notion that no one can tell them what to do. From their heights of terrain and ignorance, they look down disdainfully on regimented, sweating plainsmen. When they are conquered it is not for their riches or skills, because they seldom have either, but because it is simply more painful to

leave them free. The Fulani, the irresistible knights of the
North, never pastured their cattle on the lush all-season pastures of the plateau until the British (who wanted tin) used
a Maxim gun to pacify the pagans. The great trade routes of
the savannah carefully skirted the Plateau and all the other
mountain strongholds. Armed uprisings continued until the
mid-1930's on the Plateau, and tribal warfare has not yet
been completely eliminated in the Gwoza Hills of Sardauna
Province.

The official colonial attitude toward typical hill behavior
is well represented by the first assistant resident to adminis-
ter Lowland Division, or Kwolla Division as it was then
called. He noted that the units of people split apart as they
grew and existed without law in a state of armed neutrality.
Beside the clearly defined governmental hierarchy and orderly submission of the Hausa-Fulani emirates, the pagan
tribes seemed to be composed entirely of unruly delinquents:

There can be no punishment without authority; without respect and
reverence there can be no authority. Both qualities seem to be lacking
in the peoples of the Kwolla District, and the result is seen in the
powerlessness of the headmen and in the general conditions of dis-
order and anarchy prevailing hitherto (Fitzpatrick 1910:20).

A particularly dangerous element is the young man who "is
irresponsible, impudent, headstrong, and has all the qualifi-
cations requisite for the production of a first-rate ruffian"
(Fitzpatrick 1910:20). The indignant officer could almost as
well be speaking of Scottish highlanders, Pathan warriors, or
southern Appalachian mountaineers. Hillbillies are difficult.

It is pleasant to draw connections between isolation, self-
sufficiency, equalitarian manners, and stubborn recalcitr-
ance when freedom is at stake (cf. Lembezat 1961:38). It is
perhaps wiser, however, to remember Febvre's caution:
"When analyses are complete and numerous enough . . . it
will perhaps be possible to determine a certain number of
typical manners in which human society has adapted itself to

the various classes of mountains. . . . At present the attempt is premature . . ." (1932:200) .

Rationality and Religion

The Kofyar regard their well-integrated and efficient system of agriculture in a very matter-of-fact manner. Their ordinary conversation dwells little on crops or fields or climate. Contrary to the practice among many cultivators, Kofyar do not comment at length on farming practices and the comparative merits of fields seen along the road. They willingly answered my questions about such matters, but their own conversation is more apt to turn on recent beer drinks or the excitement of past hunting parties. When I asked who the best farmers were, the reply was usually concerned with comparative wealth, often inherited, rather than objective skill or knowledge of cultivation. The fact was that anyone who had been exposed to the prevailing cultural background of agricultural methods and who abided by social patterns of exchange and voluntary labor could be reasonably sure of producing an adequate subsistence for himself and his family.

The imponderables of farming are not by any means absent among the Kofyar. Rains may come too late or too soon, and the sight of immature millet turning brown or sorghum stalks blown down is not rare. In March and April people often speak of which villages have received rain and which are still too dry to plant. Travelers pick up earth after early storms to see how deeply it is moistened. Insects may attack the standing crops or stored grain, and stories are told of their depredations.

At a time when early drought threatened the homestead farms of Zugal, I asked the chief why this was happening. He said only, *Naan den,* "God does it," or "God puts it [upon us]." In reply to a further question about what would happen to his people, the chief shrugged his shoulders and remarked, "We will all starve." His statement was only half serious. He obviously expected no one actually to suffer hardship, much less die. Some crops might fail, but others would do well. Based on past experience, this was a reasonable assumption. When a bush field of maize is stripped by baboons or a disease wipes out a goat herd, people may point out the owner's carelessness or cluck sympathetically, but no great anxiety is aroused. These things are not a threat to survival.

The unemotional, pragmatic approach to food-getting is apparent in the paucity and simplicity of religious rites connected with agriculture. The performance of certain rituals to initiate phases of the agricultural year is prevalent among neighboring tribes. Early problems of missionaries in the Angas area revolved around converts' planting before the pagan chief had officially opened the season. The Tal mark ten stages in the cultivation and development of food crops with ceremonies in the sacred grove, and these schedule the work cycle of the entire society (cf. Nadel 1947:44). The Kofyar have fewer rites, and those that exist are mainly of a personal nature. There is no observance whatever connected with the planting or cultivation of the homestead field. Bong farmers individually make a single ridge and sow a mixture of acha, water, and a magical root before planting their bush fields. The *biyang mar* (to pierce the field) rite is preceded by a divination to see if the time is propitious for it, and it is accompanied by the standard Kofyar prayer for children, success on the hunt, and good crops. The farmer also announces that there is nothing there and that the place is "cool," that is, not magically dangerous. Communities where acha is not a staple do not perform the rite.

First-fruit ceremonies are held at the homestead, with the master tasting (*kagal*) the year's first pumpkin leaf sauce or the first roasting ear of maize, spitting some on the thatch of nearby huts or on the ground, and then giving it to the rest of the family to eat. Not every household performs this rite, and it is said only that those do it whose father did it before them. In one case I heard of, a dog tipped over and ate the ceremonial sauce, but though this prevented the ceremony no one seemed concerned about it. Fertility is not the primary object of the rite, and punishments for nonperformance are in terms of sickness for the master or rats biting the homestead occupants.

The Kofyar possess a large number of charms to protect bush field crops and fruit trees from theft. The medicine men who know these charms claim that they seldom make them for others, using them chiefly for their own fields. They are mentioned most frequently in divinatory efforts to diagnose the magical causes of illness. Patients readily confess to stealing a handful of groundnuts or some canarium fruit, but they are not required to inform the man whose food they took or to make restitution. At the harvest of late millet, two tall stalks are bent toward each other and tied at the tops to form an arch. Sheaves are brought to the cleared area near the arch and there bundled. This was said variously to increase the amount of grain harvested and to prevent quarreling among the workers. Only men may remove acha or late millet from the granaries, but there seem to be no taboos on consumption of foods.

Natural forces may act to decrease severely the harvest of an individual or a whole village. If a homestead farm suddenly declines in production, the farmer may suspect either some sin within his household or malevolent witchcraft. In the former case he may seek the cause through divination and then engage a medicine man to purify the spot (ten pe). This may also be done following a theft or the death of many domestic animals, but the rite is performed infrequently. If a witch is at work, ruining crops by magically dousing them with scalding water, nothing can be done except to hope that the offender will become ill and confess. A failure of rain may endanger the crops of a considerable area. In this case a meeting (vwak) is called by the chief, and the adult males of the entire village attend. Men talk in turn, praying to God (naan) for rain, citing the abundant crops of their ancestors, and asserting their innocence of witchcraft. There is no libation or sacrifice at this time. No one person takes on a priestly role.

Some villages have a rain maker called *wufan*. His assistance can be sought during drought for giving sacrifices and using "rain stones" and supernatural powers to bring rain. The office, hereditary in the patrilineal line, seems to have considerable antiquity. The rain maker of the ancestral village, Kofyar, bears the title *longshen* and is second only to the chief in respect. The influence of the position may well have been greater in the past. I never saw a special rain ceremony, though a dry spell in 1961 was sufficient to sizably reduce groundnut and late millet yields. A few *vwak* were held, but there seemed to be no great rise in public apprehension. Rain is said to follow a northeasterly path first laid out by a nameless culture hero. Only one annual rite (*mandyel*) is held for rain, and this takes place in Kofyar village. The ancestral graves of the rain maker and of a subsidiary lineage are honored with libations of beer. As in other rites, prayers are not only for rain and crops but for game, children, wives, and even the academic success of schoolboys. There are also discussions of witchcraft, and men say that God or the earth will "catch" people if they are indeed witches.

There is one ceremony called *ya fu yil* (catching the mouth of the earth) which is performed for the whole village. The traditional chief (*miskagam yil,* the lord of the earth) is alone empowered to do it along with another hereditary official, the *wuyil,* who may come from a neighboring village. It is a generalized fertility rite carried out only when crops have been very bad, trees have no fruit, or domestic animals fail to produce offspring. It may bring rain, but its purpose is actually to restore the goodness of the earth which has spoiled (*yil ang*). A goat is sacrificed, and its blood put on a specific stone. It is men (that is, witches) who spoil the earth, but the beneficent spirits, *moewang,* can kill witches. The blood is given to the spirits because *moewang tangkop tagam lua,* "the spirits like the blood of meat." The participants ask God to watch what they are doing because the spirits are God's creatures. All village men who attend may share the meat. The last such ceremony in Bong was about 1957.

The Kofyar have a relatively high degree of subsistence security because of the advantages of their environment, their efficient mode of agriculture, and the variety of their food crops. Their attitude toward farming is businesslike, realistic, and unemotional: crops have no spirits, and most agricultural practices are strictly utilitarian. They respond to the uncontrolled elements of the agricultural cycle with explanations in terms of divine decree or of human malevolence operating through witchcraft, and with simple magico-religious procedures. They approach ritual either as individuals executing domestic rites or as groups, with personal prayers and modest sacrifices. They lack elaborate spells, medication, and specialized priestly duties. It is possible that effectiveness in farming and relative predictability of environment lowers the need for supernatural coping techniques.[1] There seems no inherent agricultural utility in strictly regulating the timing of various events in the farming cycle. The emphasis on social solidarity and mobilization of the kin group that is seen in funeral ceremonies is generally much less evident in agricultural rites. No esoteric knowledge such as that of the *pa* divination [2] is needed for their performance. No specialized role such as that of the medicine man in healing rites is required. Perhaps a really

[1] Pospisil (1963:117) offers this suggestion in reference to Kapauku practices.

[2] Divination (*pa*) is performed with two strings of four small roughly rectangular plaques each. They are thrown down on the earth and the sequence they form is observed. Since each plaque can fall either up or down, there are sixteen possible sequences that may appear. These are named, and many of the names are cognate with those of the Yoruba *ifa* divination rite. In interpreting the sequences, reference is made to the dichotomies male-female, red-black, and favorable-unfavorable. Divination is used most frequently for uncovering the type of magical trespass a sick person has committed. The patient must then confess to a specific offense in order to recover.

serious drought would heighten the effect of ceremonies that ordinarily seem merely reverent observances. At any rate, it seemed to me that the Kofyar regarded agriculture as a subject that demanded practical application and diligence but did not engage their enthusiasm, their aesthetic sensibilities, or, to any great extent, their religious feelings.

8

Migratory Farming and Cash Cropping

The Development of Migratory Farming

ALMOST AS SOON AS the hill pagans were contacted by Europeans, it was noted that they were coming down from the hills. Fitzpatrick (1910:18) mentioned a "persistent gradual movement" southward, and he had little doubt "that in time, all these hill dwellers will find their way down to join those of their race who have preceded them in the slow advance to the Binue." The tendency to move down onto the plain was considered desirable by the new rulers because it simplified their task of pacifying and administering the isolated village clusters. After the 1930 uprising among the Kofyar, a local missionary insisted to the Resident that the hill people "simply hate the white man," and that all pagans should be forced to get out from among their rocks and live on the unpopulated plains "where they could finally find enough food to make prosperous tribes and where they could be easily controlled by Government." Though several thousand Kofyar were relocated at this time, very few settled permanently away from their hill villages. The Kofyar did not move rapidly into the lowlands as did their neighbors, the Montol and the Yergum.[1] Only recently have sub-stantial segments of the population become involved, and their particular adaptation to plains farming has been vol-untary and uniquely organized. The Kofyar pattern has been one of migration that opened up new bush farms by shifting cultivation while maintaining the old hill or plain-fringe homesteads as permanent residences. The major goal of this movement has been the production of cash crops rather than subsistence.

The first Kofyar segment to establish new bush fields were the Kwalla. As the farthest south of the Kofyar peoples, their territory adjoined sparsely populated and little-used tracts of savanna. Warfare was first eliminated in this area by the British presence, and by the 1920's, Kwalla villagers from the Chim (Tim) area were already establishing bush farms at some distance from their homes. They later moved far south-east of Kurgwi near the Goemai village of Kalong, and after ten years there returned to their original bush fallows that had regenerated. A man from one of the most southerly neighborhoods of Dimmuk is said to have established a mi-grant bush farm some ten miles away in 1930, but most of his neighbors joined in sometime later and have worked distant land for only about twenty years. They come from a low-lying area called Goebook ("muddy"), whose poor drainage makes it difficult to get good homestead crops. By 1946 it was said that the standard of homestead cultivation had fallen off considerably as people shifted their major efforts to the bush (R. L. Findlay, quoted in Rowling 1952:30). By 1961 many households had no goats for manuring the home field, and the impoverished soil of the homesteads was sandy and al-most white. Residents of a more favored Dimmuk plains neighborhood, close to the base of the hills, still maintain productive homesteads and have only begun to open bush farms since 1950.

The first hill people to farm on the plains were those of

[1] For a generalized map of migration from the Plateau, see Buchanan and Pugh (1955:78).

the seven Latok villages that were abandoned under military pressure after the 1930 killing of an English assistant district officer. Though members of the relocated group admit today that they had abundant crops on the new land set aside for them on the plain, they complained of drownings in plains rivers and, more frequently, of losing their economic trees, the oil palm and canarium. Despite yearly armed patrols until 1937, the people persisted in their demands, and by 1939 all had returned to the hills (Findlay 1945). In the early 1940's some Latok residents took up bush fields in the Kwalla-Kurgwi area and others returned to the relocation area near the Shemankar River. Though only a handful of men have moved permanently to the plain, almost the entire population of Latok village proper have some agricultural operations in the bush. Their home village site is perhaps the rockiest and the least productive in the hills.

The Kwa people had for some years farmed bush lands on the road to Dokan Kasua and east of Kwang, areas close enough for daily commuting. In 1950 the chief of Kwa took up a tract of virgin bush west of Namu. Namu is some twenty-six miles southwest of Kwa, and the men who followed the chief had to build homesteads there just as the Kwalla and Dimmuk migrants had done earlier on their bush farms. Because of their late start in acquiring bush land, Kwa people had to leap-frog about eighteen miles of country that had already been put into shifting cultivation by the Dimmuk. For people whose food supply was sometimes erratic and whose only source of cash was headloading yams and other produce from the plains to the mining camps on the high plateau, the opportunity to open new and fertile lands was highly attractive. The chief was promptly followed by his brothers and other men of Kwa, then by families from neighboring Miket, Fogol, Kwang, and Lardang. The hill people in close contact with Kwa also began to make the long trek to Namu. The trend was hardly noticeable at first. In 1955 an administrative officer could still write a trifle romantically in his touring notes: "Very few, if any, Kofyar farmers seem to be moving down into the plains, and it is to be hoped that they will not find it necessary to do so: who would live on a plain if he could live on a hill?" In fact, the chief of Kofyar had already established himself at Namu, and by 1961 twenty-three out of forty-eight households in his village were engaged in migrant farming. The idea is being taken up by more isolated villages, and in 1962 the first resident of Bong went to find a bush field on the plains.

There has never been a formal program for moving people from the hills or traditional plains villages to the new lands. The government's extensive efforts to resettle the Hill Yergum on model tracts in east Lowland Division (Meek 1957:283–291) had not even been heard of in the Kofyar area. The administration neither directly helped nor hindered the Kofyar migration, so that it took shape under purely local impetus. The rate and timing of migration, the areas selected for cultivation, the methods of farming, and the social adjustments made were all the result of individual decisions.

Why did the Kofyar choose to embark on this new endeavor? Which families went? How was their agriculture managed? How did productivity compare with that achieved on homestead farms? How were the migrant communities organized? How much new income has been achieved and what is it used for? What will be the future effects of this movement? These are questions we will try to answer in this chapter.

Adaptation of Crops and Methods

The land around Namu that is now being occupied by Kofyar bush farmers is gently rolling, threaded by small streams in shallow north-south valleys, and covered with trees ranging from high forest near water to a fairly dense orchard bush. The soil is reddish and sandy, mixed with black loam, easily worked, and seemingly of high natural fertility. The Kofyar say that it has never been farmed, and remaining patches of impressively tall straight trees suggest that it is at least in part virgin land. The first settlers asked the chief of Namu or his representative for land. Namu is a walled, nucleated town whose language and political organization are Goemai, but there is a strong tradition that it was founded by one of a pair of twins descended from Kofyar (its Kofyar name is Jebjan, "the twins"). The chief of Dimmuk has a part in the installation of the chief of Namu. Thus the Kofyar feel they have a right to claim land in the area, and the local people who farm only tracts close to their village seem happy to welcome them. As more farmers come, they mark off neighboring fields with the help of Namu authorities or of the first settlers.

Initial clearing of bush land is a difficult operation. It begins with cutting brush and small trees. When this material is dry it is piled around the bases of larger trees and fired. Efforts are made to kill all the large trees with fire so that, though they continue to stand for a few years, they will not shade the growing crops. Other firings weaken the trunks until they fall, and the entire tree may then be reduced to ashes. I have seen farms four years old that still resemble pioneer clearings with numerous standing dead trees and half-burnt fallen trunks (Plate VIIIB). After a few more years, however, farms become uniformly open and treeless. The first turning of the soil still tough with roots and grasses is merely a preparation, and only sesame is planted that year. It is followed by yams, which do best in new soil. Then comes the characteristic millet-sorghum-cowpea association interplanting. Another possible pattern is the first-year planting of yams with beniseed and sorghum among the heaps. Yams should not be planted in the same place in successive years, and a certain amount of clearing must go on so that they can be cultivated through the years. Most bush farms front on a road made by the settlers and are bordered on both sides by neighbors. They can be extended to the rear, however, and farms rapidly take on a long narrow shape. It is said that after nine years in continuous cultivation, a farm will no longer support sorghum. Some plots that I knew reliably to be from eight to ten years old were noticeably depleted, their soil considerably lighter in color than normal and of a granular consistency that flowed evenly through the fingers rather than crumbling. Cotton may be planted at this stage, alternating with either millet or groundnuts. In 1961 groundnuts and cotton were indeed beginning to appear on the older fields. It is said they would not do well in the richer soil needed for yams and sorghum. After three years of cotton and groundnuts the land is left fallow. I was told that it would regenerate sufficiently to support yams in five years, but the Namu bush farms are not yet old enough for fallowing, and I suspect they will actually require at least double this period.

Crop varieties different form those planted in Kofyar are used in the bush. It may be that rain comes later or has a longer season here. The pronounced orographic rainfall effect of the hills is absent, but the details of local climate are not clear to me. The farmers claim that the standard Kwa sorghums, if planted in Namu would be ready for harvest in the rainy season and therefore be in danger of rotting. Both the millet and the sorghum used in Namu mature late, and the sorghum variety, *swa piya* or *nogol,* is not harvested until after Christmas, more than a month after its Kwa counterpart. Cowpeas are limited to the white type. At least three major kinds of yam, *akuki, yotoro,* and *shabara,* are also grown. The Kofyar say that they begged seeds for these crops from the Namu people. The fact that crops mature at different times in the homestead farms and in the migrant bush farms allows work to be staggered and periods that would otherwise be idle made productive.

Agricultural techniques are also markedly different in the bush. There are no steep slopes to warrant terracing, and indeed the contours of the ground are so gentle that there is little problem of runoff and erosion. There is no need for the basin-listing method of ridging, and only low parallel ridges are used. Yams are planted in heaps about two feet high and two to three feet apart. The heaps are well made but lack the geometrical exactness, tidiness, and aesthetic qualities of a Tiv yam field (Bohannan 1954). The Kofyar say that they are interested in production rather than appearance, and they point out the small volume of cash cropping done in local Tiv villages. Small trees often left near the heaps give the yam vines a support for climbing. Heaps are made and the seed yams put in before the first rains. They must be weeded three or four times with the small hoe, scraping the soil up toward the apex of the mound. After the December–January harvest, the yams are stored in separate piles according to variety and covered with vines and brush. While working in the bush, the Kofyar consume quantities of the tasty and easily baked yams, selecting the smaller ones that are not good for selling. The making of new yam heaps and the leveling of old ones to make ridges for sorghum and millet is done largely during the latter part of the dry season, a slack time at Kofyar hill homesteads. The grain crops are hoed three times, once when the millet is about one foot high and again just before millet is harvested. This second hoeing is rather hasty, merely breaking the ground to allow planting of cowpeas. The final cultivation consists in burying the millet stalks, and takes place before the cowpea vines have spread widely. In a few low areas rice is grown. There are no tree crops of importance in the area.

There is no manuring of migrant bush fields. The Kofyar say simply that the land is rich and easily worked, so, "What would be the use of manure?" Rewarding crops can be harvested for some years using only the natural fertility of the soil and the ashes of trees. When a field is exhausted the easiest thing is to move on to a new patch of the seemingly boundless bush. I have seen a few goats in the bush, but they do not do well on the hot plains, according to some informants. Pigs fed on the cassava that is considered hardly worth harvesting for human food are now kept by a few households. Rubbish left in the fields is burned, but there is no collection of animal dung for manuring. A few Fulani with their herds are now moving through the country, but their presence on fields is not solicited; instead, they are thought more trouble than they are worth. The pattern, in short, is one of shifting cultivation in an extremely favorable frontier area.

Production

Intensive agriculture and shifting cultivation are both important and widespread systems of utilizing the environment for man's benefit. Both have been analyzed intensively by agronomists, botanists, and conservationists. Yet because of the many factors involved, it is seldom possible to compare the two systems point for point in a controlled manner. The Kofyar case has the virtue of demonstrating both patterns in contemporaneous use by a single cultural group with a homogeneous body of tools, knowledge, and techniques of social organization. It is the same individuals who practice both the intensive and the shifting systems. In their home territory of hills and fringes of the plain, the two systems are complementary, used for the production of different crops with differing natural requirements. The relatively recent beginning of large-scale bush farming on fresh land at a considerable distance from the old villages uses the shifting method for the growing of homestead crops that have heretofore been raised only with the aid of manuring on small permanent plots. What exactly does this mean in terms of actual production?

The migrant bush farms also devote an average of 2.94 acres to the production of yams, increasing the average in the measured sample to 10.69 acres. The total average yam crop of 792 tubers includes both those sold and an estimate of the number consumed. It is perhaps not an accurate measure because a farmer who is expanding his yam acreage will restrict his sales and consumption in order to increase his supply of seed yams. Table 14 reveals the expected relationship between production by intensive and shifting cultivation. Yield per acre under conditions of intensive manuring is 25 per cent above that of unmanured but fertile migrant-

TABLE 14

Comparative Production of Traditional Homestead and Migrant Bush Farms *

Type	Number in Sample	Average Acreage	Production per Acre (Pounds)				Total Production			
			Millet	Sorghum	Cowpeas	Total	Millet	Sorghum	Cowpeas	Total
Traditional homestead (intensive)	7	1.54	400	498	98	996	616	766	151	1,534
Migrant bush farm (shifting)	10	7.75	368	305	74	747	2,855	2,366	572	5,793

* The figures in this table are based on data gathered during the second period of field research and recalculation of earlier material and thus do not agree with those given in Netting 1965c (Table 2).

bush farms. Yet the total production of the bush farms is more than three and a half times that of the hill homesteads, even without including the important yams for which we have no comparable unit in the hills. The difference is obviously a function of land. In going out on the plains the Kofyar farmers have traded high yield for increased area in the interest of total production. Since land in large tracts is readily available, no spatial restrictions are placed on farming activities. Since no investment of labor in terracing or annual manuring is made, land may be used as long as it is fertile and then left. The level fields and the absence of rocks in the easily worked sandy soil make it possible to bring large tracts under the hoe rapidly. Shifting agriculture is by its nature extensive, and the existence of virgin land in the Namu area means that the initial stages of this process can be tremendously productive. Shifting agriculture in this frontier area can produce substantial crops of millet and sorghum for up to nine years on the same plot. Where a regular system of bush fallows has been followed for some years, as in the plains near Kwa and among the Hausa of the Anchau area (Grove 1961), the land may be cultivated for only three to four years between five-year rests, and only one or two of these years may be used for the large cereals that make heavy demands on the soil. Thus the comparison put forward here is not between average intensive and shifting systems but between an average intensive type and a shifting pattern of remarkably and perhaps temporarily high potential. After the cream of Namu fertility has been skimmed off and the supply of new land exhausted, we can expect yields to decline and the continued high productivity of the intensive farms to become even more impressive by comparison.

Social Organization

The relation of the new shifting cash cropping to social organization is significant. Though my observations of the Kofyar migrant community have been limited, I was struck by the fact that radical reorganization seems to have been unnecessary thus far. Farms in the Namu area have been settled by residents of numerous hill and plains villages, mostly from the general area of Kwa. In one neighborhood of forty-eight homesteads I found representatives of five plains and six hill communities. There is no emphasis on local groups migrating in a body. Individuals go to the bush on their own initiative, sometimes getting help from friends, but often taking up a farm in the midst of relative strangers. Though people from Kwa are in the majority near Namu, just as those from Kwalla and Dimmuk have tended to cluster south of Kwande and in the Jak-Kurgwi areas, respectively, an outsider has no difficulty being accepted. Residents of Doka and Dimmuk occupy farms among the Kwa folk. Pagan, Christian, and Moslem households cooperate as neighbors, and there is some evidence that even members of other tribes such as the Angas would be welcome. None of the localization of lineage and clan so characteristic of the Kofyar home villages (pp. 143–152, above) is apparent in the migrant bush.

The newcomers have organized themselves loosely but adequately after the patterns of traditional village life. A named ward or large neighborhood may have 15 to 60 households, and the average for five sample wards was 35.8. The headman (*mengwa*) is often one of the earliest settlers in a particular area. Among the first to take up Namu farms were the brothers of the chief of Kwa, and one of them is recognized as both neighborhood head of one ward and village head of the whole settler group. He performs liaison functions with the chief of Namu and is called in to settle land and other local disputes. Neighborhood heads do not need to come from a chiefly family. In fact, several hill chiefs have farms in neighborhoods where the *mengwa* has no traditional status whatever; in such a case the chief is granted no particular privileges and is treated just as any other migrant. The *mengwa* is elected by his neighborhood and is recognized by the Goemai chief of Namu, whose annual tribute he collects and whose instructions he carries to the people. Everyone seems quite content with this arrangement, which provides a necessary minimum of organization while not interfering with the primary business of independent cash cropping.

The migrants, though frequently spending longer periods in the bush each year, insist almost to a man that they do not plan to transfer their permanent residences to Namu. Funeral feasts, the treatment of illness, marriage, and seasonal activities are still conducted primarily in the home villages. Taxes are paid at home, and the traditional political life of lineage and clan has not, to the best of my knowledge, been transferred to the migrant area. There is certainly a trickle of permanent migration from the more crowded Kofyar areas, but even the poor and very rocky Latok community of seventy-one homesteads has had only three of its members transfer residence to the plains.

Of perhaps greater importance than the minimal political association established among the migrants is the expansion of work group patterns. Extensive farming requires a large cooperative group for effective hand cultivation, and the traditional Kofyar voluntary work party has proved highly adaptable. Whereas many plains households depended on their homestead farms and had little occasion to employ the voluntary work group (*mar mwos*), the new conditions of the migrant bush area encouraged such efficient mobilization of labor. Not only cultivation of growing crops is done by large groups of neighbors in return for beer, but harvesting and the threshing of grain are also provided for in this way. One wealthy farmer had a total of six work group sessions rewarded with beer to supplement the labor of his large family. The same spirit of competition and excitement pervades the voluntary work parties in Namu, enhanced perhaps by the addition of a drummer who accompanies the work. Since strong young men and women in their late teens and twenties form the major element in such groups, an amazing amount of work may be accomplished.

It appeared to me on my brief acquaintance with the

migrant bush farm area that the increased emphasis on voluntary work groups was the only minor adjustment required
of Kofyar social organization in a situation of extensive shifting cultivation. Only when I came to examine data on family composition after leaving the field did I discover that
another factor might also be significant. Figure 10 shows a

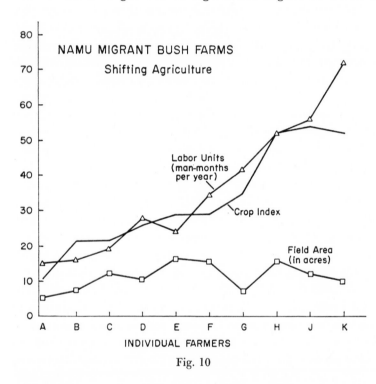

Fig. 10

crop index of total production varying directly with labor
units (resident man-months per year) and seemingly unrelated to farm area. This is contrary to the pattern of intensive homestead farming, seen in Figure 6, where it is land
area and not available labor that correlates directly with
production. The conclusion would seem to be that production can be expanded by shifting cultivators through a
greater labor input rather than by an increase in farm size.
This is true only within limits. A field that has been long in

use will give declining yields irrespective of the work expended on it. This was, in fact, the situation of Kadaura (K in Fig. 10), in 1961, in farming an old field where his large family group was not effective in raising production. He was, accordingly, opening a new farm where labor could be more profitably invested.

If an enlarged resident labor force pays dividends in terms of production, then the average number of adult workers in households engaged in migrant farming should be significantly greater than the number of adults per households that

TABLE 15

AGRICULTURAL SYSTEM AND HOUSEHOLD ADULT LABOR FORCE

Agricultural System	Number of Households	Total Number of Adult Workers	Average Number of Adult Workers per Household *
Traditional home farming only	313	924	2.95
Migrant and home farming	98	415	4.23

* The difference in average number of adults per household is found to be significant at the .001 level by use of the *t* test.

cultivate only the traditional homesteads. Comparative figures for adult workers in households that farm only at home and other households that maintain migrant farms in addition to their homesteads are shown in Table 15.

Why should labor units of the resident family be important when large voluntary work groups are readily available for the major tasks of the farming year? It would appear that certain jobs usually done by the resident family household have a crucial effect on yield. Pioneer clearing and burning are most often done by the farmers themselves. The dry season preparation of yam mounds and cereal grain ridges is important. One man complained to me that the person left in charge of his farm did not weed thoroughly, and the result was a marked decline in production. Guarding the ripening crops from animals and birds is also a significant contribution. The presence of more women in the household allows greater and more frequent brewing and is thus indirectly related to the numbers of neighbors who can be enlisted for a voluntary work party.

If more permanent labor is indeed an advantage, how can it best be assembled? One method is to plow back profits from the farm into bride price, thus increasing the female work force by additional wives. This has indeed been done. Of ninety-eight household heads interviewed, thirty-eight (39 per cent) had married at least one wife since beginning

TABLE 16

KOFYAR FAMILY TYPE AND AGRICULTURAL PRACTICES

Family Type	Traditional Homestead Farm	Both Homestead and Migrant Bush Farm	Total
Nuclear and incomplete	311	43	354
Polygynous	290	63	353
Total	601	106	707

migrant bush farming, and a total of fifty brides had been taken. When the proportion of polygynous marriages among traditional homestead farmers and migrant farmers is compared (using a different sample which includes marital data), it appears that an increased rate of polygyny correlates with the cultivation of migrant holdings. Sixty-one per cent of the migrants censused were polygynous, as compared to 45 per cent of the married men who cultivated only at home. The difference, as shown in Table 16 is significant at the .05 level on the basis of a chi-square test.

The profitability of additional wives is dramatically illustrated by the marital history of a three-generation chiefly family in a plains village. Whereas his grandfather had eight wives and his father twelve, the present chief has a total of fifty-six wives. The opening of the migrant farms has afforded opportunities both for the accumulation of cash and further wives by the chief himself and for the year-round employment of many wives in the brewing and selling of beer to increasingly affluent fellow villagers.

Though wives may be advantageous in the migrant situation, it is also necessary to be able to call on the labor of adult males for the heavy clearing, prolonged hoeing, and transporting crops. The simplest way to accomplish this is to retain grown sons as part of the household work group. Instead of dividing into nuclear units characteristic of the

TABLE 17

KOFYAR VILLAGE HOUSEHOLD COMPOSITION OF HOME
AND MIGRANT FARMERS

Type of Farming Practiced	Number of Households	Average Number of Workers per House- hold	Number of Extended Families	Extended Families (Per Cent)
Home farmers	18	3.50	3	17
Migrant farmers	30	5.03	12	40
Total	48	4.46	15	31

family engaged in intensive homestead cultivation, the migrant family stays together, sons bringing their brides into the paternal household and remaining there to rear their families. Though the movement to plains migrant farms is of recent origin, there are already signs of this tendency.

Table 17 shows that not only do Kofyar village migrant farmers have a larger number of adult workers per household than their counterparts who farm only at home, but they also have a markedly higher incidence of the extended family. A larger sample including 588 households (Table 18) shows that whereas 28 per cent of all nuclear family households were practicing migrant farming, 62 per cent of all extended families were engaged in such supplementary activity.

TABLE 18

KOFYAR HOUSEHOLD TYPE AND AGRICULTURAL PRACTICES

Household Type	Traditional Homestead Farm Only	Both Homestead and Migrant Bush Farm	Total
Nuclear	387	151	538
Extended	19	31 *	50
Total	406	182	588

* The proportion of extended family households among migrant farmers is significantly higher than that of traditional homestead farmers (using the χ^2 test, $P < 0.001$).

An extended family of Kofyar village forms a single household economy, though its members may be divided at any particular moment between home and migrant bush. Peak labor needs occur at slightly different times and promote a shifting of the major work force. At the seasons of heaviest work in the bush, the entire group, with the exception of a woman or older person guarding the traditional homestead, goes to the migrant farm. At times of homestead farm cultivation or village celebrations, the situation is reversed. Occasionally a nursing mother (who would normally live apart from her husband) remains for an extended period on the bush farm, but other family members move back and forth according to the demands of work and take turns watching over bush huts and livestock during slack seasons. While younger adults undertake the most strenuous chores, children and the elderly also serve as guards and caretakers. The master of the homestead directs cooperative work, arranges for the sale of produce, divides food, and gives money as needed to the other adult males of the family. He is also responsible for providing tax money and bride price for the sons and brothers who reside with him. A single household economy is thus maintained in contrast to the separate economic units formed when a household undergoes fission.

It would appear, then, that shifting cultivation of cash crops as adopted by the Kofyar can best be managed by a large resident labor group. This is because (1) production can be raised by a larger labor input rather than an increased land area, and (2) the successful maintenance of cultivation on widely dispersed lands requires alternate spreading and pooling of productive efforts. Almost all members of an extended family, regardless of age, can contribute to the success of such an enterprise. The economically rewarding goal of a larger labor group can be attained both by marrying more wives and by extending the elementary family by the inclusion of adult male relatives and their wives who would normally establish independent households.

Instead of deserting their intensive homesteads and emigrating permanently to the new lands, most Kofyar have chosen to maintain both farms. Production in the two operations is complementary. The old homestead provides subsistence crops that might also be harvested on the migrant farm, but the economic trees and domestic animals of the home territory cannot readily be transplanted to the migrant locations. With most of subsistence assured, the migrant farmers can concentrate their efforts on cash crops. Labor needs also mesh nicely because of the varying maturation rates of crops planted at home and in the distant bush. Though exact figures are lacking, it is probable that the greatly increased production among migrants is based on a higher total labor input. Some of this is merely the shifting of effort from low-yielding bush fallows near the traditional villages to high-yielding migrant fields. But it is also my impression that individuals put in rather longer days of work and, more importantly, that the formerly idle dry season months of January through March are now being put to productive uses. Clearing, threshing, and the major work of yam mounding go on at this time. Ceremonial and hunting activities formerly pursued during these months are necessarily curtailed.

Wage Labor

The enlarging of a family group by marriage and birth is a slow process. Voluntary labor groups are not usually used for the time-consuming, arduous work of felling brush and breaking new land. The making of yam heaps and hoeing for swamp rice are also individual matters. One solution has been the acceptance by the Kofyar of wage labor, a practice almost never found in connection with agriculture in the home communities. Young and often single Kofyar men will work for cash or for the promise of help in acquiring their own crop land plus seed yams with which to begin planting. Some of the wage labor comes from the hills above Kofyar where Mushere, Sura, and Angas live close to the subsistence level and have few opportunities for getting money. Thirty out of a sample of 98 migrant bush farmers employed workers in 1961. Of these workers 52 were Kofyar, 19 came from outside Kofyar territory, and the origin of 8 was not recorded. The largest number of laborers hired at one time was five, and usually the group was of two or three. Since farm work is highly seasonal, the Kofyar have no permanent employees, and no one in the sample was hired for more than a month. The average length of wage labor work was 8.7 days, and 18 out of 30 instances were 5 days or less. Payment is given on the completion of a job for which the price has been settled in advance. The Kofyar do not think in terms of daily wages, and an effort to compute such figures gives a range from 6d. to 3s. 3d. per day, with an average for 30 cases of 1s. 7d. Workers are fed while they are employed. Most of the Kofyar youth are working with the objective of eventually taking up their own farms, and they regard wage labor as a temporary means to this end.

The availability of paid workers may have an indirect effect on intensive homestead farming. Men from the hills who have opened migrant bush fields have been so busy that they have neglected the hoeing of their homestead farms preceding the rains. As clearing progresses and returns from cash crops become available, they are able to hire men to make the bush yam heaps and thus free themselves for the early cultivation at home.

The Market Economy

The swift, continuous shift by part of the Kofyar population from traditional subsistence agriculture to vigorous migrant bush farming needs an explanation. The movement appears to be spontaneous and based on the decisions of individuals rather than the action of corporate groups. I suspect, though I cannot prove, that there have been different motivating factors actively influencing this process. Those people who set up bush farms in the 1930's and 1940's were suffering from restricted land resources and resulting food scarcity at home. Residents of the more swampy areas of Dimmuk and the rock-strewn Latok valleys went earlier and in greater numbers than their more fortunately situated neighbors. The chief of Miket told of competition among a growing population for homestead farm sites in the days before the bush area was available. The migrant farms have furnished a safety valve for increased pressure on subsistence resources.

The recent upsurge in migrant activity has been due not to the need for food but to the desire for cash. As soon as an area was brought under British colonial control, a system of taxation was instituted. The first collections were assessed in horses or sheep and gathered by the chief from his people. This was replaced as quickly as possibly by a tax in money on each adult male. The pacification of the area was accompanied by the penetration of Hausa merchants, generally from Goemai country. Thus both the necessity for tax money and the desire for cloth, beads, and other newly available articles sent the Kofyar in search of cash. The hill people found in sylvan products such as palm oil and locust beans a source of money. They could also dispose of a small surplus of domestic animals and sauce crops such as groundnuts, peppers and bitter tomatoes. There had been small markets of indeterminate age in Doka and the Goemai section of Kwalla on the edges of Kofyar territory. In 1931 a Hausa trader settled in Dimmuk and began a market at the request of the chief. Until this time the limited commerce in iron and salt into the hills had been handled by trading partners on a barter basis. The Kwa people who lacked both economically useful trees in appreciable numbers and land for growing increased crops resorted to a middleman-porter role in order to get cash. Ames (1934) reported that men from Kwa bought yams in Kurgwi and salt in Awe, carrying them to markets on the high plateau for resale. The presence of mining camps employing considerable numbers of wage laborers made possible the selling of farm produce at a profit. This trade is maintained to some degree, and there is a brisk commerce in locally grown foodstuffs headloaded to the high plateau. On a March visit to the large Mangun market in Sura country, I counted forty-eight Kofyar from eleven different vilages, most of them selling home-grown foodstuffs. They had walked from six to nine hours up hill paths to reach the market.

Only with the opening of roads, however, has there been a really sizable outlet for bulky farm produce. In 1943 Lowland (then Shendam) Division was visited by one lorry once a month, and this followed a circuitous route from Pankshin to Shendam. Roads were built using local labor in the late 1940's, and some lorries began to go from Shendam to the western side of the Shemankar. Though bridges were almost totally lacking, and culverts are still the exception rather than the rule on Kofyar roads, there has been a growing volume of dry season motor traffic since 1950. A new all-weather road opened in 1958 gives easy access from Jos and the mine fields to Dokan Tofa on the edge of Kofyar. The United Africa Company opened a buying point in Lowland Division in 1951, but much of the produce trade was handled independently through Hausa middlemen or Ibo lorry owner–traders.

The Mernyang group from Kwa and the neighboring hills

began migrant bush cultivation around 1950. The development was obviously for cash cropping purposes. It was not the poorest men who led the way but the men of substance. The chiefs who certainly had no need for food wanted cash for the clothing and prestige goods they had seen outside the area. They grew crops for sale, concentrating on native cereals and beans that could be bagged and stored easily and on the new crop, yams, which was in demand by the labor force on the plateau. Coco yams, which do not keep well, and small grains such as acha and eleusine, unknown in larger markets, were not grown. To sell their crops in quantity the Kofyar migrants had to have lorry access to their farms. They built a road into their area so that grain and yams could be loaded directly onto the lorry at each farm. The Kofyar point to their road as a sign of involvement in the market economy and contrast this with the lack of any road by an older Tiv community which is still subsistence-oriented.

Actual sale of migrant farm products was originally to non-Kofyar traders who visited individual farmers. Hausa men, often working out of Kurgwi, bought grain, especially during the rainy season. Ibo lorry drivers and owners from Jos, Lafia, and elsewhere soon entered the trade, and they employed agents to tour the area on bicycles, arranging deals during the dry period of open roads. Kofyar men sometimes assisted in these transactions, being given one to four shillings per bag for each sale they contracted. The larger migrant farmers began to market their yams and sorghum themselves in Jos. By hiring a lorry the farmer could retain the entire market price minus transport costs and eliminate the middleman's profit. It was only a step from this to buying small lots of produce and collecting sizable shipments for resale. In 1962 six Kofyar men were independent traders, the first having begun the preceding year. The chief of Kwa, Doedel, who had initially begun migrant farming near Namu was, by 1961–62, affluent enough to purchase a lorry, which commuted constantly between the bush farms and Jos. The Kofyar are proud of these developments. They claimed

in 1962 that the Hausa merchants who took grain on consign-
ment (*lap kaat,* "to take a debt") and paid only after it was
resold were losing their share of the market to Kofyar. The
Kofyar traders are men who have accumulated capital either
in migrant bush farming or other enterprises, and their policy is to deal only in cash. Kofyar also prefer to do business
with other Kofyar because wealth is then retained by local
rich men, who can be expected to dispense beer liberally to
all. The increased prosperity will also reflect favorably on
the whole community and, as Kofyar say, "cause our name to
grow."

Produce moves in different directions and at different
times in response to prices, availability of transport, and
personal needs. Early millet, valued chiefly by the Kofyar as
a brewing staple, is sold for the most part locally in Dimmuk
or Kwa markets. It varies in price from 3*d.* to 4*d.* per *mudu* [2]
just after the July harvest to 8*d.* in the wet months immediately before the harvest. Sorghum fluctuates more narrowly,
from 3*d.* in January to 6*d.* before the new crop has come in.
Beans may be sold in December to raise money for taxes at
only 16*s.* a bag (2*d.* a *mudu*), but by the end of the dry
season they may reach £3 5*s.* (over 8*d.* a *mudu*). Yams vary
from £2 to £3 a hundred to from £4 to £5, depending not
only on supply and demand but on the size and quality of
particular lots. Prices in general are best at the beginning of

[2] The *mudu* used for measuring grains, beans, and groundnuts in
Northern Nigeria is a shallow metal bowl. When used in the marketing
of food products, it is heaped to overflowing. These bowls, called
kwanu in Kofyar, come in varying sizes with no distinguishing marks.
The most commonly used is the *bali,* which holds on the average 2.8
pounds of early millet, 2.9 pounds of sorghum, 2.6 pounds of shelled
groundnuts, 2.2 pounds of rice, and 2.6 pounds of cowpeas. There is a
seasonal variation in the price per *bali mudu,* but a further price dif-
ferential is introduced by using larger measures when grain is plentiful
and smaller ones when it is scarce. This is a recognized practice among
middlemen buying Kofyar migrant bush farm crops for resale in the
cities. It is also reported that an unwary seller may be cheated when
the buyer surreptitiously exchanges a smaller for a larger *mudu* during
the course of measuring.

the rains in April and May, when lorries can still negotiate the Namu road but remaining marketable surpluses are not large. The months just before harvest, from July to November, would be even better, but the Kofyar lack both suitable storage facilities and motorized transport. The 7s. cost of sending a 250-pound bag of grain from Namu to Jos would be considerably increased if it were necessary to negotiate the first thirty-five miles on foot or by bicycle.

I do not have sufficient data to estimate profits in the commodity trade. One young Kofyar man buying beans and sorghum in February, 1962, figured that he would pay £3 5s. and £1 13s. 3d. per bag, respectively, and sell them for £4 and £2 5s. in Jos. Deducting transportation costs, he would make a profit of 8s. on a bag of beans and 3s. 4d. on sorghum. He was buying from boys taking small lots to market to get "salt," that is, small household necessities, and he gave them the going market price without haggling. He hoped to collect a full lorry load by the close of the dry season.

Such important features of a market economy as a price system, standard weights and measures, entrepreneurs, a nonagrarian population, and adequate transportation are already present in the larger environment of the Kofyar. The growth of migrant farm cash cropping is an adaptation to the opportunities of the market. This appears most strikingly in a comparison of budgets. An analysis of income and expenditure indicates the differing market participation of cash and subsistence farmers, both in regard to money received and the increased use of cash in certain areas. Tables 19 and 20 contain individual budgets with sums received and disbursed, grouped according to various significant areas of economic activity. Both the Bong and the Kofyar villagers whose budgets are summarized are hill homestead intensive cultivators, while the mixed hill and plain farmers at Namu maintain migrant as well as home farms.[3]

[3] The budgets were collected by privately questioning homestead heads on a number of specific items that they could possibly have bought

TABLE 19

BUDGETS OF SUBSISTENCE AND CASH CROP FARMERS: INCOME

Group	Number	Food Crops	Tree Crops	Animals	Beer	Loans	Crafts, Labor	Other	Total
Bong home farmers	1	£ 2	£ 3 15s.	£1 6s.	£5	£4			£16
	2	5s.		£1 12s.	£2		£4 10s.		£ 7 18s.
	3		£ 1 5s.	11s.					£ 1 16s.
	4	£ 2 10s.	£ 6 5s.	13s.	£2	£2			£13 3s.
	5	5s.	£ 1 3s.	7s.					£ 1 15s. 3d.
	6	£ 1 17s. 6d.		6s.					£ 2 3s. 6d.
	7	£15 19s.	£10		£2 5s.	£4 10s.			£32 14s.
	8		£ 5	9s.	£2	8s.			£ 7 17s.
	9		£ 1 6s.	15s.				£ 1 5s.	£ 3 13s.
	10	10s.	£ 3						£ 3 10s.
Kolyar home farmers	11	£ 2 15s.	£ 1 13s.	8s. 6d.	£2		£1 10s.		£ 8 6s. 6d.
	12	14s.	5s.	14s.	£1 5s.				£ 2 18s.
	13	£ 1 11s.	£ 3 3s.	£1 17s. 6d.	£1 10s.				£ 8 1s. 6d.
	14	£ 4 19s.	£ 1 8s.	£1					£ 7 7s.
	15		10s.	£1 11s.	£1 5s.	£1	£3 8s.		£ 7 14s.
	16	5s.	12s.	5s.		£3			£ 4 2s.
Namu migrant bush farmers	17	£35 15s.	£ 4	£2 10s.	£1 10s.	£1 10s.		£20 *	£65 5s.
	18	£ 8 9s.		£8 2s.	£2 7s.	£6			£24 18s.
	19	£32 7s.	£ 3 3s.	8s.	£3			£11 *	£49 18s.
	20	£ 4 12s.	4s.	3s.	£2 10s.	£1	10s.		£ 8 19s.
	21	£51 9s.		12s.					£63
	22	£22 15s.	£ 2 5s.					£ 8 *	£33
	23	£24 9s.		9s.		£3			£27 9s.
	24	£16 4s.		2s.		£5			£23 4s.
	25	£26		17s.					£26 17s.
	26	£21 10s.		£1 15s.					£23 5s.

* Bride price received.

TABLE 20

BUDGETS OF SUBSISTENCE AND CASH CROP FARMERS: EXPENDITURES

Group	Number	Tools	Cloth	Food	Meat	Beer	Animals	Loans	Bride Price *	Other	Tax	Total
Bong home farmers	1	15s.	15s.	15s.	4s.	£5	£2 10s.	£1	£2	1s.	£2	£14 8s.
	2	10s.	£2 16s.	10s.	4s.	£1 10s.	£1 7s.	11s.		4s.	£2	£9 12s.
	3	8s.	8s.	6s.	3s. 9d.	£1				5s.	£2	£6 5s.
	4	£1 16s.	£2	£1	£1 10s.	£3 10s.	£1 18s.		£1 5s.	£1 5s.	£2	£12 9s.
	5	2s.	5s.		£2	£1 10s.				7s. 1d.	£2	£7 9s.
	6	6s.	7s.	1s. 6d.	7s.	£1			£1 5s.		£2	£3 2s. 6d.
	7		7s.	5s.		£1 15s.	£5 18s.	£1	£31 3s.	£4 1s.	£4	£43 7s.
	8	9s. 9d.	5s.	2s. 6d.	3s. 2d.	£1			£2		£2	£8 4s.
	9	14s. 6d.	5s.	6d.		£1	6s. 9d.			1s.	£2	£8 5s.
	10	£1 6s.	8s.	5s.	2s.	£1		2s.	£3		£2	£8 3s.
Kofyar home farmers	11	10s.	£3 8s. 6d.	17s.	£1 10s.	£3	12s. 3d.			£1 9s. †	£2	£13 6s. 9d.
	12	4s.	17s.			£1 5s.	6s. 6d.	6s.		6s.	£2	£5 10s. 6d.
	13	8s. 6d.	£2 1s. 6d.	5s.	10s.	£4					£2	£9 11s.
	14	4s.	£4 9s.	£3	£1 2s.	£3	5s.		£2 12s.	£5 19s. †	£2	£22 11s.
	15		£1 5s.	£1	£2	£1 10s.		£1	£13	£2 15s.	£2	£25 5s.
	16	£1	5s.	10s.		10s.	5s.	£1		£1	0 ‡	£3 15s.
Namu migrant bush farmers	17	5s.	£3 13s.	10s.	£1	£2 15s.		£4 10s.	£1	10s.	£6	£20 3s.
	18	16s.	£2 8s.		£4			£6		£2 2s. †	£2	£20 4s.
	19	13s. 6d.	£3 19s.	7s.	£2 8s.	£4 10s.				£15 7s. §	£4	£31 9s.
	20	13s.	£1 19s.	10s.	15s.	£2	12s.	£1		2s. †	£2	£8 19s.
	21	14s.	£12	£2		£5					£6	£35 9s.
	22	15s.	£3 15s.	£1	£3	£5	15s.	£5		£6 5s. †	£2	£32 15s.
	23	18s.	£2 10s.	£2	£3	£7		£3	£12	£12 16s. ‖	£2	£48 13s.
	24	7s.	£2 6s.	£1		£1	£1 9s.	£9		£1 7s. ‖	£4	£17 10s.
	25	8s.	£4 5s.		10s.	£3		£4		£1 12s. ‖	£8	£21 8s.
	26	15s.	£4 1s.	5s.	£1	£2			£2	£2 4s. ‖	£4	£16 5s.

* Either payment to father or return to divorced husband.
† School fees.
‡ Old man, not compelled to pay tax.
§ Bicycle.
‖ Labor, paid wage work.

No effort was made to balance the respective budgets. It was difficult to learn how much cash remained after the previous year's tax was paid, and informants were reluctant to say how much was still on hand in their houses. Eight out of ten Bong budgets show expenditures exceeding income. This is due partly to the underestimation of income and partly to the fact that a standard expenditure for tax was included though many people had not yet sold the produce or animals to obtain this money. Certain items in Bong budgets were influenced by the presence of the anthropologist. Number 2 worked on building my house and so acquired cash he might not otherwise have had. Number 7, an ex-chief on whose land I lived, obtained loans from me which supported some of his heavy bride price payments. In general, the questions on expenditures were more detailed than those on income, and I believe that the total expenditure figure is a more accurate indication of money that actually passed through the hands of an individual household

or sold during the year extending from November, 1960, to the tax collection in November, 1961. I asked for the amounts of money earned selling such products as sorghum, millet, and peppers, palm and canarium oil, goats, sheep, and chickens, and combined these figures in the broader areas of food crops, tree crops, and animals for tabulation purposes. Some categories include economic activities of different kinds. In some cases expenditures for beer include sums for purchasing brewing millet. Animals are bought both as investment (*long,* wealth) and more frequently for sacrifices connected with curing rites. Though sacrificial animals are eaten, the Kofyar do not group them with animals or meat acquired solely for eating. If I overlooked a particular area in my questioning (for example, transport costs for plains farmers, tobacco purchases in the hills) , information on that was not volunteered. In selecting the individuals to be interviewed about their budgets, I tried to get a cross-section representing young and old, rich and poor, early and more recent bush migrants. The sample is thus not random, but in reviewing the group I do not see any major signs of bias in it. None of the Kofyar interviewed keep written records, and the figures given are based solely on memory. When asked to explain abnormally high or low quotations, the informant could usually account for them plausibly, and the sums mentioned in various categories have a certain consistency. For items like beer, which include a multitude of two- to sixpence purchases over many months, the total given can be thought of only as a rough estimate.

head over the course of a year than that given for income. This holds for the subsistence farmer, but I am inclined to think that the opposite is true for the Namu cash cropper. The selling of his products is done in large lots, and he is paid with a lump sum that is easily remembered. His statement of income is perhaps therefore more accurate than the recollection of expenditures.

The budgets given are not a trustworthy indication of the total household economy. Money earned by women through selling their own farm products (groundnuts, beans, sauce crops), beer, or craft goods (pottery, baskets, cotton thread) is kept by them and used for sauce materials, their own and sometimes their children's clothing, beer, and livestock. Husbands have no share in their wives' earnings. Though their incomes may not be large, women have no tax to pay and seem often to have more cash on hand than do men. Small items of wearing apparel that I sometimes sold as a favor to friends were invariably paid for more promptly by women. It is also a fairly common practice to borrow from a woman in order to pay taxes. Women, however, do not have access to proceeds from the sale of major cereals or tree crops, bride price, or trading in nonindigenous goods. They may own animals, but usually not more than a few chickens and perhaps a dog or a goat. Unfortunately I do not have budgets for women.

Tables 21 and 22 compare the average sums received and spent in the various categories by Bong and Kofyar home farmers and by Namu migrant bush farmers. No average has been listed where the item occurs in fewer than half the budgets sampled. The figures on average income make clear the economic advantages of cash cropping. The average income of the ten migrant bush farmers is more than five times that of Kofyar village nonmigrants. Even if certain nonrecurrent items such as the return or payment of bride price were eliminated, Namu farmers' average income would still exceed thirty pounds a year. Unlike the subsistence farmers, whose expenditures appear to exceed income in thirteen out

TABLE 21
Average Incomes of Subsistence and Cash Crop Farmers

Village	Sample Size	Food Crops	Tree Crops	Animals	Beer	Loans	Total
Bong	10	£2 5s.	£3 2s. 11d.	11s. 11d.	£1 6s. 6d.	£1 2s. 6d.	£9 1s. 1d.
Kofyar	6	£1 18s.	£1 5s. 2d.	19s.	£1		£6 8s. 2d.
Namu bush	10	£24 5s. 2d.	19s. 2d.	£1 9s. 10d.	18s. 8d.	£1 13s.	£34 11s. 6d.

TABLE 22
Average Expenditures of Subsistence and Cash Crop Farmers

Village	Sample Size	Tools	Cloth	Food	Meat	Beer	Animals	Loans	Tax	Other	Total
Bong	10	12s. 9d.	16s. 11d.	6s. 7d.	9s. 7d.	£1 14s. 6d.	£1 1s.		£2 4s.	10s. 8d.	£11 18s. 11d.
Kofyar	6	8s. 7d.	£2 3s. 6d.	£1 6s.	17s.	£2 4s. 2d.	4s. 9d.	7s. 8d.	£1 13s.	£1 18s. 2d.	£13 6s. 6d.
Namu bush	10	12s. 8d.	£4 1s. 7d.	£1 1s. 2d.	£1 17s. 4d.	£3 4s. 6d.		£3 5s.	£4	£5 8s. 4d.	£25 1s. 6d.

of sixteen cases, the bush cash croppers have only one out of ten in this position. Evidently income has increased more rapidly than it can be spent, and an average surplus of almost ten pounds annually is indicated for bush farmers. The increase is largely accounted for by the greater quantities of food products marketed. Income that comes from such varied sources as field crops, tree crops, domestic animals, and beer on the intensive farms is concentrated on cereals and yams in shifting cash cropping. No tree produce whatever is harvested in the Namu area, but some migrant farmers own economic trees at their homes.

An increased income has contributed to a changed pattern of consumption among the migrant cultivators. In all areas except tools and animals they substantially exceed the averages of the Bong sample. The Namu migrants spend 4.8 times as much on clothing as their Bong counterparts and almost four times as much on meat. Food expenditure, most of which is for salt, goes up somewhat, and twice as much money is available for beer. The standard of living has obviously risen, both as indicated by such traditional markers as meat and drink and along the relatively new scale of wealth and status as reflected in dress. There is obviously some demand to share the newly acquired cash with other members of the community, and the sampled bush farmers have made loans averaging £3 5s. The higher average tax payment by Namu farmers reflects the extension of the family to include more adult males, a phenomenon previously analyzed in the section on social organization of migrants. Significant sums have also been devoted to goods and services that have no place in the traditional system. Bicycles that are useless in the hills become valuable assets when there is a need to travel back and forth to distant plains farms. Several of the Namu farmers are also paying school fees for their children.

Expenditures of the Kofyar village men who have continued to farm only at home have tended to rise along the same lines as their migrant fellows (the first four men on the

Namu list are Kofyar residents), but there has been no accompanying increase in income. The Kofyar farmers, perhaps influenced by the example of those who have profited in the bush, buy more cloth, beer, food, and meat than do Bong people. Yet chiefly because they have fewer economic trees, they have less money to finance these purchases. Bong is an isolated village whose children do not generally go to school. Kofyar has had a primary school for some years, and a few local children have gone on to higher schools where tuition is correspondingly increased. Even if we do not consider bride price that may be the result of long-term savings, it appears that Kofyar farmers will not be able to satisfy their newly acquired needs without recourse to new sources of income. This makes it probable that migratory bush farming will continue to attract home farmers until only those with particularly large homestead fields or those too old for the heavy work will be content to abstain from cash cropping. Given the present situation with most trades and crafts closed to non-Moslems, and with cash available only for arduous porterage or distant mine field labor, migrant farming provides a most welcome alternative to the Kofyar. They remain independent, doing work they know in the company of family and peers without permanently leaving their ancestral homesteads. The sale of produce can bring in sizable amounts of cash by the second year and requires no capital investment. They have the rewards of pioneering with the security of doing it in their own back yards.

We may only speculate about what the next step may be. Variable factors that cannot now be calculated, such as the extent of virgin bush land remaining, the rate of new migration, and the ability of heavily worked soil to regenerate, will all be important in determining the future of the adaptation to shifting cultivation. Permanent migration from the hills has thus far been negligible because of the economically valuable tree crops there, the social solidarity of the lineage group in respect to land, and the religious attachment to the graves of forefathers. *De facto* moves may take place gradually as household heads spend successively longer periods on the bush farm. This process is speeded by the scarcity and poverty of land in some hill and plains communities. The crowded communities at the foot of the hills have already witnessed some permanent out-migration. The unoccupied bush furnishes an outlet for a growing population that the Kofyar must take advantage of in order to avoid serious problems within their traditional territory. It is to be hoped that as bush land is filled and households establish permanent residence there, some of the effective techniques of intensive agriculture will be adapted for use in the plains environment.

9

Conclusions

IN THE BODY of this work I have attempted to provide data on the subsistence adaptation of the Kofyar and a provisional analysis of their cultural ecology. The general theoretical approach is that of Julian Steward. It includes the isolation of related features of environment and human exploitation and the empirical connection of this subsistence situation to certain cultural patterns. These interrelated factors together form the ecosystem. The method has proved useful in accounting for structural features among hunting and gathering populations. I have tried to demonstrate that it is also effective in explaining the functional relationship between resources and technology and a limited range of cultural features in a preliterate agricultural society. In an effort to refine Steward's approach, I have considered a single people in a small area with a relatively consistent natural setting and made a detailed investigation of their means of production. My evidence for demonstrating functional relationships among variables came from synchronic description and analysis, cross-cultural comparison, and historic change. I have sought to explain the distribution and cooperative organization of people as adaptations to the demands of the agricultural system. Certain of these social features are also seen to change in response to an altered environment and technology.

Kofyar farming is relatively unique in tropical Africa because of its highly developed knowledge and techniques which permit remarkable permanence of cultivation and are functionally interdependent with a substantial density of population. It is based on the intensive cultivation of cereal staples on approximately an acre surrounding the residential homestead plus shifting cultivation of larger, more distant bush fields. Crucial to this system are several natural and technological factors:

1. Dependable rainfall due to the orographic effect when moist south winds encounter the steep southern escarpment of the Jos Plateau.

2. Hill soils with good mineral supplies from decomposing rock.

3. Effective conservation of soil and water by bench terracing and the type of ridging known as basin listing.

4. Development and maintenance of soil fertility by annual manuring and crop rotation.

5. Knowledge and wide use of a variety of cultigens with different growing seasons, providing insurance against crop failure, and varying requirements, allowing the utilization of different microenvironments.

The Kofyar can thus support a population averaging close to 300 persons per square mile and reaching an estimated 1,200 per square mile in some areas. For most Kofyar, heavy and dependable yields eliminate the annual season of hunger that is familiar in much of Africa. The Kofyar prevent erosion and retain soil nutrients in ways not practiced by their tribal neighbors. Lacking mythical histories and linguistic and archaeological evidence, it is impossible to trace the origins of this highly developed agricultural system. It seems probable, however, that its practice allowed the Kofyar to expand their population while remaining in the spectacularly rugged area that effectively shielded them from

Hausa-Fulani and Jukun imperial armies and slave raiders. Chapter 3 contains a systematic description of an integrated set of farming techniques and the agricultural knowledge in which they are grounded.

Ecological relationships to the system of food production can be traced in a number of areas of Kofyar culture.

Settlement Pattern

The prevailing dispersed settlement of the Kofyar, with households occupying discrete clusters of huts in the middle of homestead fields, is an efficient device for maintaining intensive agriculture. It allows homestead residents to tend their small plot carefully and regularly as well as protecting it from pests and other types of damage. Time is not wasted in travel to and from the field, manure is easily applied, and harvested crops need not be transported far.

In the past, defensive measures did not require nucleation into walled villages, as was common in Northern Nigeria. Other inducements to the clustering of residence, such as markets with specialized artisans and traders, were not traditionally present in the area.

Household Organization

In the intensive farming of homestead plots, production is directly related to land area but is not affected by higher labor input. Thus a small resident group provides sufficient labor, and the nuclear family proves adaptive. Population grows by fission and the formation of new households with their own farms rather than by expansion of existing family units. This again is traceable to the need for close, on-the-spot supervision of homestead fields, protection from pests, and the maintenance of goat herds for manure.

In shifting cultivation, such as that practiced by the Kofyar on migrant cash crop farms, the size of the resident labor force becomes crucial to production, while land area is a largely independent variable. Needs for clearing the land, making yam heaps, weeding, and guarding the crops increase labor requirements. The work force is supplied by marrying more wives, hiring workers, and retaining sons or brothers and their wives as part of the household unit in the form of an extended family. The extended family is shown to be more frequent among migrant farmers than among those who remain at home.

Division of Labor

Because households are typically small and independent, men and women may substitute for one another in many domestic tasks. Rigid division of labor is also lacking in agriculture where hoeing requires all able-bodied workers and especially strenuous tasks such as tree cutting are seldom required.

Labor groups of various sizes appropriate to different tasks are mobilized on a territorial basis (neighborhood, village) and by voluntary means (exchange, beer party, named association of contemporaries). Such localized, flexible units are not subject to limitations of size or geographical dispersal that might affect kin-based work groups.

Residence and Kin Groupings

Individual rights in land, plus the advantages of agricultural cooperation suggest that patrilineal kin groups have expanded by budding within a limited, permanently cultivated area. Lineages and clans are still largely localized in one or more adjoining neighborhoods.

Clan and lineage segments retain a corporate character only as long as their members maintain common village residence and continue to use land in the area. Nonlocalized clans exist in name only. The assumption of land in a different village may ultimately bring a shift in kinship affiliation to the landowner's lineage.

The self-sufficiency of village units and the existence of nonarable areas between settlements contribute to the independence of villages and the lack of any wider traditional political integration.

Land Tenure

Land rights are concentrated in the individual who by an investment of labor first builds up the permanent productivity of the soil and grows economic trees. Since homestead land remains an economic asset indefinitely it cannot be assigned on a usufruct basis as is commonly done under systems of shifting cultivation.

Leasing and loaning are an adjustment to unequal ownership of land and the need to reallot land to suit the needs of a changing population.

Because the homestead farms are too small to be divided into economically viable segments, they must be passed on entire to a single heir. This entails some sons' moving off to other sites, either owned or leased, in response to the needs of a growing household and the desire for autonomy in the control of farm produce. The homestead then is inherited by the son who remains in occupation.

Land is considered a productive resource only as long as it is farmed. Leased land brings only negligible rent to the owner, and complete alienation by sale is permitted only under exceptional circumstances by the lineage of the owner.

Land boundary and inheritance disputes increase in proportion to land scarcity.

Conceptualization

The direct production of their own food by small, independent households leads the Kofyar to internalize conscientious work and careful husbandry as personal values.

The dependability of agriculture and the success of conventional methods fosters a practical, unemotional attitude toward farming.

Magico-religious rites connected with agriculture are usually simple and personal. Communal ceremonies are irregular and are held only in the event of a natural disaster.

Change to Cash Cropping

Methods of shifting agriculture are being adapted for growing major crops in an area of fertile soil, level terrain, and readily available vacant land.

The goal of increasing production for market is most rapidly and efficiently attained through extensive, shifting cultivation.

Decisions to enter cash cropping take place on an individual basis and are not administratively stimulated or restrained. To the migrant farmers, traditional village and kin ties are largely irrelevant. Common residence in a bush area is the basis for agricultural cooperation. Leadership in migrant communities comes from the earliest settlers.

Early migrant farming was an effort to increase subsistence crops by persons from areas of poor or scarce land. More recently the wish for a money income has appeared as the dominant factor in opening new land. Budgets reveal that cash is used to increase consumption of traditional foods (beer, meat), for productive investment (wives, bicycles, labor), and for new goods and services (cloth, medicines, transport, school fees).

The Kofyar have spontaneously adopted the cash cropping pattern and creatively adapted indigenous productive techniques. They continue to maintain traditional intensive farms, but population pressure plus the requirements of a market economy will probably increase their dependence on shifting cultivation. The rapid exhaustion of vacant land may stimulate a further and not fully predictable change in agricultural techniques and accompanying social adjustments.

The above conclusions are offered with varying degrees of validity. Statistical evidence is brought forward to support the hypothesis of differing labor requirements in intensive and large-scale shifting agriculture. Changes in family organization are then viewed as adaptations to these labor needs. The arguments offered in relating division of labor, work group organization, and features of land tenure to intensive agriculture are inductive, but an attempt is made to include sufficient data so that other interpretations of the facts may be made. The localization of residential and kin groupings may well have historical roots related to the need for common defense. I regard the ecological explanation of these phenomena as well as the discussion of Kofyar attitudes and religious practices as speculative and perhaps suggestive, rather than definitive. My information on cash cropping is based on census and budgetary material collected by me or under my supervision. Since I spent only a limited period of actual participant observation with the migrant farmers, details of their agriculture are perhaps less fully documented than those of the hill Kofyar. Although I am certain that a substantially increased money income results from cash cropping, I have looked only at the more obvious social correlates and made no attempt to analyze the economic, sociological, or psychological factors that predispose individuals to undertake this new productive activity.

The informing concept behind this discussion of Kofyar land and life is that human society cannot be fully understood without attempting to relate significant features of its environment, its subsistence techniques, and its social organization. If the approach of cultural ecology can demonstrate these functional connections through various lines of empirical evidence, then it is a worth-while tool of social science. As Leach (1961:306) notes, "Every anthropologist needs to start out by considering just how much of the culture with which he is faced can most readily be understood as a direct adaptation to the environmental context, including that part of the context which is man-made." The value of this approach lies also in its ability to rule out ecological interpretations in areas where explanation in terms of psychology, social structure, or political norms may be more useful. The compelling interest of ecological analysis is in its revelation of meaningful order and pattern uniting a wide range of human activities with the ecosystem, showing both their purpose and their integration.

The study of Kofyar cultural ecology offered here is preliminary, contenting itself with interrelations and avoiding
questions of causality and origin. This is largely due to the
essential circularity of process, the intricate feedback mechanisms of the system. Moreover, I cannot at this time adequately handle the priority of the factors involved or
separate dependent from independent variables in their complex interplay. I suspect, however, that certain variables
from the Kofyar case have a wider application: that, for
instance, where an agricultural population increases within
a favorable but territorially restricted environment there
will be a marked tendency toward intensive cultivation in
which both production per acre and labor expenditure per
unit produced are forced upward. Thus demographic growth
and resulting food scarcity are the initial spurs to increased
food production by intensive methods. In these circumstances dispersed settlement, nuclear family households, and
individual land tenure all become adaptive. There is no
absolute necessity about their emergence, but they seem to
meet the problems created by the new farming technology in
an effective manner and to provide a certain selective advantage in biological terms. This does not mean that alternative
cultural solutions will be rapidly eliminated, but rather that
societies that react differently will be somewhat more limited
in their growth and in the opportunities they can utilize.

These hypotheses suggest that in relatively simple farming
societies like the Kofyar a set of environmental parameters
and a given agricultural technique together create certain
conditions which directly influence social organization. Assumed here is the principle of least effort, that "the best
general rule to the behavior of primitive farmers is that they
work to get the maximum return for the minimum effort"
(Nye and Greenland 1960:129). Institutions and groups respond to adaptive pressures from the environment-technol-
ogy sector to the extent they are involved in productive labor
or other tasks of subsistence. It is the investigator's job to
specify the extent of this involvement.

Discussions of ecological adaptation are often generalized as the processes of cultural evolution, and, in fact, Sahlins and Service (1960) refer to its as "specific evolution." I would prefer to regard the interpretation of Kofyar cultural ecology as merely an attempt at functional analysis in which some but not all of the relevant variables are isolated. There is nothing irreversible about the nature of the intensive agricultural adaptation. The Kofyar are now in the process of changing their farming techniques, entering the cash economy, and finding a place as prosperous peasants in a national state. The relations of these changes to family organization, kinship, locality, law, and world view are anything but simple. The values and ethics of the intensive terrace farmer may perhaps preadapt him for a successful role in the economy of the new Nigeria, but this is the sort of speculation that charts new research.

I admire the Kofyar, both what they have been and what they are becoming. For the men and women I know, change is not frightening. Fortunately they retain the freedom to choose among several alternatives in the pursuit of the good life. Their confidence is borne of a past in which they shaped a stubborn landscape to human dimensions and a future where new fields await their hands.

Appendix

KOFYAR KIN TERMS

Kofyar Kin Term	Kin Type	Abbreviation
pakaam	grandfather	(GF)
nankaam	grandmother	(GM)
nda, fup	father	(F)
na, noegoen	mother	(M)
koen	mother's brother, sister's child	(K)
emnoegoen	sibling	(sib)
la	son	(s)
reb	daughter	(d)
cik	grandchild	(gc)

KOFYAR KIN TERMS
(Lardang Variant)

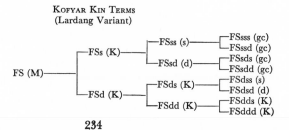

234

KOFYAR KIN TERMS
(Bong Variant)

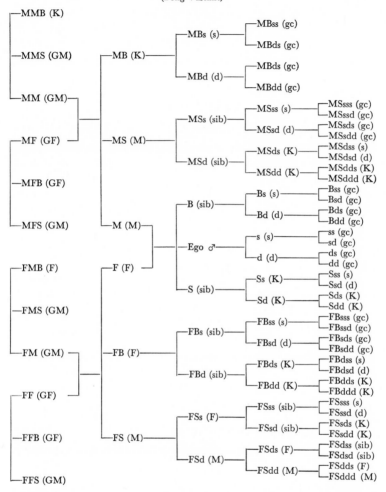

References

Allan, W.
1965 The African Husbandman. Edinburgh, Oliver and Boyd.
Alland, A., Jr.
1966 Medical Anthropology and the Study of Biological and Cultural Anthropology. American Anthropologist 68:40–51.
Ames, C. G.
1934 Gazetteer of Plateau Province, Jos. Jos Native Authority.
Barrau, J.
1958 Subsistence Agriculture in Melanesia. Honolulu, Bernice P. Bishop Museum Bulletin 219.
Barth, F.
1956 Ecologic Relationships of Ethnic Groups in Swat, North Pakistan. American Anthropologist 58:1079–1089.
1961 Nomads of South Persia. New York, Humanities Press.
Bartholomew, G. A., Jr., and J. B. Birdsell
1953 Ecology and the Protohominids. American Anthropologist 55:481–498.
Bates, M.
1953 Human Ecology. In Anthropology Today, A. L. Kroeber, ed., pp. 700–713. Chicago, University of Chicago Press.
1961 The Forest and Sea; A Study of the Economy of Nature and the Ecology of Man. London, Museum Press Ltd.
Baumann, H., D. Westermann, and R. Thurnwald
1940 Völkerkunde von Afrika. Essen, Essene-Verlaganstalt.

Baumhoff, M. A.
  1963 Ecological Determinants of Aboriginal California Populations.
        Berkeley, University of California Press.
Beardsley, R. K.
  1964 Ecological and Social Parallels between Rice-growing Com-
        munities of Japan and Spain. *In* Symposium on Community
        Studies in Anthropology, V. E. Garfield, ed., pp. 51–63. Seattle,
        American Ethnological Society.
Biebuyck, D., ed.
  1963 African Agrarian Systems. London, Oxford University Press
        for the International African Institute.
Bohannan, P.
  1954 Tiv Farm and Settlement. Colonial Research Studies, No. 15,
        London, Colonial Office.
Booth, A. H.
  1960 Small Mammals of West Africa. London, Longmans.
Boserup, E.
  1965 The Conditions of Agricultural Growth. Chicago, Aldine.
Buchanan, K. M., and J. C. Pugh
  1955 Land and People in Nigeria. London, University of London
        Press.
Cansdale, G. S.
  1961 West African Snakes. London, Longmans.
Carneiro, R. L.
  1961 Slash-and-Burn Cultivation among the Kuikuru and Its Implica-
        tions for Cultural Development in the Amazon Basin. Anthro-
        pologica Supplement No. 2:47–67.
Chisholm, M.
  1962 Rural Settlement and Land Use. London, Hutchinson.
Clark, C., and M. Haswell
  1964 The Economics of Subsistence Agriculture. New York, St.
        Martin's Press.
Clarke, G. L.
  1954 Elements of Ecology. New York, John Wiley & Sons, Inc.
Collins, P. W.
  1964 Towards a Reconstruction of Functionalism. Paper read at
        the 63rd Annual Meeting of the American Anthropological
        Association, Detroit, Michigan.
Collis, W. R. F., J. Dema, and F. E. A. Lesi
  1962 Transverse Survey of Health and Nutrition, Pankshin Division,
        Northern Nigeria. West African Medical Journal 11:131–154.
Conant, F. P.
  1962 Contemporary Communities and Abandoned Settlement Sites.

Annals of the New York Academy of Sciences 96, Art. 2, pp. 539–574.

1965 Korok: A Variable Unit of Physical and Social Space among the Pokot of East Africa. American Anthropologist 67:429–434.

Conklin, H. C.

1957 Hanunoo Agriculture. FAO Forestry Development Paper No. 12, Rome, Food and Agriculture Organization of the United Nations.

1961 Study of Shifting Cultivation. Current Anthropology 2:27–61.

Curwen, E. C., and G. Hatt

1953 Plough and Pasture. New York, Henry Schuman.

Dale, T., and V. B. Carter

1955 Topsoil and Civilization. Norman, University of Oklahoma Press.

Dalziel, J. M.

1937 The Useful Plants of West Tropical Africa. London, Crown Agents for the Colonies.

Davidson, B.

1959 The Lost Cities of Africa. Boston, Little, Brown.

Demangeon, A.

1962 The Origins and Causes of Settlement Types. In Readings in Cultural Geography, P. L. Wagner and M. W. Mikesell, eds., pp. 506–516. Chicago, University of Chicago Press.

De Schlippe, P.

1956 Shifting Cultivation in Africa. London, Routledge and Kegan Paul.

Edgerton, R. B.

1965 "Cultural" vs. "Ecological" Factors in the Expression of Values, Attitudes, and Personality Characteristics. American Anthropologist 67:442–447.

Eggan, F.

1954 Social Anthropology and the Method of Controlled Comparison. American Anthropologist 56:743–763.

Elgood, J. H.

1960 Birds of West African Town and Garden. London, Longmans.

Evans, E. E.

1956 The Ecology of Peasant Life in Western Europe. In Man's Role in Changing the Face of the Earth, W. L. Thomas, ed., pp. 217–239. Chicago, University of Chicago Press.

Evans-Pritchard, E. E.

1940 The Nuer. London, Oxford University Press.

Fairbairn, W. A.

1943 Forestry in Plateau Province. Farm and Forest 4:182–192.

Febvre, L.
1932 A Geographical Introduction to History. London, Kegan Paul.

Findlay, R. L.
1945 The Dimmuk and Their Neighbors. Farm and Forest 6:138–142.

Fitzpatrick, J. F. J.
1910 Some Notes on tthe Kwolla District and Its Tribes. Journal of the African Society 10:16–52, 213–221.

Floyd, B.
1965 Terrace Agriculture in Eastern Nigeria: The Case of Maku. Journal of the Geographical Association of Nigeria, 7:91–108.

Forde, C. D.
1934 Habitat, Economy, and Society. London, Methuen.
1947 The Anthropological Approach in Social Science. The Advancement of Science 4:213–224.

Freeman, J. D.
1955 Iban Agriculture. Colonial Research Studies, No. 18, London, Colonial Office.

Fried, M. H.
1952 Land Tenure, Geography and Ecology in the Contact of Cultures. American Journal of Economics and Sociology 11:391–417.

Froelich, Jean-Claude, P. Alexandre, and R. Cornevin
1963 Les populations du Nord-Togo. Paris, Presses Universitaires de France.

Gardi, R.
1956 Mandara. Zurich, Orell Fussli Verlag.

Geertz, C.
1963 Agricultural Involution: The Processes of Ecological Change in Indonesia. Berkeley, University of California Press.

Gluckman, M.
1941 Economy of the Central Barotse Plain. Livingstone, Northern Rhodesia, The Rhodes-Livingstone Institute.
1963 Order and Rebellion in Tribal Africa. New York, The Free Press.

Goldschmidt, W.
1959 Man's Way. New York, Holt.
1965 Theory and Strategy in the Study of Cultural Adaptability. American Anthropologist 67:402–408.

Goody, J.
1957 Fields of Social Control among the LoDagaba. Journal of the Royal Anthropological Institute 87:75–104.

240   REFERENCES

Gray, R. F.
1963   The Sonjo of Tanganyika. London, Oxford University Press.
Gray, R. F., and P. H. Gulliver
1964   The Family Estate in Africa. London, Routledge and Kegan Paul Ltd.
Greenberg, J. H.
1955   Studies in African Linguistic Classification. New Haven, Compass Publishing Company.
Grove, A. T.
1961   Population Densities and Agriculture in Northern Nigeria. *In* Essays on African Population, K. M. Barbour and R. M. Prothero, eds. London, Routledge and Kegan Paul.
Gulliver, P. H.
1955   The Family Herds. London, Routledge and Kegan Paul.
Gunn, Harold D.
1953   Peoples of the Plateau Area of Northern Nigeria. Ethnographic Survey of Africa, Part 7. London, International African Institute.
Hallowell, A. I.
1949   The Size of Algonkian Hunting Territories: A Function of Ecological Adjustment. American Anthropologist 51:35–45.
Harding, Thomas E.
1960   Adaptation and Stability. *In* Evolution and Culture, M. D. Sahlins and E. R. Service, eds., pp. 45–68. Ann Arbor, University of Michigan Press.
Haswell, M. R.
1953   Economics of Agriculture in a Savannah Village. Colonial Research Studies, No. 8. London, Colonial Office.
Helm, J.
1962   The Ecological Approach in Anthropology. American Journal of Sociology 67 (6):630–639.
Hodgkin, Thomas
1960   Nigerian Perspectives. London, Oxford University Press.
Hogben, S. J.
1930   The Muhammadan Emirates of Nigeria. London, Oxford University Press.
Irvine, F. R.
1953   A Textbook of West African Agriculture, 2nd ed. London, Oxford University Press.
Johnston, Bruce F.
1958   The Staple Food Economies of West Tropical Africa. Stanford, Food Research Institute.

Jungraithmayr, H.
1964 Die Sprache der Sura (Maghavul) in Nordnigerien. Afrika und
      Übersee 47:8–220.
Kopytoff, I.
1964 Toward Composite Theories of Witchcraft. Paper read at the
      7th International Congress of Anthropology and Ethnology,
      Moscow.
Krader, L.
1955 Ecology of Central Asian Pastoralism. Southwestern Journal
      of Anthropology 11:301–326.
Kroeber, A. L.
1939 Cultural and Natural Areas of Native North America. Berkeley,
      University of California Press.
Lattimore, O.
1940 Inner Asian Frontiers of China. New York, American Geo-
      graphical Society.
Leach, E. R.
1961 Pul Eliya: A Village in Ceylon. Cambridge, Cambridge Uni-
      versity Press.
Lehman, F. K.
1963 The Structure of Chin Society. Illinois Studies in Anthropology,
      No. 3. Urbana, University of Illinois Press.
Lembezat, B.
1961 Les Populations Paiennes du Nord Cameroun et de l'Adam-
      aoua. Monographies Ethnologiques Africaines, Part 9. London,
      International African Institute.
Linton, Ralph
1936 The Study of Man. New York, Appleton-Century Company.
Livingstone, Frank
1958 Anthropological Implications of Sickle Cell Distribution in
      West Africa. American Anthropologist 60:533–562.
Lounsbury, F. G.
1964 The Formal Analysis of Crow- and Omaha-Type Kinship
      Terminology. In Explorations in Cultural Anthropology,
      Ward H. Goodenough, ed., pp. 351–394. New York, McGraw-
      Hill.
Malinowski, B.
1935 Coral Gardens and Their Magic. New York, American Book
      Company.
Manners, R. A.
1964 Colonialism and Native Land Tenure: A Case Study in
      Ordained Accommodation. In Process and Pattern in Culture,
      R. A. Manners, ed., pp. 266–280. Chicago, Aldine.

Meek, C. K.
   1925   The Northern Tribes of Nigeria. London, Kegan Paul.
   1931   Tribal Studies in Northern Nigeria. London, Oxford University Press.
   1957   Land Tenure and Land Administration in Nigeria and the Cameroons. Colonial Research Studies, No. 22, London, Colonial Office.

Morgan, W. B.
   1953   Farming Practice, Settlement Pattern and Population Density in South-eastern Nigeria. Geographical Journal 121:320–333.

Murdock, G. P.
   1959   Africa. New York, McGraw-Hill.

Murphy, R. F., and J. H. Steward
   1956   Tappers and Trappers: Parallel Process in Acculturation. Economic Development and Cultural Change 4:335–355.

Nadel, S. F.
   1942   A Black Byzantium. London, Oxford University Press.
   1947   The Nuba. London, Oxford University Press.

Netting, R. McC.
   1963   Kofyar Agriculture: A Study in the Cultural Ecology of a West African People. Ph.D. Dissertation, University of Chicago.
   1964   Beer as a Locus of Value among the West African Kofyar. American Anthropologist 66:375–384.
   1965a Heritage of Survival. Natural History 74 (3):14–21.
   1965b A Trial Model of Cultural Ecology. Anthropological Quarterly 38:81–96.
   1965c Household Organization and Intensive Agriculture: The Kofyar Case. Africa 35:422–429.
   1967   A Word List of Kofyar. Research Notes, No. 2. Department of Linguistics and Nigerian Languages, University of Ibadan.

Nicholas, R. W.
   1963   Ecology and Village Structure in Deltaic West Bengal. The Economic Weekly, Special Number, July, 1963, 1185–1196.

Nimkoff, M., and R. Middleton
   1960   Types of Family and Types of Economy. American Journal of Sociology 66:215–223.

Nye, P. H., and D. J. Greenland
   1960   The Soil under Shifting Cultivation. Technical Communication No. 51. Commonwealth Bureau of Soils. Harpenden, Commonwealth Agricultural Bureau.

Odum, E. P.
   1959   Fundamentals of Ecology. Philadelphia, W. B. Saunders Company.

Oliver, S. C.
1962 Ecology and Cultural Continuity as Contributing Factors in the Social Organization of the Plains Indians. University of California Publications in American Archaeology and Ethnology 48 (1) :1–90.

Perham, M. F.
1946 The Economics of a Tropical Dependency. London, Faber and Faber.

Phillips, J.
1959 Agriculture and Ecology in Africa. London, Faber and Faber.

Platt, B. S.
1955 Some Traditional Alcoholic Beverages and Their Importance in Indigenous African Communities. Proceedings of the Nutrition Society 14:115–129.

Polanyi, K.
1953 Semantics of General Economic History (revised). New York, Columbia University Research Project on Origins of Economic Institutions. Reprinted in M. H. Fried, ed., Readings in Anthropology, vol. 2 (1959), pp. 161–184. New York, Crowell.

Porter, Philip W.
1965 Environmental Potentials and Economic Opportunities—A Background for Cultural Adaptation. American Anthropologist 67:409–420.

Pospisil, L.
1963 Kapauku Papuan Economy. Yale University Publications in Anthropology, No. 67.

Prothero, R. M.
1961 Population Maps and Mapping in Africa South of the Sahara. In Essays on African Population, K. M. Barbour and R. M. Prothero, eds., pp. 63–82. London, Routledge and Kegan Paul.

Pullam, R. A.
1962 The Concept of the Middle Belt in Nigeria: An Attempt at a Climatic Definition. Nigerian Geographical Journal 5:39–52.

Redfield, R.
1953 The Primitive World and Its Transformations. Ithaca, Cornell University Press.

Richards, A. I.
1939 Land, Labour, and Diet in Northern Rhodesia. London, International Institute of African Languages and Cultures.

Rowling, C. W.
1952 Plateau Land Tenure. Kaduna, Northern Nigeria Regional Government.

Sahlins, M. D.
  1961 The Segmentary Lineage: An Organization of Predatory Expansion. American Anthropologist 63:322–345.
  1962 Moala. Ann Arbor, University of Michigan Press.
  1964 Culture and Environment: The Study of Cultural Ecology. *In* Horizons in Anthropology, Sol Tax, ed., pp. 132–147, Chicago, Aldine.
Sahlins, M. D., and E. R. Service
  1960 Evolution and Culture. Ann Arbor, University of Michigan Press.
Sauer, C. O.
  1963 Land and Life. Berkeley, University of California Press.
Scudder, T.
  1962 The Ecology of the Gwembe Tonga. Manchester, Rhodes-Livingstone Institute.
Sears, P. B.
  1957 The Ecology of Man. Eugene, Oregon System of Higher Education.
Smith, M. G.
  1955 The Economies of Hausa Communities of Zaria. Colonial Research Studies, No. 16. London, Colonial Office.
  1960 Government in Zazzau. London, Oxford University Press.
Stenning, D. J.
  1957 Transhumance, Migratory Drift, Migration: Patterns of Pastoral Fulani Nomadism. Journal of Royal Anthropological Institute 87:57–73.
  1958 Household Viability among the Pastoral Fulani. *In* Developmental Cycles in Domestic Groups, Jack Goody, ed. Cambridge, Cambridge University Press.
Steward, Julian
  1937 Ecological Aspects of Southwestern Society. Anthropos 32:87–104.
  1938 Basin-Plateau Aboriginal Sociopolitical Groups. Bureau of American Ethnology, Bulletin 120.
  1955a Theory of Culture Change. Urbana, University of Illinois Press.
  1955b Irrigation Civilizations: A Comparative Study. Washington, D.C., Pan American Union.
  1965 Some Problems Raised by Roger C. Owen's "The Patrilocal Band. . . ." Brief communication in American Anthropologist 67:732–734.

Stewart, Omer C.
1954 The Forgotten Side of Ethnogeography. *In* Method and Perspective in Anthropology, R. F. Spencer, ed., pp. 221–248. Minneapolis, University of Minnesota Press.

Thistleton, G. F.
1960 Nature Study for Africa: Mammals. London, Evans Brothers.

Thomas, F.
1925 The Environmental Basis of Society. New York, Century.

Thornton, D., and N. V. Rounce
1936 Ukara Island and the Agricultural Practices of the Wakara. Tanganyika Notes and Records 1:25–32.

Udo, R. K.
1965 Disintegration of Nucleated Settlement in East Nigeria. Geographical Review 55:53–67.

Vayda, A. P.
1961 Expansion and Warfare among Swidden Cultivators. American Anthropologist 63:346–358.

Vayda, A. P., and R. A. Rappaport
1968 Ecology, Cultural and Non-cultural. *In* Introduction to Cultural Anthropology, J. A. Clifton, ed., pp. 477–497. Boston, Houghton Mifflin.

Wagner, P. L.
1960 The Human Use of the Earth. Glencoe, The Free Press.

Wallace, A. F. C.
1961 Culture and Personality. New York, Random House.

Wedel, W.
1941 Environment and Native Subsistence Economies in the Central Great Plains. Smithsonian Miscellaneous Collections 101 (3).

White, C. M. N.
1963 Factors Determining the Content of African Land Tenure Systems in Northern Rhodesia. *In* African Agrarian Systems, D. Biebuyck, ed., pp. 364–373. London, Oxford University Press for the International African Institute.

White, Stanhope
1941 The Agricultural Economy of the Hill Pagans of Dikwa Emirate, Cameroons. Empire Journal of Experimental Agriculture 9:65–72.

Wilson, M.
1963 Effects on the Xhosa and Nyakyusa of Scarcity of Land. *In* African Agrarian Systems, D. Biebuyck, ed., pp. 374–391. London, Oxford University Press for the International African Institute.

Winans, E. V.
  1965a The Political Content of Economic Adaptation in the Southern
         Highlands of Tanganyika. American Anthropologist 67:435–
         441.
  1965b Ecology and Selected Problems in African Ethnology. Anthro-
         pological Quarterly 38:167–180.
Wissler, Clark
  1926 The Relation of Nature to Man in Aboriginal America. Lon-
        don, Oxford University Press.
Wittfogel, K.
  1956 The Hydraulic Civilizations. In Man's Role in Changing the
        Face of the Earth, W. L. Thomas, ed., pp. 152–164. Chicago,
        University of Chicago Press.
Wolff, H.
  1954 Nigerian Orthography. Zaria, Gaskiya Corporation.
Worsley, P. M.
  1956 The Kinship System of the Tallensi: A Revaluation. Journal
        of the Royal Anthropological Society 86:37–75.
Young, R., and H. Fosbrooke
  1960 Smoke in the Hills. Evanston, Northwestern University Press.

Index

Acha, 47, 60, 63, 64, 74, 80, 81, 82, 86, 88, 90, 91, 98, 99, 106, 128, 130, 133, 136, 214; planting, 70–71, 72; harvest, 75; threshing, 75; varieties, 83; production compared, 92; preparation for food, 101; weight consumed per person, 104; sowing with, 188
Adoption, 169; to lineage membership, 148
Adult workers, 133
Agricultural cycle, 8, 65, 66, 182, 191
Agricultural extension: lack of, 54
Agricultural system: variables in, 134
Agricultural techniques and knowledge, 57, 77, 198, 227, 232, 233
Agriculture: methods for the study of, 7; anthropological investigation of, 8; contrast with horticulture, 55*n;* field preparation, 65, 206; planting, 67–69, 70, 81, 133, 142; hoeing, 69–73 *passim,* 125, 133, 142, 199, 228; transplanting, 69, 74; interplanting, 71–72; harvesting, 74, 133, 142; weeding, 74, 133, 206, 227; threshing, 75, 128, 210; Kofyar and Chokfem compared, 130; yields, 132; mechanization, 133, 142–43; dangers to, 187; native interest in, 187; rites, 191; yields contrasted, 200–2; origins of, 226; clearing, 227; and religion, 229; and values, 229. *See also* Crops; Fallowing; Manuring
Ancestor, eponymous: burial place, 148
Ancestor, of Kofyar peoples, 149
Anchau town, 202
Angas peoples, vii, 4, 26, 188, 203, 211; language, xiii; and Kofyar languages, 38; reputed origin, 44; agriculture, 130; household type, 130
Animals, domestic. *See* Domestic animals
Animals, wild: indigenous species, 35; as pests, 86
Ankwe. *See* Goemai peoples
Anthropogeography, 5–6
Archaeology, need for, 24
Architecture, 39
Assistance, mutual. *See* Labor
Authority system: as adaptive variable, 17
Awe town, 213
Axes, 56

Bambara groundnuts, 74, 100, 102
Barbers, 123
Barlow, Assistant District Officer, killed by Kofyar, 49